# THE CRUCIBLE;

OR,

# TESTS OF A REGENERATE STATE.

DESIGNED TO

BRING TO LIGHT SUPPRESSED HOPES, EXPOSE FALSE ONES, AND CONFIRM THE TRUE.

BY

REV. J. A. GOODHUE, A. M.

WITH

An Introduction

BY REV. EDWARD N. KIRK, D. D.

Examine yourselves, whether ye be in the faith; prove your own selves.
COR. 13:5.

BOSTON:
GOULD AND LINCOLN,
59 WASHINGTON STREET.
NEW YORK: SHELDON AND COMPANY.
CINCINNATI: GEORGE S. BLANCHARD.
1860.

ELECTROTYPED BY W. F. DRAPER, ANDOVER, MASS.

Printed By R. M. Edwards.

# PREFACE.

---

THE volume now offered to the reader is the result of no transient thought or feeling. The subject of which it treats has for years enlisted the author's deepest anxiety. In commencing, however, to express his thoughts through the press, he contemplated only a brief article for some periodical; but the subject so expanded under his hands, as to render it impossible to stop short of the present extended discussion.

Three classes of religious experience are here portrayed *in separate form*, in order to exhibit a more distinct image of each, and enable the reader, with less liability of mistake, to determine to which his own experience belongs. To do this fairly, he must test his experience, not by statements taken apart from their connection, but as interpreted by the whole description. This remark is particularly applicable to the second part, the tone of feeling in which, though in appearance approaching very near to that of the third, of which it is the counterfeit, will yet be found to differ vitally from it. The self-distrusting and tender-hearted will, doubtless, feel afflicted by the perusal of this part, but will find their solace in the others. Though the discussion can be critically understood only by a comprehensive view of its three parts, yet, for practical purposes, either may be selected, to the omission of the others, according to the mental state of the reader. It is believed that each will be recognized as representing a distinct and actual experience. Whether they are rightly assigned, is submitted to the answer of all genuine Christian experience, and the Word of God. If the second part is not a faithful portraiture of closely, and, for the most part, successfully counterfeited conversions, — which are commonly admitted to exist, — it is hoped that others will be incited to draw more truthful pictures, suggested by wider observation and experience. It would be legitimate to expect that against this portion of the discussion the most common objection will be made, since in this direction error most prevails.

The convictions of the writer are the product of no theory, except such as he has been forced to adopt from the teachings of the Scriptures and the facts of religious experience. It may be added, too, that the more widely his observation has extended, the more thoroughly have the positions which have been submitted become established. He does not flatter himself that, upon a subject so various as that of religious experience, his views will, in all respects, meet the approval of his brethren. If he knowingly differs, it is only because love for the truth and for souls is stronger than desire for their approval. It is only asked that points of difference may be examined as seriously as they are submitted.

In addition to kind suggestions and encouragement from many of his brethren, the author desires to make special mention of his indebtedness to Rev. Edward N. Kirk, D. D., who, in repeated interviews, has favored the writer with the valuable results of his extended experience in this department of labor.

Though this work has been prepared under the pressure of deep and strong convictions, yet the author is not ignorant that the subject furnishes occasion for almost unlimited investigation. Nor does he claim to have arrived at such results as are still to be desired in this direction. If this humble endeavor shall be used by the Master to save men from self-deception, and advance the interests of genuine piety, or if it shall serve to incite others to a more just and adequate treatment of this too much neglected subject, it will subserve the end desired.

# CONTENTS.

## PART I.

## UNRECOGNIZED REGENERATION;

## OR, FAITH WITHOUT HOPE.

### CHAPTER I.

#### ASPECTS OF UNRECOGNIZED REGENERATION.



### CHAPTER II.

#### CAUSES OF UNRECOGNIZED REGENERATION.

##### SECTION I.—WHY UNRECOGNIZED BY THE SUBJECT.

### SECTION II.—WHY UNRECOGNIZED BY OTHERS.



## CHAPTER III.

### RESULTS OF UNRECOGNIZED REGENERATION.



## CHAPTER IV.

### REMEDY OF UNRECOGNIZED REGENERATION.

# PART II.

# UNRECOGNIZABLE REGENERATION;

## OR, HOPE WITHOUT FAITH.

## CHAPTER I.

### ASPECTS OF UNRECOGNIZABLE REGENERATION.



## CHAPTER II.

### CAUSES OF UNRECOGNIZABLE REGENERATION.

#### SECTION I.



#### SECTION II. — FALSE TREATMENT.



#### SECTION III. — DECEITFULNESS OF SIN.

#### SECTION IV. — SATANIC INFLUENCE.

## CHAPTER III.

### RESULTS OF UNRECOGNIZABLE REGENERATION.



## CHAPTER IV.

### REMEDY OF UNRECOGNIZABLE REGENERATION.



# PART III.

## RECOGNIZED REGENERATION;

### OR, FAITH AND HOPE.

### POSSIBILITY AND MODE OF RECOGNIZING REGENERATION.

## DIVISION FIRST.

### PRELIMINARY DISCUSSION.

## CHAPTER I.

### POSSIBILITY OF RECOGNITION — BY THE SUBJECT OF IT — BY OTHERS.

## CHAPTER II.

### MODE OF RECOGNITION. — GENERAL PRINCIPLE STATED AND ILLUSTRATED.



# DIVISION SECOND.

### GENERAL PRINCIPLE APPLIED TO THE RECOGNITION OF REGENERATION BY THE SUBJECT.

## CHAPTER I.

### PRELIMINARY.

## CHAPTER II.

### SPIRITUAL CONSCIOUSNESS THE PRIMARY EVIDENCE.



## CHAPTER III.

### SUPERIORITY OF SPIRITUAL CONSCIOUSNESS.



## CHAPTER IV.

### PECULIARITIES OF THE CHRISTIAN CONSCIOUSNESS.



## CHAPTER V.

### SECONDARY SOURCE OF EVIDENCE.—REASONING PROCESS.

#### SECTION I.—PRELIMINARY.

## SECTION II.—PECULIARITIES OF THE REGENERATE CHARACTER.

# DIVISION THIRD.

## GENERAL PRINCIPLE APPLIED TO THE RECOGNITION OF REGENERATION BY OTHERS.

## CHAPTER I.



## CHAPTER II.



## CHAPTER III.

### TREATMENT OF INQUIRERS AND YOUNG CONVERTS.

# INTRODUCTION.

THIS work addresses itself to all serious persons, but particularly to those whose office requires them to guide and test the religious experience and hopes of others; and even they who may not agree with all its positions, will find it worthy of their serious attention.

To facilitate the reader's progress, it may be observed that the discussion accords, in its scope and spirit, with Pres. Edwards's treatise on "The Affections," to which we may refer as a standard. The differences between them will be found in their immediate aims, sources, and modes of treatment. Starting from the common ground, that there is a real and a spurious conversion, they contemplate the subject from different points of view. Aiming, in common with Mr. Edwards, to prevent false conversions, to confirm true Christian hope, and to present definite tests of regeneration in others, the writer of this essay had also in view a class of persons to whom the other makes little or no reference; that is the class he describes as having experienced an unrecognized conversion, and to which, probably, Mr. Edwards himself belonged for many years, as also Mr. Brainard, whose memoir he wrote.

In bringing the matter of regeneration to a practical test, the two authors employ different methods: Mr. Edwards, to some extent, enters into the theological elements of the subject; considering those portions of it which lie back of all consciousness and observation; such as the agency of the Holy Spirit, and those unconscious changes in our nature which that agency produces. But this essay is distinguished by making consciousness the primary evidence of one's own regeneration; the spiritual sense the primary medium of testing another's conversion; and, auxiliary to both these, incidental peculiarities, which, however important, appear to have been overlooked by other experimental writers.

Comparing the two treatises by their effects, there will probably also be found a striking contrast. Edwards's essay is almost universally discouraging to young believers; and the reason seems to be, that he presents tests rather of sanctification than of regeneration — of mature life, rather than of infantile existence. He wrote rather from his own eminent experience, than from that of Christians generally, — which, unhappily, presents but little corresponding to his attainments. So far as his work aims to promote holiness, this is well; but if regarded simply as designed to test the existence of piety, it is so far defective. Mr. Goodhue has aimed, on the contrary, to hunt out the feeble, halting, undeveloped life of piety, of which, for various reasons, so many examples do actually exist in the world; and also to exhibit, as fully as possible, the symptoms of an ordinary regenerate state, for the confirmation of the true believer. Some may, indeed, object to his carrying the regenerated person back to former and first experience; they would think it better to urge him to higher attainments. But, our author would reply, the fact is, you cannot get their past experience out of their way. It has become, by perversion, a hinderance to their progress ; for they are constantly laboring to go through the first stages, which they have already passed. They want to get as new what can never be new to them again. They are afraid to act as Christians, lest they should be hypocrites. They must know that their former exercises were Christian, in order that they may advance intelligently, confidently, and joyfully. And he considers it no small evil that such persons may do much injury unintentionally, by holding up some advanced stage of sanctification as a model for others in the stage of conversion. The cases are not unfrequent of persons directing inquirers, from their own experience, in a way which is painfully superficial and defective, however sincere. A person converted in early life, but not regarding himself as converted, once met a clergyman, who gave him this direction: "Go to work as if you were a Christian." He took the advice, and soon was filled with heavenly peace. But the evil in the case was, that he regarded that as his conversion; and from that time his counsel to inquirers of all grades was, to go to work as if they were Christians — a counsel which differed widely from that call to repentance which takes for granted we are not Christians. It is a great evil to confound the expansion of piety with its commencement — the fruit with the blossom.

Although this treatise is eminently practical, yet it involves principles of great importance, which have probably never yet received a due consideration. A part of the feebleness of the church consists in its having so much natural religion added to its fellowship — so much natural religion that has never been transmuted into spiritual religion. Perhaps on this account the book may meet opposition, and from none more strongly than from those whose zeal is for numbers rather than for godliness, and those who regulate the admission of members to the church by social feelings and considerations, or even by the exercise of a natural judgment, rather than by spiritual tests.

The discussion of this subject by the author is valuable, because, while he concedes to unregenerate men as much religion as any of them claim to possess, at the same time he clearly exhibits to them the fact that natural religion is not spiritual religion; that it is not that piety which God's spirit has formed, or which he will acknowledge as fitting its possessor for heaven. And these views have an increasing importance, as revivals of religion increase, because there will be a growing tendency to bring into the church multitudes who have gone no farther than to have their natural religious sensibilities quickened. Indeed, the first impression produced, on hearing the third part of this work read, was that this is a timely discussion in reference to two classes — "the elders in Israel," and this community generally, in which natural religion is so extensively confounded with godliness, and where the instincts of our apostate nature are taken by so many for "fruits of the Spirit."

The subject of "second conversion," here brought to view, is one demanding a thorough discussion; and the author has fairly introduced that discussion.

No one will question the simplicity and loftiness of his aim. Like his great predecessor, he has sought to attract and charm the reader, not by ornaments and glowing periods, but by clearly presenting the mighty theme in its own colors.

For many years his soul has been burdened with what he considers a grand defect of the church —

the inability of Christians to discern suppressed piety, and to discriminate between the true and the false.

And if any, on reading the first part, should fear that he is lax, lenient, and superficial, it may be suggested to them to suspend their judgment until the second part shall have been read. Indeed, a just opinion of the whole work cannot be formed until the third part has been read: it is the main portion of the discussion.

In requesting this Introduction by one more extensively known than himself, the author asks for no patronage to his person, or partiality to his book. He simply asks the servants of Christ to examine his views; and, in compliance with his wishes, I simply and cordially say, they are worthy of a serious examination.

And may our glorious Lord bless the author and the reader, and employ this essay to advance his kingdom.

EDWARD N. KIRK.

5 STANIFORD ST., OCTOBER, 1859.

# PART I.

## UNRECOGNIZED REGENERATION;

OR,

## FAITH WITHOUT HOPE.

# UNRECOGNIZED REGENERATION.

## CHAPTER I.

### ASPECTS OF UNRECOGNIZED REGENERATION.

It is a well-known fact that there are many professing Christians who do not know when they were converted.[1] They have been led gradually to believe they are Christians, without reference to any change which they could call a new creation. Regeneration being an instantaneous work, it follows that they must have been in a regenerate state, in many instances, for a series of years, without its being so understood by themselves or others. An eminently pious deacon, who has been an honored member of a Baptist church for forty years, writes: "I remember at nine years of age being much troubled about my sins, but nothing definite as to any change in my feelings. Yet I do remember when I felt much better, more happy, enjoyed prayer more. I never made known my feelings, and never supposed I was a Christian. I became acquainted with wild and wicked boys, and my serious impressions by degrees wore off; and, till about thirty years of age, their return was rare as angel visits. I lived through several

1 The term conversion is used for convenience, not in its strict, but popular sense. It is regeneration, strictly, we are about to discuss.

revivals of religion, and was very anxious, at times, to experience a change of heart which should be so manifest that I should never have occasion to doubt. But, after all, I was obliged to go back twenty-one years, gather up the little fragments of evidence, bring them before the church, and let them decide. Contrary to my expectation, they declared themselves satisfied to receive it as a Christian experience." This is not a solitary case. Such examples constitute a class of persons by no means small.

An interesting question now arises. If there is a class of Christians who have been in a regenerate state for a series of years without its being so regarded, is it not probable that, in every Christian community, there is a corresponding class still in this condition? If so, are there no means by which they can be known and relieved, and the condition prevented on the part of others? It is believed that they may be known, and that a better understanding of the aspects of the condition, its causes, its results, and the proper remedy, would subserve the desired end.

We shall call the state unrecognized regeneration. The subjects of it are persons whose religious character is a puzzle, and a source of constant perplexity. They have come to years of maturity under Christian influences; they are often the children of pious parents; they may have been taught in the Sabbath School; may be constant and seemingly interested attendants upon public worship; but never assume a decided position in matters of religion. In times of revival, and by particular providences, they are awakened, but nothing more. By some they are said to be gospel-hardened. To their friends they are a wonder and an anxiety. To most, it is strange that they should be the subjects of so much pious influence—be brought so near, but never enter, the kingdom of heaven. To a few, most intimate with them, but not venturing to express the opinion, they seem to be Christians in all but the name. Their apparent condition is that of being almost persuaded.

This is their outward history. Their inward history is unwritten. Were it known, it would be found to be peculiar, exceedingly varied and distracted, and mostly of an unhappy nature. They are strangely sensitive to the providences and claims of God. They are penetrated with a lively sense of their personal sin and guilt, and great unworthiness. They sometimes pray, especially in affliction; but, for the most part, prayer is neglected. At times they partially enjoy prayer; but oftener it is a burden; while its neglect is a source of pain. They have a high perception of the nature and value of true religion; but never think they are Christians, though greatly desiring to be such. They can neither enjoy religion, nor abandon it. They are sensible that they are wicked, yet dare not ask or hope for forgiveness. Their ideal of the Christian character surpasses human attainment.

We cite, as an example, the case which first arrested the attention of the writer. It was that of a lady, thirty years of age, of sound mind, and an honest regard for religious things. She stated that no Christian had conversed with her upon the subject of religion for fifteen years, yet she betrayed an apprehensiveness of spiritual things truly remarkable in an unconverted person under no special religious awakening. To the inquiry, whether she had at any time been made the subject of religious impressions, she replied that she had not. This seemed incomprehensible, that one should be so tender and perceptive spiritually, without having been awakened. It being urged that she must have had religious exercises, she acknowledged that when young she became *excited* in a revival; but added, that it amounted to nothing, and soon passed away. Yet her exercises proved to possess all the features of a genuine Christian experience. She had never formed the habit of prayer. When urged to commence it, and trust the promise of God, she reluctantly resolved to attempt it. Soon, without additional convictions, she became hopeful that she was a child of God; and has since manifested a growing Christian character, yet not essentially unlike what she had possessed from her early youth.

This will suggest to every Christian minister many persons in respect to whom he is constantly anxious and perplexed, and a solution of whose religious condition would be truly grateful. The hypothesis submitted is that they are in a regenerated state, which is unrecognized by themselves and others.

The first of the several aspects of this condition we shall call *unconscious regeneration.* The declaration of many persons, that they do not know when they were converted, implies that at the time of conversion they were unconscious of any religious exercises. But this supposition is not warranted in the large majority of cases, if it is in any. We are not prepared to assume that such a change as that of the new birth is ever experienced without a consciousness of some religious exercises.

The example first adduced assumes this general form. The individual would doubtless say, that he never knew when he was converted. Yet the idea cannot be that at that time he was not conscious of any religious exercises. He says: "I found myself often in the fields, and other retired places, trying to pray. I remember being much troubled about my sins; remember when I felt much better, enjoyed prayer more." The meaning, therefore, of the statement is, that while he was conscious of religious exercises, he did not suppose he had become a Christian.

This is doubtless the true explanation of most, if not all, similar examples. In many cases we cannot obtain evidence that the persons were conscious of all the exercises commonly connected with conversion, though in almost all cases a consciousness of some of them is discoverable. To meet the case of Christians who believe they never had any conscious religious exercises in conversion, which we do not know to be impossible, we have introduced the supposed aspect of unconscious regeneration.

The second aspect is *unobserved regeneration.* The supposition here is, that the person, though not unconscious of religious exercises, yet takes no observation of them. Were his attention called to them, he would perceive that an important work was being wrought. They are like the evaporation of water, or the gradual infection of the atmosphere, of which, though not unconscious, we take no note.

This aspect differs from the former, in that the one is supposed to be a process which cannot be observed, while the other may, but is not. If any given cases are regarded as belonging to that class, the question would arise whether they should not be referred to this.

The third aspect is *unremembered regeneration.* To this class belong those instances in which the process was not an unconscious one, nor unobserved, but had passed, with many other mental phenomena, into oblivion. Instances of this kind differ from the last, in that the unobserved cannot be recovered to the mind, while the unremembered often can be. The former have left no trace behind, and are lost; the latter, having left their footsteps, can be retraced. The unobserved could once have been saved from perpetual oblivion; many of the unremembered can be still. Frequent examples which might be supposed to belong to the first and second classes, if examined, would be found to take their place under this; or some of the exercises of any given case may belong to one class, and some to another.

In this class of cases persons may be assisted by other Christians, in many instances, in reviving their exercises. In the second example cited, the individual declared it was so long since they occurred, that they had been forgotten; but, upon being interrogated, she was able to recall the outlines of a Christian experience. One who is conversant with the phenomena attendant upon regeneration, the order and circumstances in which they commonly occur, will be able essentially to aid in the recovery of experiences which otherwise would never be restored. The recovery of one exercise leads to another, until most or all are recalled, — enough, at least, to prove that all existed.

The fourth aspect is *unidentified regeneration*. In this state the individual is not unconscious that a change has been wrought; it is not unobserved, nor forgotten, but is unidentified as the change desired. The exercises constitute an important era in the history of the person, but he never supposes that from them he must date the beginning of his spiritual life.

Cases of this class are numerous, if we include those Christians who have always regarded the process of obtaining evidence that they were Christians as the process of regeneration, which are by no means identical or simultaneous, but are often widely separated. During the interval, of course, the persons must have been in a state of unidentified regeneration. Multitudes of intelligent Christians are of this number, regarding their conversion and their indulgence of hope as simultaneous, while they are separated by perhaps a space of years.

The fifth aspect is *unacknowledged regeneration.* This is that of unidentified regeneration, advanced a step nearer to recognition. The individual has had inward impressions and outward intimations that his exercises may have constituted a work of grace, but has cultivated the habit of refusing to acknowledge them as such. He sometimes wonders whether it may not be so; but, when interrogated, positively disclaims it. In this class there is even an unwillingness to accredit what evidence exists that they are regenerate persons. They express themselves confidently and positively. They *know* they have not been converted. They think it absurd to raise the question, and utterly useless to examine their exercises to ascertain whether they give evidence of a change. It seems to them as useless as it would be to raise the question whether they may not even now be saints in glory, and about as much an insult to their reason. This is the farthest extreme of unacknowledged regeneration, which exhibits many shades of variation. Its central idea is a decided unwillingness to acknowledge having been converted, or to entertain the thought.

The difference between this and former aspects is, that in this the persons have had some evidence that they are Christians, while in the former they have had no such apprehensions. In this, evidence is resisted; in those, it is simply wanting. In both, the fact of regeneration is denied, but with more of vehemence in the latter case, in order to resist affirmative intimations and impressions. The more strongly such intimations are presented, the more vehement becomes the denial. All reasoning towards a favorable conclusion from the nature of their exercises, is met with reasoning in the opposite direction; all light thrown in upon their understandings is lost in clouds and darkness. Having been enlightened by the Spirit, they have spiritual weapons with which to contend against their own internal impressions, and the intimations of others. Their prevailing disposition is utterly to condemn themselves, to disown all their exercises, and deny the existence of any source of encouragement.

Abundant individual examples illustrating this aspect of unrecognized regeneration might be cited; but a single one, of an extreme nature, must suffice. A lady, thirty years of age, having previously been made a subject of grace without entertaining hope, upon being awakened anew by the sudden death of a friend, came to regard herself as being in a most reckless and lost condition; as even given over to hardness of heart, and a reprobate mind. Her statements were of the most contradictory nature. She declared that she had no feeling; she could not shed a single tear; she had no interest for herself whatever; no sense of sin, or of her lost condition, and no desire to be a Christian. Yet her feeling was of that unutterable kind which finds no vent in tears. Her interest for herself was so intense, that, though in perfect health, she believed she was about to die, and in a few days be finally and forever lost. Her lost condition was so deeply realized, that she conceived herself to be in the very jaws of death and hell. Upon subsequently obtaining evidence of acceptance with God, she was obliged to refer her real conversion to a date fifteen years previous.

# CHAPTER II.

## CAUSES OF UNRECOGNIZED REGENERATION.

### § I.—Why unrecognized by the Subject.

At this point the question will arise, What reason is there to suppose that the class of persons under consideration are regenerate persons? The answer to this question must be deferred until we shall have considered, in its several aspects, the causes and results of unrecognized regeneration. We shall treat first, and mainly, of regeneration as being unrecognized by the subject of it; and secondly, of its being unrecognized by others.

1. *Unconscious Regeneration.* — If a state of unconscious regeneration is a possible or actual condition, it must be accounted for upon the supposition that the mind is capable of undergoing important changes unconsciously; that the soul is the subject of many phenomena, which are so electric and subtle that we are incapable of observing them, and that our mental sensitiveness is not sufficiently delicate to warn us of their existence.[1] It must be supposed, too, that among these phenomena is that of the new birth,—the most important of all mental changes, — and that this may occur in so silent and hidden a manner, and in such harmony with the natural workings of the mind, as to elude the consciousness

[1] For a discussion of the possibility of undergoing mental changes unconsciously, see Sir William Hamilton's Lectures, Vol. I. Lect. XVIII.

If there are pious persons who never had any initial experience of religion of which they were conscious, — not an experience which they did not observe, but one which they could not observe, because unconscious of it, — this is the only possible solution of the casė. Sometimes persons of this description seem to think that their regeneration was gradual; or that, being very religiously inclined from their earliest recollection, they have somehow grown up by degrees into true piety. But the doctrine of gradual regeneration, or of a naturally pious tendency which only needs to be cultivated, is deserving of no sympathy. The assertion that many Christians do not know when they were converted, should be so guarded as to avoid conveying such an impression. Nor are we warranted in encouraging the supposition of unconscious regeneration, even with the solution which has been offered, since facts do not appear to demand it.

An eminently pious gentleman, who was accustomed to say that he had from his earliest recollection been very religiously disposed, and that he could not point to the era of his conversion, upon being questioned concerning his earliest religious impressions, was able to recall, at the age of eight, first, deep convictions of sin; then the loss of those convictions, and a quiet state of mind; then occasional seasons of darkness and gloom, and subsequent tenderness of conscience in regard to offending God. He had no recollection of any special peace, or happiness, or enjoyment of prayer; although, at that time, these, and all the essential features of conversion must have existed, — it being the only point at which any outlines of an initial experience could be discovered. Whether he was unconscious of the essential exercises which he could not recall, or did not observe, or afterwards forgot them, cannot be known.

2. *Unobserved Regeneration.* — We are by no means accurate observers of all that transpires within us. Mental and moral phenomena are often experienced in so brief a period, as to have transpired ere there is time to note them. We pass from one mental state to another so silently, that we do not observe the transit nor the change. Occupied with the new condition, we do not realize that we are not the same we were an hour ago. So it may be with the exercises attendant upon regeneration.

The *naturalness* of the work is another reason why it may be unobserved. The Holy Spirit, in changing the heart, operates in perfect harmony with the workings of the mind. Its delicate machinery suffers not the slightest interruption or derangement. A man is never more free than when, under the influence of the Holy Spirit, he becomes a disciple of Christ. He is so free that he is conscious of no divine interposition. Hence his attention is not turned to the process, as anything extraordinary; the natural idea being, that an extraordinary effect must be contrary to nature, and not in harmony with it.

The *intensity* of the work is another cause of its being unobserved. A work of grace, at the highest point of its intensity, so penetrates and absorbs the whole man, that it is not possible he should be simultaneously a subject and an inspector of it. The powers of reflection are merged in the change which the soul is undergoing. In regeneration, the sinner is in the solitary presence of a sovereign God, and when in that presence he recognizes no other. The guilty creature, adjusting his case at the bar of an offended God, cannot at the same time make a record of the proceeding; he cannot be criminal and recorder at the same august tribunal. The work of regeneration, therefore, not only *may*, but *must* be unobserved while it is being performed. Observation is taken, and reflection made upon it only subsequently, by at least a brief space. This being so, circumstances may conspire, as we shall see hereafter, to protract this space to a longer or shorter period.

Another cause of unobserved regeneration is, that it ordinarily occurs in early youth, when the mind is unaccustomed to take note of its own phenomena. On this account, the liability that the change will remain unobserved is greatly increased. In childhood, too, the exercises are not upon so large a scale as in adult age. In consequence of these causes combined, it would not be strange if the phenomena attendant upon regeneration in childhood were not so observed as afterwards to be recalled.

3. *Unremembered Regeneration.* — We do not retain in our memories all the events of our inward history. Sometimes the most important pass into oblivion, while the more trivial abide. Only such remain as are deeply engraven upon the mental tablet. Whether they are thus engraven depends not upon their actual importance, but upon our conception of it. If the event of regeneration be not understood, then, with others which slightly impress us, it may be forgotten. Occurring, as it does, to a large extent, among the young, the ignorant and obscure, and being also mysterious in its nature, it would not be surprising if its infinite moment should sometimes fail to be apprehended. The precious pearl may fall into concealment in the midst of mental rubbish. It may glitter at the first, but soon become tarnished and defaced. Had the attention been called to the exercises, their peculiarities

pointed out, and explained to be the signs of spiritual life, they might have been saved from a long forgetfulness. The orphan has forgotten the countenance of his departed parent, because he did not realize that it would ever be to him, of all the world besides, the face of faces.

4. *Unidentified Regeneration.* — The apostle John says: "He that believeth on the Son of God, hath the witness in himself." So also Paul, to the Romans: "The Spirit itself beareth witness with our spirit that we are the children of God." Through what causes, then, is it that the subject of a work of grace may be conscious that a change has been wrought in him, and have observed and retained it in his memory, and yet not identified it as the change desired? An answer requires a brief account of the witness of which John speaks. This may be considered as consisting of two parts, which we shall call the subjective and objective. The subjective witness consists of a direct impression, or assurance, produced in the soul of the believer by the Holy Spirit, to the effect that he is born of God. This assurance is mysteriously wrought into the consciousness, through the exercise of the mental and moral faculties. Its design is to impart a living sustentation to the hope of the believer, which shall support him amid all unfavorable indications.

In the first place, we do not know that it is God's pleasure always to give the witness, in this form, simultaneously with the believer's act of faith. We cannot tell but that, in exceptional cases, he may have purposes to accomplish which shall require him to withhold, for a time, this assurance. He perfectly adjusts the economy of grace to the varied condition and disposition of every individual, and may see that it is best, in some instances, to adopt a soul into his heavenly family, and make him an heir to the society of saints and angels, without at once apprizing him of it. It may be to subserve the purpose of greater dependence, more thorough humility or repentance, or to qualify the individual for a peculiar service.

In the second place, we remark that the witness, in the form of direct assurance, may be given, but the testimony in great part suppressed. This may be caused by the imperfect working of our mental faculties. In consequence of some jar or disturbance among them, or their sluggish action, the influence of the Spirit may not find so free access to the soul of the believer, as to create and sustain a confidence that he is prepared for a glorious immortality. A self-distrusting and unhopeful mental temperament also frequently contributes to the same effect. This is often strong enough to remove every gleam of hope that is shed upon the soul. It induces a mental habitude of despondency and gloom, which presents, in many cases, an insuperable barrier, humanly speaking, against the gentle inworkings of the Holy Spirit seeking to bear witness with the soul that it is born of God.

Another cause of unidentified regeneration may be found in the supposition that the witness is sometimes *misunderstood.* We have thus far spoken of a direct, inwrought assurance. This has no connection with the understanding. The feeling of hope produced by it is an essential part of the new being. It is simply a living, spiritual consciousness of oneness with Christ. The witness, in this form, has no need to be comprehended. That which is liable to be misunderstood consists of those feelings created in the soul by the Holy Spirit, which, when reflected upon, or put upon the stand and interrogated, may be regarded as bearing witness to the believer that he is born of God. Of these there are two classes, — first, those spiritual graces which are the *fruits* of regeneration; and secondly, those feelings which are incidental and peculiar to the Christian state. The former may be called the *characteristics*, the latter the *signs* of regeneration. These, especially the latter, are liable to be misunderstood. Every minister of the gospel finds persons in exercise of Christian feelings, without any idea that such is their character. When informed that the feelings they possess are common to all true Christians, and never attendant upon an unrenewed state, the announcement is received as incredible.

Nor is there any absurdity, but, on the other hand, a perfect naturalness in the supposition that such may be the case. It may result through man's natural misapprehension of spiritual things. Christ was not seldom unknown by the men to whom he presented himself. "He came unto his own, and his own received him not." He was often unrecognized by his disciples, when in personal intercourse with them. Jacob, at Bethel, said, "The Lord is in this place, and I knew it not." The subject of regeneration, though well instructed in religious things, invariably finds the Christian state to be quite diverse from his previous conception. Hence, when he first comes to the exercise of Christian feelings, he ordinarily discredits them, they are so unlike his natural ideal; and for a brief period he conceives of himself as having gone back into a state worse than the first. Sometimes, rather by way of exception, he receives confidence at once, proceeding from the fact that his condition is so new and unanticipated; but soon, from the same cause, he plunges into the depths of doubt and despondency. The soul must become somewhat used to its new kind of life, before it can acquire the habit of relying upon it as the life desired. It is disabused of its false conceptions only with the greatest difficulty. Indeed, it is never perfectly done in this world. Our Saviour had constantly occasion to remove from his disciples their carnal notions of spiritual things.

This originally false conception of the spiritual graces may abide with the newly-converted soul for a period of time, greater or less, according to the tenacity with which it has been held; and especially may it be so if the subjective witness be withheld or suppressed.

This misapprehension is, however, quite as likely to exist with reference to what we call the *signs*, as the characteristics of regeneration. There are certain exercises of mind, incident and peculiar to the Christian state, which it is natural should be misconceived. This arises from want of instruction and information in regard to the peculiarities of the inward Christian character. The true Christian has many feelings which he is ashamed of, and ought not to possess. Hence he discloses them with reluctance, and only as duty requires. The prevailing view, therefore, of the peculiar mental states of the Christian is a disproportionate one. Greater prominence is given to their happy and inviting aspects, than to those of an opposite character. The fact, for instance, that the Christian is ordinarily penetrated with a sense of personal sin and guilt, does not hold so prominent a place in the expressions of Christians as in their hearts. Such a sense of sin is an essential feature of a regenerate state. It is one of those feelings which, if put upon the stand and interrogated, will bear witness to the believer that he is born of God. But the fact is not adequately understood. So deficient is the common impression respecting it, that young Christians are often alarmed because they possess this feeling. They understand it as witnessing *against* and not *for* them. So, also, with the believer's painful sense of his short-comings in all spiritual attainments. This feeling is a symptom of a regenerated state, while at the same time it conduces to suppress the hope of the believer, and, when combined with other causes, often does it effectually.

When regeneration occurs, as it ordinarily does, in early life, the youthfulness of the subject contributes to the same result. If the subjective witness, which does not require reflection, be suppressed, then the objective, which does require it, is likely to fail of being understood. Of the examples in illustration of this aspect of unrecognized regeneration, most are instances of conversion in very early life. Conversion has been unidentified by these persons, from the want of a discernment of their exercises by others, and of suitable encouragement and instruction, especially as to their own experience. In numerous instances it proceeds from the reluctance of parents to encourage their children, when very young, lest they should be deceived. In some instances it arises from positive discouragement, when the child is inclined to hope. In general, the cause is want of encouragement, occasioned by the difficulty of discerning the minute exercises of young children, and by their natural reluctance freely to express to their parents their religious feelings. An example representing this class, is that of a lady who had remained in a state of unidentified regeneration from the age of twelve to twenty-six. At that early period she was the subject of religious impressions; but, on account of her youth, her mother feared to encourage her. Hence, possessing the self-distrusting and humble spirit of every new-born soul, and naturally thinking that her mother knew better than herself whether she were a Christian, she regarded her exercises as of no account, and remained for fourteen years waiting, in vain, to receive a new experience.

5. *Unacknowledged Regeneration.* — Regeneration involves enlightenment as to one's own character, and all spiritual things. It produces also thorough honesty, great humility, and entire self-distrust. These combine to render a work of grace unacknowledged by the subject of it. They so completely penetrate the soul as to oppress the witness struggling to bear its testimony, and also to overbalance the other graces of faith and trust in Christ. They are so prevalent, and hold such dominion in the heart, that the testimony of outward observers as to the spiritual state of the individual is of no avail. The various features of the new man are out of due proportion. The graces which look self-ward are too strong for those which look Christ-ward. The former, unbalanced by the latter, assume a morbid action. All the symptoms which exist in the case are unfavorably interpreted. Out of deep sincerity and self-enlightenment produced by the Spirit, an extreme fear of self-deception arises. This feeling, unrestrained by trust in Christ, assumes unlimited sway in the soul. It forbids all acknowledgment of renewal by the Spirit until every shade of doubt is removed; and this intensifies shades into the darkness of night.

Sometimes this feeling assumes the form of a desire to be thorough, which is cherished by the individual as of supreme importance. He must be so thorough, that to advance becomes impossible. Or, if advancement should occur, it would be unacknowledged as such, unless he realized in it his ideal of thoroughness.

This condition has various shades of positiveness. The graces are less unevenly balanced in some cases than in others. In all instances, while no influences from without are interposed, it is self-perpetuating and self-strengthening. The longer it continues, the more confirmed it becomes. The greater the growth, the greater the disproportion. The more the habit of discrediting Christian feelings is cherished, the more difficult it is to abandon it. The state is ordinarily entered into, from causes which have been mentioned, in early youth, and grows with the person's growth to perfect maturity.

In many instances the subject of unacknowledged regeneration is deeply awakened at the recurrence of every revival through which he passes. He makes a serious and honest effort to realize his ideal of a Christian character, but in vain. These repeated, unsuccessful efforts to become a Christian, not only reäct upon and confirm his belief that he is not a Christian, but tend to produce a belief that he never can be.

In other but rare instances, the individual resorts to pleasure-seeking, to irreligious society, *apparent* hostility to religion, fault-finding with Christians, with the providences of God, and the doctrines of the Bible, — all to stifle the monitions of his quickened conscience. He manifests, also, seeming opposition to revivals of religion, the basis of which is not hatred of true religion, but rather envy of those who possess it. His opposition to revivals is aroused, not because of his conviction of their uselessness and mischievousness, as he alleges it is, but because he cannot, with others, be a sharer in the benefits which he is conscious they confer.

The consideration that he resorts to pleasure-seeking, to irreligious society, and that he opposes revivals of religion, which he supposes is based upon actual hatred of them, reäcts upon his belief that he has never known the grace of God. It does so naturally. Having been spiritually enlightened, he has a lively sense of the exceeding wickedness of these things; and this produces a deep conviction that he is in an unregenerate, if not a reprobate, state. The supposition that he is not a Christian, has caused him to elevate his standard of piety above the actual into the ideal. This gives to his religious sense an unrestrained and morbid action, which assists to remove beyond the region of the possible the idea of his being in a regenerate state. Thus it is that when this state has been once induced, it perpetuates and confirms itself.

An instance illustrating the self-perpetuating nature of this condition is that of a gentleman, forty-five years of age, who gives evidence of having been renewed at the age of fifteen. From that time, according to his confession, he has been almost constantly the subject of deep and strong religious emotions. Repeatedly, in times of revival, he has been openly an earnest seeker of salvation. Pious friends have prayed with him and for him, and still his condition remains the same. His exercises at the age of fifteen exhibit all the appearance of a genuine work of grace. His apprehension of spiritual things is apparently as profound and clear as that of the most intelligent and devoted Christians. His sense of his sinfulness and lost condition without a Saviour, possesses a thoroughness seldom witnessed. No self-righteousness or self-reliance is to be found in his feelings. He has often been an agonizing suppliant for salvation, both in public and in private; and yet the idea of his having been converted, is rejected as repugnant and absurd. His feeling of sinfulness and unworthiness has become so dominant in his mind as to prevent the recognition of his being already in the hands of a compassionate Saviour. His repentance seems to be truly profound and sincere, without the least conception that he has been forgiven. The graces of faith and hope are crushed by the dominion of conviction of sin and of self-condemnation. The one class of feelings, by long-continued exercise, have become so strong, and the other, by as long-continued neglect, have become so weak, that the perpetuation of the condition, without some special divine interposition, seems inevitable. His sense of his utterly lost condition has so increased as to cause him to demand a more exalted work of grace to meet his necessity than it is the privilege of mortals ever to receive. The experience which he conceives he must have, to warrant the belief that he has been renewed, is such as no Christian would profess to have enjoyed; and his conception of this experience has become the more vivid with every successive, and, as he supposes, fruitless awakening.

Illustrations of the causes which produce and perpetuate a condition of unacknowledged regeneration in its milder degrees of positiveness, might be given, but space will not allow.

The assertion that persons in a state of unacknowledged regeneration sometimes resort to pleasure-seeking, to irreligious society, to fault-finding with Christians and the providences of God, and even assume, for a time, an *attitude* of hostility to religion, will be received with distrust by most, and perhaps rejected by many, as absurd and injurious to true religion. The position, therefore, from which the statement is made must be fully apprehended. Such a declaration would not be warranted were not the conviction of its truthfulness produced by the force of irresistible facts; nor would it be made were it not believed that its proper understanding and use will subserve the well-being of many souls.

There is nothing in the position to disparage the power of the gospel, and nothing contrary to the supposition that such persons are in a regenerate state, which is unacknowledged; but, on the other hand, we find in it an argument for both. It shows that true religion, even when unrecognized and unacknowledged by the possessor of it, and consequently when its force is greatly impaired, has yet sufficient power so to quicken man's conscience, and the demands of his religious nature, as to put him forever more in a state of disquietude until the monitions of conscience are obeyed, and these demands met by a hearty embrace of the gospel. The individual resorts to pleasure-seeking, not because his regeneration, though unacknowledged, has so *little* effect upon him, but because it has so much. It creates a felt want in him which spiritual things only can supply. He seeks to satisfy it in other ways, but in vain. His renewed nature allows him no satisfaction till he comes back and seeks it at the same source that had power to produce its renewal.

This is according to the testimony of those who have been in this condition. A gentleman having had such an experience for several years, says of himself: "I resorted first to the reading of novels, with which to satisfy myself, but in vain; then to works of the most solid and instructive kind, with the same result. I did this, too, under a sense of guilt, knowing that true religion only could ever satisfy my wants, the truth of which has been fully proved." The case of a lady is present to the writer's mind, who sought to suppress the uprisings of the new life within by endeavoring, through the aid of infidel writers, to destroy in her mind the authority of the Bible, upon the ground that it contained inconsistencies in its statements. She declared it contradicted itself, and she did not believe it was true. But the assertion was made in a manner indicating that she was stung to the heart by a quickened conscience, whose power she was attempting to resist. A gentleman, also, who is now an influential member of a Christian church, relates at length his experience as having been of this peculiar kind, from the age of twelve to thirty-three. He represents himself as having been driven by the unacknowledged spiritual cravings of his soul to endeavor to satisfy himself with the doctrine of Universal Salvation, with Infidelity, Atheism, and irreligious society, until he was obliged to return for peace to the source from which he had departed.

We have said, also, that there is nothing in the position to invalidate the belief that such persons are in a regenerate state. The departures from a proper Christian course which have been cited, are not so serious as many instances of transient apostasy recorded in the Scriptures, even by inspired men. It will be said that David and Peter quickly came to repentance. The testimony of this class of persons, also, is that they have had no peace until, sooner or later, they were constrained to do the same. They have, also, no internal disrespect for true religion, even where the attitude of hostility is assumed. We cite the case of a lady who, though religiously educated, appeared for several years to be an opposer of religion. She confesses that all the while she had a lively internal sense of its worth, and of her guilt in not embracing it. The appeals of the gospel always had a particular claim upon her. When her husband was converted, she felt that she could no longer endure his society. Yet she confesses, upon a review of her feelings, that she had no dislike of true religion, but a real desire to possess it; and that her seeming opposition was simply dissatisfaction and disquiet because she could not secure the treasure which others were obtaining.

### § II. — Why unrecognized by others.

We shall present now some of the reasons why regeneration is often unrecognized by others than the subject of it. The first is, that a change of heart is not in all cases accompanied by a corresponding change in the outward life. So far as morality and an external regard for religion are concerned, there is, in many instances, no occasion for outward change. This is the case with children, among whom unrecognized regeneration commonly occurs. It is often felt that when they are converted they ought to become men and women, instead of being Christian children. Parents frequently look for too much evidence in the outward life of their children, and regard too little their change of feelings. They are, almost uniformly, from the influence of natural affection, either too ready or too reluctant to credit their conversion. They imagine that conversion will at once remedy all the defects of previous parental discipline, and prevent farther trial with them. They not unfrequently require them to manifest more of the spirit of religion in the family than they exhibit themselves. If this is not realized, their conversion is unacknowledged, and greater evidence is desired. The feelings of the child being thus crippled and discouraged, the desired change does not appear.

Sometimes the conversion of the young is put to tests unduly severe. From fear of self-deception, all encouragement to profess religion is withheld until they shall prove their ability to maintain a more godly life without the aid of a profession than mature Christians do with it. The result is, that they are unrecognized as being Christians, their new life is oppressed, and the evidence they exhibit becomes less and less.

This occurs in times of revival. Even when the utmost watchfulness is exercised, the young and the naturally retiring will come in the press behind and touch the hem of the Saviour's garment, unrecognized by all but the Saviour himself. There is a tendency, also, to accredit conspicuous conversions, and discredit the opposite. Other things being equal, the more conspicuous they are, the more credit they obtain, though on that account no more deserving.

The want of a well-cultivated discernment of the religious characters of men, is also a reason why regeneration is unrecognized. If sole reliance is placed upon the phenomena of the outward life, the work of grace will often occur unobserved. With the young, the retiring and obscure, the observation must be directed to the feelings of the heart. To be able always to discover the workings of the Spirit among such, requires a facility for ascertaining the temper of the heart when the channels of communication are very imperfect.

Another reason why regeneration is not recognized by others is, because it is not recognized by the individuals themselves. If a person does not claim to be a Christian, he is not commonly regarded as such, especially if he insists that he is *not* a Christian. Every truly converted person has at the first a reluctance, arising from self-distrust and sense of unworthiness, to profess having been converted. If this reluctance prevails, the person is passed by as still unrenewed.

Another reason why regeneration is unrecognized by others is, that it is not always accompanied by the external fruits, such as professing religion and performing its outward duties. That such fruits should be looked for, is legitimate. But the cases we are considering are exceptions. If the fact that one is born again is not recognized by him, then we should not expect him to act as if he recognized it, but should anticipate a suppression of the proper fruits. This suppression of the fruits reäcts unfavorably upon the inward life, and this, in turn, diminishes the fruits, and so impairs the outward evidence. If a person does not regard and treat himself as a Christian, but as being still unrenewed, and if he is so regarded and treated by others, it must hinder rather than nurture and develop his Christian growth and activity.

## CHAPTER III.

### RESULTS OF UNRECOGNIZED REGENERATION.

THE consequences attendant upon unrecognized regeneration can be appreciated only by a distinct apprehension of the condition, and by personal labor with those who are suffering from it. They vary according to the aspect of the case. Common to all its aspects is a dwarfed condition of the new creature, the loss of Christian happiness, growth, and usefulness, and, in many instances, the casting of doubt, gloom, and fear over the subsequent Christian life.

One of the results not least to be lamented, is, that from this source proceed false and practically injurious sentiments respecting Christian experience and the character of unconverted men. For example, relief from this condition, which, from an apparent similarity, is commonly regarded as conversion, is, in a large proportion of cases, gradual, characterized by no marked exercises of mind. The individual is a Christian already, in all but merely taking to himself the name. There is, therefore, simply a gradual transition of the mind to a state of conscious trust and repose in Christ. This causes Christians to remark that regeneration is sometimes a gradual work, as in their own experience. The fact that they suppose they became Christians gradually, without any severe mental struggle, causes unconverted men to hope to do the same, which prevents their earnest seeking.

In other instances, the transition from an unrecognized to a recognized state of regeneration is more sudden and marked, but wanting in a growing conviction of sin. The individual has been convicted already. The process consists now chiefly in a struggle, often severe, to surrender himself into the hands of Christ, to be disposed of according to his mercy. This gives rise to the erroneous and injurious sentiment that conversion *may* take place without conviction of sin.

Those also who regard their transition to a recognition of their spiritual state, and to a consciousness of trust in Christ, as their initial experience, conceive of all their previous history as being of an unrenewed character. This occasions false views of an unregenerate condition, and inappropriate treatment of unconverted persons. They are regarded as being penetrated with a sense of personal sin and need of a Saviour, and as requiring only to be invited and urged to accept of Christ. They are taught that there is no need to wait for conviction. They must simply resolve at once to forsake their sins, and serve Christ, and do it deliberately, as they would undertake any worldly business. The error is, that they conceive the condition of unconverted men to be the same with that of themselves when in a state of unrecognized regeneration. They suppose them to possess the same spiritual power to comply with these directions, while they are yet dead in sin.

Such labor with unconverted men is either ineffectual, or results in false conversion. When directed to persons in the unrecognized state, it often produces what is supposed to be conversion, and on this account is thought to be suited to the unconverted. These effects of unrecognized regeneration are widely spread. Two classes of exercises are erroneously regarded as conversion. The one are false experiences, which this kind of treatment is calculated to produce when applied to unconverted persons; the other are those which constitute the transition from an unrecognized to a recognized regeneration. The result is a diversity of sentiment as to the legitimate phenomena of conversion, and the proper means to be used for securing it.

Not unfrequently persons having gradually come to a recognition of their regenerate state, and understanding from reason and Scripture that regeneration is not a gradual change, are harassed with anxiety and fear lest they have never experienced a genuine work of grace.

These are some of the general results of unrecognized regeneration. That aspect upon which most unhappiness is attendant, and which is most to be deplored, is the unacknowledged state. There being in this the nearest approach to recognized regeneration, the Christian life has more maturity than in the others, and suffers greater abuse. The internal witness demands a hearing, but is positively refused. The testimony of others, also, is rejected. Christ, in his grace, has redeemed the sinner and made him his; but he persists in disowning the relation. In this he sins against light, and suffers correspondingly.

The subject of unacknowledged regeneration has a profound conviction that he is hell-deserving, mitigated by no ray of hope or trust in an atoning Saviour. He can neither enjoy the dead calm of indifference and hardness, as do the unregenerate, nor the sweet and lively peace of penitence and forgiveness, as do those in a healthy regenerate state. He is in the position of a burdened, anxious, hopeless sinner, constantly being slain by the law, but never made alive in Christ. The Providence, the Word, and the Spirit of God, all combine with his own conscience to declare his condemnation, while he sees in them no atonement, and no redemption for his guilty soul. He esteems Christ, and the expiation he has made for sin, as being good, but inapplicable to him.

One of the most unfortunate results of this condition is the difficulty with which relief from it is obtained. Any new and marked experience which might serve as the basis of present evidence and hope, is inadmissible. The person must fall back upon evidence already received, which he is especially unwilling to do. He has solemnly and repeatedly resolved that he will never cherish the slightest hope upon the low ground he now occupies. He must have new light, an irresistible demonstration that he is born of God. But this is impracticable. He cannot receive sudden and striking evidence, and with the greatest difficulty can he be induced to cherish that which is feeble, that he may obtain stronger. He is like a young tree, which, having for a long time been bent to the ground, cannot easily be made to grow erect.

The subject of unrecognized regeneration is one whose inner being has been quickened by the Spirit. He differs from the unregenerate in that he is not hardened and indifferent, but possesses a nature deeply sensitive to spiritual things. His conscience has a peculiar keenness of edge and of action. The natural stupefaction and deadness of soul, caused by sin, are broken up. He has been endowed with spiritual sight, and sees deeply his need of salvation by Jesus Christ. The disclosure which has been made to him of his inward corruption, and the just displeasure of God, constantly agitates the depths of his soul. His inmost being is pervaded with a sense of guilt, and is greatly disquieted, not only by his own conscience, but by the providences, the government, the Word, and the Spirit of God. Such a man cannot be simply respectful to religious things, like the unenlightened. His agitated nature will impel him to some kind of religious action.

In the state of unacknowledged regeneration, this inward compunction induces a melancholy seriousness, and repeated struggles for deliverance and peace. In the other states, in some exceptional cases, the person is impelled by the same cause to an opposite course of life. He seeks for peace, by striving, not to obey, but to stifle the dictates of his quickened conscience. He tries not to hearken to the utterances of God, which are constantly falling upon his ear from within and without, but to silence them. The result is, he lives a life of contention with God and the monitions of his own enlightened nature. He betakes himself to apparent opposition to religion, to immoral practices and irreligious society, not because he despises things that are good, but to quell the commotions of his troubled soul. Thus he lives on, in utter abandonment of religious things, except as he is impelled, by the disquiet of his quickened but unadjusted nature, to oppose them, until, being unable to maintain the contest longer, he is brought, by some particular providence, and by the Spirit of God, to cease the strife, and yield himself to Christ in a sweet submissiveness unfelt before.

An instance in illustration is that of a lady, already mentioned as endeavoring to suppress the uprisings of the new life within, by seeking to find out inconsistencies in the Bible. When afflicted by the death of a child, her heart rose in opposition to God's dealing in the event. She declared it was unjust. He had no right to deprive her of her child. She could not and would not endure it.

But her opposition, too keen to be continued long, was soon broken, and melted into the sweetness of complete submission, which resulted in a public profession of religion, her original experience being referred to a period seven years prior to these events.

It may be asked how such a manifestation differs from that of an unconverted person under like circumstances. A parallel instance of an unconverted mother afflicted by the death of an only child, will illustrate. Instead of that distinct, keen perception of the hand of God dealing with her in the event, and that sharp scrutiny of his justice, which indicated a more than natural sense of the divine sovereignty over the guilty creature, this unregenerate mother turned herself about in a natural manner, to see by what means she might, ere long, be prepared to meet the child. Her first concern pertained to her relation to the child, and not to God; while, in the other case, it was the opposite. In the one instance, the end aimed at was a matter of selfishness; in the other, it was one of right and wrong between God and the creature. The one case indicated spiritual ignorance and indifference to the divine purpose; the other, great light and keen sensitiveness. The result, in the former instance, was submission and peace with God; in the latter, a fruitless issue of the blind and selfish effort to be prepared to meet the child.

Frequently these opposite results, assuming, from the same cause, at one time the form of opposition to God, and at another that of earnest seeking of him, are commingled together. Conscious unrest impels, now to one course, and now to the other. The strong man armed, and the stronger than he, are both striving to sit upon the throne. There is warfare, but no victory. The graces of the gospel and their opposites — loving and hating, seeking and rejecting, believing and denying, praying and opposing — are constantly arrayed against each other. The individual has in himself all the forces and unhappy consequences of a most orderless and unsuccessful warfare, which makes him, to Christian observers, a puzzle, a source of inexplicable perplexity and anxiety.

In this peculiar frame there is less despair of an adjustment of the moral forces of the soul, than where they are all combined in a false direction. In such a case, the individual employs in vain all his powers to realize his ideal of what it is to be a Christian. His sky is covered from day to day with unbroken cloud and gloom. But in these examples, black clouds and gleams of sunshine, wind and rain, are mingled together in utmost confusion. But the result is a speedy clearing up of the moral heavens into a cloudless and sunny firmament.

We record here, in illustration, the instance of a lady, at the age of twenty, who had been in the unrecognized state for seven years, but had now come into that particular phase of it just described. Possessing naturally marked peculiarities of mind, and being in a peculiar religious condition, her manifestations of feeling were of the most complicated nature. She gave expression at one moment to feelings, with reference to spiritual things, most revolting and absurd, and at another evinced an uncommon apprehension and tenderness. Her mind was filled with unbelief, objections, and obstacles, which were made to appear the more hideous, because illuminated with occasional gleams of spiritual light. It seemed as if Satan himself were putting forth his last effort to retain dominion of the soul, against the strivings of the Spirit of God. Though she gave expression to feelings such as to dissipate all hope, yet the traces of spiritual light and susceptibility which were mingled with them, produced the conviction that such a state of commotion must soon find a happy termination. So it was. As the contrary forces of tide and tempest agitate the ocean, and produce its purification and tranquillity, so the conflicting and raging elements of her soul soon wrought out the purity and peace of forgiveness and reconciliation with God.

A state of unrecognized regeneration is not a normal and healthy regenerate condition. Its results are, in general, of an unhappy nature, its influence being felt in various ways throughout the subsequent Christian life. In many instances, however, it is overruled for good, being used as discipline for securing the person's advancement in holiness, and his qualification for eminent Christian service. It has been remarked that transition from this to a recognized state of regeneration is commonly regarded as original conversion. This transition is not always effected at once. Sometimes a partial relief occurs, sufficient to enable the person to profess religion, and perform Christian duties, while yet his enjoyment is impaired, in consequence of the unhealthiness of the previous state. This sometimes continues through life, and sometimes is followed by another experience, which has been called a "Second Conversion," or the attainment of a "Higher Christian Life."[1]

[1] A volume recently issued, entitled the "Higher Christian Life," is devoted to a discussion of this experience. While the volume contains much that is stimulating, and otherwise useful to the Christian, it appears to view the subject of which it treats from a false position. What the author calls "second conversion"— not meaning by it a second regeneration — is treated as if it were a legitimate experience superinduced upon a healthy regenerate state, constituting a higher Christian life, attainable, either gradually or suddenly, by all. The representation is, that one element of salvation is experienced in original conversion, and another equally important

The proper view of this experience is, not that it is legitimate and necessary, nor perhaps that it deserves, in all respects, to be called a higher Christian life, but that it is compensatory, rendered necessary by a previous unhealthy or imperfect experience, and hence constitutes a higher attainment when compared with the previous condition, but not necessarily so when compared with a uniformly developed Christian character. The sudden development of a particular feature before suppressed, may give to it unusual prominence, while the character, as a whole, may not be unusually developed.

In regeneration, the person becomes a new creature in Christ, though upon an infantile scale. He has the beginning of a well-proportioned Christian character. The germ of all the graces is there, — the germ of trust in Christ for sanctification, as well as trust for justification. It is impossible that one should be produced without the other. A consciousness of either may be wanting, and hence its growth, through lack of cultivation, be suppressed, and the new creature become disproportioned. Trust in Christ for sanctification, may be more liable to this than trust for pardon. Circumstances may conspire to suppress this feature, while the others are developed. Subsequently, influences may combine to cause this previ-

in second conversion. In the first, the sinner trusts in Christ for justification, in the second for sanctification.

That such examples of Christian experience occur, is not questioned. The objection to the view taken of them by the author cited, is, that it presents the Christian character out of its due proportions, by giving to this feature of experience too prominent importance, and thus depreciating the original and only conversion. It is objected, also, that it represents the original work of the Spirit in conversion as incomplete, and the introduction of an entirely new element subsequently as essential.

ously suppressed grace to reäct from its confinement, and come forth into unusual prominence.

In unrecognized regeneration, the whole character is suppressed. In the case of unacknowledged regeneration, of long continuance, deliverance is liable to be delayed perhaps during life, and the injury never compensated in this world. In less confirmed stages, and in other aspects of the unrecognized state, reäction into a happy condition more frequently occurs. In such cases it is easy to conceive that the subsequent growth may become more vigorous, in consequence of the previous depression. Consciousness of trust in Christ for justification being more easily attained than that of trust for sanctification, this feature is likely to be recovered first from its oppressed condition; or the recovery of the two may be simultaneous. The restoration of the former is commonly regarded as original conversion, and the restoration of the latter, "second conversion," while regeneration is prior to them both. In such cases, the result of this unusual spiritual discipline may be an uncommon Christian attainment, especially in the direction of trust in Christ.

One cause of this, in unrecognized regeneration, is the fact that the first experience being unmarked by any recognized crisis, the person is obliged to base the evidence of his conversion preëminently upon faith, and not upon sight. Since he cannot fall back upon a marked initial experience to sustain his hope when weak, he is compelled to derive his evidence, to a greater degree than usual, from the constant presence of Christ, as would be better for those also who have been favored with a marked original conversion. There is, however, no uniformity in these exercises. All experiences are subject to great variation.

Facts show that unrecognized regeneration often results in the happy experience which is sometimes called "second conversion." A case in point is that of a gentleman who, having experienced religion at the age of eight, without recognizing the fact, spent a series of years in trying to settle the question whether he had ever been born again. Not being able to determine it by reference to the past, nor by obtaining a new and diverse experience, he was led by the Holy Spirit to resolve to leave that question evermore with God, and rely for his evidence upon a life of daily humiliation and penitence, trust in the atonement of Christ, and devotion to his cause. And the result is, entire freedom from doubt, and such a uniform and heavenly peace of mind, in trusting in the mercy of God through Jesus Christ, as is rarely attained.[1]

[1] The examples cited in the volume mentioned above, of persons who have experienced "second conversion," appear to be, originally, cases of unrecognized regeneration. Jonathan Edwards was, doubtless, converted in his boyhood, at a time of revival in his father's congregation, though he did not indulge hope for several years afterwards, and only as he attained to new experience. The religious history of Martin Luther contains evidence that the divine life was begun in his soul at the age of eighteen, though he did not recognize it until, in subsequent years, he had attained to a new and more marked experience. The exercises attendant upon his narrow escape from death by the thunderbolt, do not bear the marks of original conversion, but rather of the first stage of his transition from an unrecognized to a recognized and healthy regenerate state. At this time he obtains a consciousness of trust in Christ for justification, and at a subsequent period, for sanctification. The author of the "Higher Christian Life" regards the occasion of the thunderbolt as the time of his original conversion, and the latter occasion as his "second conversion;" whereas, his real conversion had, doubtless, taken place prior to the first event. The error, which is a common one, consists in regarding his coming to a full consciousness of his regenerate state, as the point of conversion. Edward Payson is mentioned as having experienced "second conversion," just before the close of life. His was originally a case of unrecognized regeneration, which may have been instrumental, in part,

Andrew Fuller seems to have afforded an example of unacknowledged regeneration, — having had intimations of his conversion, but rejecting them, and refusing to acknowledge himself as having been born again, until he had attained to a high degree of sanctification, through the instrumentality of a subsequent marked experience. By a similar discipline, God seems to have qualified John Owen, Thomas Halyburton, and numerous others, for the eminent service to which they were called. In harmony with these examples of "second conversion," so called, those which have come under our observation, are uniformly instances of originally unrecognized regeneration.

The view to be taken, therefore, of unrecognized regeneration, in its connection with this happy experience, is, that while it is not a condition to be desired, yet, like affliction, it is sometimes overruled, and perhaps appointed of God, for a special end. What is unfortunately called "second conversion," also, is not a legitimate or possible experience in a healthy regenerate state, but is compensatory in its nature, or a resultant from a previously suppressed condition, and is commonly, if not always, connected with unrecognized regeneration, — since the causes which suppress one grace are likely to suppress another. A legitimate and healthy experience, doubtless, consists of a uniform development of all the Christian graces, in the proportions in which they are originally produced by the Spirit in regeneration.

of the gloom which pervaded his Christian life, while it did not prevent his usefulness, but was perhaps overruled, and even designed, for its promotion. God may have seen that this discipline was necessary to his eminent service, and hence allowed him to attain to a cheerful view of himself just at the close of life, when his labors were done. Similar remarks are applicable, also, to Baxter, James Brainerd Taylor, and Adelaide Newton.

This question must now be considered: What evidence is there that this class of persons are in a regenerate state? It is to be remembered that they are not supposed to be in a healthy regenerate state, but in one which is oppressed for the want of nutriment and culture. Hence the evidences cannot be so full and clear as where there is a healthy and growing Christian life. The condition is exceptional, and not one which God designs man should ever occupy, except as he ordains all things that are.

First, we remark, that an unrecognized regenerate state is a *possibility*, involving no absurdity, while abundant causes exist for producing it. And, moreover, we should expect just such phenomena to be attendant upon it as are exhibited.

Secondly: These persons are thoroughly enlightened as to their sinfulness, their helplessness, and their need of salvation by Christ. They have a perception of spiritual things, which harmonizes with that of all Christians. This is one of the signs of a renewed condition. "The natural man receiveth not the things of the Spirit, . . . . neither can he know them, because they are spiritually discerned." These, then, are not natural men.

They are not only enlightened, but, for the most part, are humbled and penitent. They possess a tenderness of spirit, and sensitiveness to religious things, not common to the unrenewed heart. Nothing is more evident than that their natural pride has been bowed, though at times, as with every Christian, it rëacts and rises again. It is no more true that they are sinful, and neglectful of duty, and sometimes disobedient, than that they are penitent on account of it. This is the universal testimony of those who have for any length of time been subject to this condition, even such as have been at times rebellious. The pangs of guilt and sorrow have followed hard upon the footsteps of disobedience. Their natural hardness and stupidity are removed. The fallow ground of their hearts is broken up from its lowest depths. This is their permanent condition, and one which cannot be predicated of unregenerate men. The minds of these never settle down into natural stupidity and indifference. The uniform testimony of the unrecognized is that they are susceptible of religious impressions at all times; are always stirred by Christian exhortation and appeals, and by the preaching of the gospel; and are repeatedly anxious in seasons of revival, which, for a series of years, is not the case with unregenerate men. If awakening does not soften the soil of the heart, it hardens it.

Thirdly: Their *lives*, in most cases, correspond with the supposition that they are renewed persons. In a very large proportion of examples they possess as much of the spirit of the gospel as most professing Christians. Where phenomena of a different kind exist, they may be as well accounted for as can many unfavorable appearances in the lives of acknowledged Christians.

Fourthly: They create the same peculiar response in the hearts of others that is awakened by the Christian state, accredited as such upon common grounds. This response is elicited, though the judgment in regard to them is confused by other causes.

Again: When such persons are brought into a healthful Christian state, the process does not in all respects bear the marks of original conversion. It is commonly mistaken for it, but is essentially unlike it. It is better understood upon the supposition of a previous unrecognized regeneration. In some cases, the process involves no marked change; in others, the exercises are not so deep and strong as would otherwise be expected; in others they are strangely violent, and of unexpectedly brief duration. There is no growing conviction of sin. There are no new convictions in kind. Relief is obtained differently. It comes rather in the form of renewed consecration to God, than of original brokenness of heart, submission, and acceptance of Christ. There is more of the creature's action, and less of the display of God's sovereignty. In the one case, the individual deliberately and earnestly resolves to *come* to Christ, to trust him and serve him; in the other, he is *brought* to Christ in a way that he knows not. When the subject of unrecognized regeneration is brought out of that condition, he manifests, also, greater maturity, more spiritual knowledge and strength, than would be expected in case it were his real conversion. In many instances, also, persons of this class have more striking evidences of their conversion than do the newly-converted, which serves to free them permanently from the doubts to which others, especially young Christians, are commonly subject. The previous state of unrecognized regeneration is compensated by unusual confidence. In short, it is according to the uniform confession of such persons, when they have examined their exercises, that at that time they had no vital change in their views or feelings. It is a change only in degree. Such persons also, in after-life, most commonly are in doubt about this as being their conversion. They think it possible they might have been converted before, yet conclude to disown it. Besides, at some period in their former lives, exercises having an appearance of true conversion are, for the most part, if not always, discoverable.

Finally: This is confessedly a peculiar religious condition, and one which, it is believed, can be accounted for only upon the hypothesis here submitted. It differs from that of unrenewed men in general, and from what the Scriptures call an enlightened, but reprobate state, to which some of its features have a seeming correspondence. It is evident that these persons are not among the reprobate, because they possess tenderness of heart, humility and penitence, and are also frequently, and doubtless always, eventually, brought into a healthful Christian state. And moreover, it is believed that this hypothesis will not only explain all the peculiarities in the case, but also furnish a key to the legitimate phenomena of regeneration, which is greatly to be desired as the means of reducing to unity and harmony the diversity of sentiment which exists in regard to the proper features of conversion, and the means to be employed for securing it.

## CHAPTER IV.

### REMEDY OF UNRECOGNIZED REGENERATION.

In considering the remedy to be applied to this unhealthy religious condition, we shall inquire as to the means of preventing it, and then as to the means of its removal. So far as means for preventing it exist, we remark that they lie chiefly in the hands of the religious guardians and teachers of the young. The state of unrecognized regeneration ordinarily originates in the conversion of children, and commonly in times of revival. It is the tendency of the multiplied facilities for the religious instruction of the young, to increase both the number and the earliness of early conversions. The result is, that, of all the real conversions which occur, a larger proportion take place in youth and childhood, at the present time, than ever before. It has been shown that children, when truly converted, are less likely to make it known than adults; and that their conversion, for a variety of reasons, is more liable to be overlooked by others.

The causes of unrecognized regeneration among children, are found in the characteristics of childhood, and in the nature of true conversion, and will always exist. No improvement of their religious education will prevent it. The prevention is to consist chiefly in the application of instruction and encouragement at the time of conversion. Nor can these be applied subsequently with the same effect. If they are withheld just when most needed, their loss can never be repaired. We do not mean that young persons, when first converted, need to be informed that they are Christians. This would be inappropriate, and worse than useless. They require to be nurtured in accordance with the fact that they are infants in the kingdom of grace. This necessitates the cultivation of a careful discernment of an initial experience, as it exists in children and youth, combined with a closer watchfulness over the feelings of the young at the time of their interest in religious things. So safe a judgment cannot subsequently be formed as to whether a change has taken place.

The *remedy* of unrecognized regeneration pertains to the treatment appropriate to those who are still in this condition. But the question will first arise, how these persons may be known. To this it is answered, that they may be known by their *peculiar language.* All Christians speak a peculiar language, but these a peculiar dialect of it. They may be as readily distinguished, both from unconverted men and from professing Christians, by their language, as Christians are from unconverted men. The chief peculiarity which modifies their expressions is their belief that they are *not* converted. This is common to all persons of this class. If they are interrogated, or if it is intimated that they may have been converted, their belief assumes the form of a positive denial, made in a tone of peculiar sensitiveness. They have deep feeling about it. When asked if they do not *desire* to be Christians, they answer that they do not know as they have any special desire; or, they do not think they have much desire; or, they have not such as they ought to have. They freely acknowledge that they ought to be Christians, but do not think they ever shall be. They do not think religion is for them. If interrogated about former exercises, they disclaim having had any, or such as were of any account. They had convictions when quite young, and were for a while interested; but their convictions soon wore off, and their interest died away.

These expressions differ from the language of unconverted men. *They* acknowledge that they are not Christians, but do not assert it with so much positiveness and depth of feeling. They think they *do* desire to be Christians very much, and at some time they shall be. They have always intended it, and have thought a great deal about it, but have neglected it. When they have a more convenient season, they mean to attend to it, and become true Christians.

The reason which persons in the unrecognized state uniformly give for not believing they are Christians, is, that they do not *live* like Christians. If the suggestion is made that they may have been converted in early life, they declare positively that it is not possible they should have been converted and have lived as they have done. The idea is revolting to their spiritual sense. This feeling these persons retain after being brought out into a recognized state. They have been so long accustomed to look upon their previous life as unregenerate, that it is almost impossible for them to change their views.

These remarks will suffice to assist somewhat in identifying this class of persons. A safe judgment, however, can be formed only by a minute acquaintance with their entire religious history. Personal experience and observation, moreover, are requisite to furnish facility in detecting this peculiar religious condition. The subject will be prevented also from awakening false hopes in the unconverted. If a person, not having hitherto indulged hope, is inclined to think that possibly he may be in the unrecognized state, this will be proof that he is not so; since those who are in this condition uniformly disown it. Nor is the case at all applicable to those who have once indulged hope, but lost it.

Many individuals of this description are brought into a state of spiritual healthiness, in times of revival, under the same treatment that is applied to unconverted persons, this being well suited to certain aspects of this condition. Others pass through repeated revivals without any happy result beyond a new awakening, because of their need of treatment specially suited to their peculiar state. Not unfrequently, also, God uses affliction to accomplish this result; but this often loses its appropriate effect, for the want of being accompanied by a special application.

Proper treatment will vary according to the state in which an individual may be found. In many instances of simply unidentified regeneration, the person is, to all intents and purposes, a Christian, except that he does not so regard it, and of course does not profess it. What he needs, therefore, is to be led to look upon himself as being in a regenerate state, and act accordingly. This is usually best accomplished by instructing him as to the nature of his religious exercises, showing that they are of a spiritual character, that his peculiar feelings are the feelings of all true Christians. He has not been accustomed so to regard them, and will be surprised, on a comparison of his feelings with those of acknowledged Christians, to discover their similarity. This will give him a new view of himself; and he will gradually come to cherish hope, and be ready to perform any known duty. Any means by which such persons can be persuaded to take upon them the *duties* of a Christian, will be of service. Sometimes it is necessary for them to begin to *act* like Christians, to produce a feeling that they are such. The action begets evidence, and then the evidence and the action strengthen each other. They may therefore be urged to make a public profession of religion without delay, since the longer it is deferred the more reluctant they will be to perform the duty. To exhort and pray with and for such persons as if they were unconverted, serves only to promote the feeling that they are not converted, which stands directly in their way.

In other instances of merely unidentified regeneration, there seems to be needed, and often occurs, a renewed conviction of sin, humbling of pride and submission to Christ, the exercises being frequently even more deep and strong, though of shorter duration, than in the first experience. This occurs where there has been long neglect of personal religious duties, such as secret prayer and attendance upon the means of grace; also where there has been departure from a proper mode of life, apparent opposition to religion, and a resort to irreligious society or immoral practices. Hence appropriate treatment in these cases will be mostly similar to that which is adapted to unconverted persons. It differs from the last described, in that no intimation should be given to the individual that he may previously have been converted. He should be led to see his sin, espeially what light he has rejected and privilege abused, which will be the prominent features of his convictions.

One important element should be introduced into the treatment of a person in this condition, which is not appropriate to an unconverted state. He should be urged to a committal of himself to one final struggle for his salvation, which, if it do not succeed, he will expect to be his last. He should be led, if possible, to resolve to commence an effort which must continue till he finds or is lost. He should be persuaded now, once and forever, to cast his soul upon the mercy of God, through Jesus Christ. He will be reluctant to make the committal, and will, perhaps, repeatedly decline; but the point must not be yielded. If it be gained, there is ground of confidence in a speedy and happy result. There is special reason to believe that the Spirit will use the means, because God already has the soul in charge. A work has been begun which must be completed. This will be felt by one who labors with such an individual, as it is never felt with regard to an unconverted person not specially under the Spirit's influence.

This is presented rather as an illustration, than as a rule to be followed. It cannot be determined beforehand, in any given case, precisely what treatment would be appropriate. Treatment appropriate to one case would not be to another, and what might be successfully employed by one person could not by another. We have presented the illustration, because such treatment has in many instances been attended with happy results.

One thing in connection with this subject must be mentioned in passing. It is, that many of the representatives of this class of persons are in a condition which encourages personal labor with them at any time. Some need to be brought under the influence of powerful religious awakening. But many are at all times in a position well suited to constitute the starting-point of a work of grace among a people. They have constantly within them the germs of a revival. If these are developed, and the individual brought into a recognition of his regenerate state, it has the effect upon others of a real conversion. Special labor with unconverted men under ordinary circumstances, does not necessarily give promise of success. We may secure from *them* pledges and promises, but shall not have such a guarantee of their fulfilment as exists in connection with the persons under consideration.

It remains only to speak of the treatment appropriate to those who are in an extreme state of unacknowledged regeneration. And here we confess our ignorance of the means best adapted to their relief. They seem to baffle all efforts put forth in their behalf. No revival is suited to their case; for they are already deeply, and even morbidly, awakened to a sense of their lost condition and need of Christ. New awakening only confirms their unhappy condition. All prayer, instruction, encouragement, and labor, they turn to their disadvantage. Their morbid state converts everything it feeds upon into nutrition for its own unhealthiness. If they are regenerate persons, they will be saved at the last; but whether they shall ever be brought into a healthful Christian state in this world, and by what specific means, we have yet to learn. We know not but they may die as they are, and, like the righteous in the twenty-fifth chapter of Matthew, be welcomed into the kingdom prepared for them from the foundation of the world, while denying their preparation to be the recipients of such a heavenly boon at the hands of a gracious Saviour. We leave them at the disposal of a Being whose judgments are unsearchable, and his ways past finding out.

# PART II.

## UNRECOGNIZABLE REGENERATION;

OR,

## HOPE WITHOUT FAITH.

# UNRECOGNIZABLE REGENERATION.

## CHAPTER I.

### ASPECTS OF UNRECOGNIZABLE REGENERATION.

It has been already stated that there are many professing Christians who do not know when they were converted. It is added now, that there are also others who do not know they *never* were converted. The former were said to be in a state of unrecognized regeneration. These are the subjects of what we shall call *unrecognizable regeneration*, it being the opposite of the former, — the one being true regeneration taken for false; the other, false taken for true. We shall use the term unrecognizable as conveying this idea, denoting a merely assumed regeneration supposed to be recognized as genuine. This *is* an unrecognizable regeneration.

The persons who compose this class must be distinctly borne in mind. We do not mean all who believe they are Christians, and are not; but only those who, without sufficient cause, suppose themselves to be such upon an evangelical basis. They are not intentional deceivers, but self-deceived. They are naturally honest, but spiritually hypocritical.[1] They think they are Christians, not know-

[1] For the distinction between natural and spiritual honesty, see Third Part, page 198.

ing that their piety is feigned. Nor do they think so unwittingly, merely cherishing a vague fancy or idle whim, that they are converted. A religious change is experienced, closely resembling the new birth in form, but in spirit essentially diverse.

That a class of persons who are self-deceived exists, is commonly admitted as probable. Our Saviour declares that many will say in that day, "Lord! Lord!" to whom he will say, "I never knew you." The most important inquiry is, Who are they that compose this class? Can they be known? and can anything be done for their relief, or to prevent the self-deception of others? To meet these inquiries is, in the main, the present design. We shall seek to accomplish it by considering the *aspects*, the *causes*, the *results*, and the *remedy* of a state of unrecognizable regeneration.

We shall describe some of the features of unrecognizable regeneration by contrasting it with the unrecognized, to which, in each of its aspects, it stands opposed.

The self-deceived professor of religion, in contrast with the subject of *unconscious* regeneration, represents himself as possessing a *highly positive* consciousness of being under the Spirit's influence. Instead of being *un*conscious, he is *more* than conscious. He brings spiritual things almost into the region of the sensible. His mind localizes them. It assigns to them exact limits and definite forms. The change he has experienced does not seem so subtle and refined that it is almost impossible for him to realize it, but distinct and marked. It is manifest to him that he is very different in all respects. His experience is not vital, pertaining to the temper of the heart, but one of form. It is a change of attitude in the religious affections, and not of quality. This involves motion, and hence an approach to what is physical and sensible,—it being characteristic of the natural man, as did Nicodemus, to take carnal views of spiritual things. Not having been taught by the Holy Spirit the peculiar dialect of the Christian, the language which the individual uses to describe his change is common and unspiritual. He expresses himself in such language as, having "found a hope," or as having just "started" or "set out" to be a Christian.[1] A hope, instead of being a mysterious life in the soul, he conceives of as something which he has discovered and taken into his possession. His beginning to be a Christian is a "starting" or "setting out" to go somewhere. Or if he uses terms which Christians employ in relating their exercises, he impregnates them with the same common, natural spirit. This is because the natural man comprehendeth not the things of the Spirit. And he cannot express what he does not comprehend.

In other instances, the exercises of the false professor are purely intellectual. His experience is in the head, and not in the heart; in his views, rather than affections. It does not reside in the consciousness, but in the understanding. It is on this account that such persons, in relating their experience, are often spoken of as being very clear, seeming fully to comprehend the work wrought in them, as they can any matter of intelligence or process of reasoning,—intellectual operations being more easily comprehended than heart-changes. The mysteries of godliness not having been brought before their minds, they relate what they suppose to be God's dealings with them by his Spirit, in an easy, familiar, business-like manner. They

[1] These and like expressions are unspiritual language, and constitute, at least, an unfavorable symptom, inasmuch as they denote an erroneous, natural *conception* of spiritual things.

can distinctly mark the bounds and progress of his mysterious operations within them, from the beginning to the end. Sometimes, however, such persons do remark that they cannot describe their feelings, the reason evidently being that they have none to describe,—difficulty of utterance arising not from mysteriousness, but destitution of inward experience.

The subject of unrecognizable regeneration seems to himself to have strong faith—so strong that it is almost turned to sight. It appears in this respect remarkable, and quite in advance of the faith of most true Christians. He thinks he is sensible, also, that his prayers are heard and answered—thinks he has the precise things asked for, and in the manner marked out. He asks and receives favors from God as he would from any earthly friend, comprehending the process with the same ease.

The false professor speaks as if he had a *full* consciousness of the forgiveness of his sins. It is quite clear to him that they are *all* forgiven. He thinks he has a *perfect* consciousness of loving Christ, and of being loved by him. He is as sensible that he loves Christ, and that Christ loves him, as he is that he loves his earthly friends, and is loved by them. His love for Christ, and his conception of Christ's love for him, are of a temporal and carnal nature. There is nothing incomprehensible or mysterious in them. His religious sense easily and perfectly embraces both. Indeed, it embraces his whole duty to God, and all God's dealings with him.

In unrecognizable regeneration we have the opposite of that which is *unobserved.* In this false work the individual very *distinctly* observes the process which he is undergoing. He looks at it, and reflects upon it, as leisurely and unconcernedly as if another, and not himself, were the subject of it. He inspects his anxieties and fears, his sense of sin and of God's displeasure, his repentance, and faith, and joy, and love, as coolly as if they were events of outward occurrence with which he had no vital connection. He notes the process of being slain and made alive in Jesus Christ, as he would that of having an outer garment adjusted to his person, his inner life being scarcely more affected by the one than the other. He is more interested in his experience as a matter of personal history, than of right and wrong between himself and God. He conceives of it more as a desirable era in his career, than as an adjustment of a serious difference between himself and his Maker, and hence is more careful to mark it.

The subject of spurious conversion thinks he can almost perceive his exercises with the natural eye. The presence of Christ is conceived of as that of his almost visible appearance in human form, near the person or by his side. He speaks of the spiritual light that breaks in upon the soul, as if it were a physical illumination.[1] A young person, in relating her experience, declared that her room, at night, was actually lighted up, so that objects became visible. She united with the church, but in a twelvemonth was excluded — her light having gone out.

In other instances, the person has visions of spiritual things. Instead of walking by faith, he walks by sight. He has visions of Christ and heaven; and because of these, he believes he is a Christian. A lady, desiring to make a profession of religion, stated that she seemed to herself to be knocking earnestly at the gate of the heav-

1 We do not mean here that loveliness and beauty which sometimes come over nature when the sinner is forgiven, but something *conceived* of as a physical illumination, though, of course, understood not actually to be such.

enly city. She saw the gate presently thrown wide open; saw the golden streets, and the Saviour himself extending his arms, and inviting her to come in, a welcome guest. The narration affected her to tears; but in half a year her vision vanished, and all appearance of piety with it.

A young man, upon a sick-bed, supposing his end was near, professed to have met with a change. He conceived of himself as sailing off from the shore in a boat, which was fastened to the land by several cords, representing the ties that bound him to earth. He imagined himself as letting go of these, one after another, until he saw the last cut asunder, when his transport became intense. His unexpected recovery, however, soon dissipated whatever evidence he gave that he was prepared to die. In other instances, the individual observes the work of grace by the hearing of the ear. Passages of Scripture are distinctly uttered to him. Something seemed to say, "Thy sins be forgiven thee;" or he heard some other consoling Scripture.[1]

[1] These manifestations are to be understood as occurring in the crisis of the work, and as constituting to the person's mind the leading points of his evidence. In most instances, if the individuals are interrogated as to whether they rest upon these things as evidence, they answer in the negative, and perhaps honestly, though, after all, they are the primal source of their hope. They occur simultaneously with the removal of the burden, and commonly constitute its instrumental causes, which indicates that the work is not of the Spirit.

The reader will understand that this is the portraiture of a false conversion, so far as it forms a contrast with unrecognized regeneration, — the main idea being that the spirit of the one is too much suppressed to be healthy, while that of the other is too prominent to be true.

The question may arise whether some of these manifestations may not be found in a real conversion. We answer, that if any particular passage is interpreted according to the spirit of the whole description, it will be found to be inconsistent with that supposition. These are the manifestations which false conversion commonly assumes.

Sometimes the person who is in a state of unrecognizable regeneration, does not rely so much upon having definitely observed the original change. He hastens over his first experience, puts off examination of it, and dwells upon present intentions and plans for holy living in the future. Though he cannot point to any definite period when the change occurred, yet he thinks he distinctly observes in himself Christian feelings, evidences, and fruits.

The various phases of this aspect of the subject can be made familiar to the mind only by practical observation. The tones and inflections of the voice, to be understood, must fall upon the ear.

Persons who are deceived by a spurious conversion, often have a very distinct *recollection* of their experience. Exercises of which they are so sensible, and which they so definitely observe and comprehend, are not likely to be forgotten. Not being so profound, refined, or mysterious, as to baffle the understanding, they are conveniently retained in the memory. In unrecognized regeneration, the event is sometimes forgotten, because less importance is attached to it than it deserves; while here, for the opposite reason, it is very carefully remembered. Occasionally persons of this class seem to have laid up their religious experience in the memory with great care, for the purpose of thinking it over at their leisure, which they do with evident complacence and satisfaction. Their first exercises are the ground of their hope, and as such they are careful to preserve their recollection. They are so plain and easy to be understood, too, that they love to run them over. They say they remember precisely how God brought them along, as if they understood it well. It is flattering to their self-complacence and vanity to think that God should take special notice of them, and that they should have so clear an experience, and be able to understand so perfectly the Spirit's operations with them, while others often are so much in the dark. Hence they are careful to preserve these grateful recollections. They remember their experience better than they remember Christ.

The self-deceived professor also believes he distinctly *identifies* his experience as being a gracious work. It precisely meets his ideas of what a religious experience should be. This is, in part, because he is anxious to regard his conversion as genuine. He desires the comfort and ease of feeling that his case is all right with God, and will give him no more concern. This feeling overrules his honesty of heart. His self-righteousness predisposes him also to think more highly of his exercises than he ought. He conceives it altogether probable, beforehand, that they are sound and good. He has no suspicion that his heart is so vile as to deceive him. Besides, his experience is his own production, and would, of course, be according to his ideas of a proper one. Nor has he, on account of his spiritual blindness, any view of a genuine one, with which to compare it. He compares his own production with his own standard, and must of necessity suppose he identifies it. Hence his experience is of a model character. Its features are all good, and none are wanting. The spiritual frame is complete. He has kept all the Saviour's commandments, and asks, "What lack I yet?" The frame is also clothed with beautiful graces. The new man is well to look upon. He takes particular satisfaction in gazing upon his comely proportions; thinks he identifies the new creature as being a true, spiritual man, and he thanks God for it;—thanks God that he is not as other men are, especially that he is not like poor publicans.

The false professor believes he distinctly identifies the

work of the *Spirit* in his conversion. He sees clearly that God designed that certain events which occurred in his history should be used by the Spirit to bring him to Christ. The death of a friend, the loss of his property, or some other affliction, mysterious to him at the first, he came to see were just such as were needed by the Spirit as the means for accomplishing his gracious work. Or, he recognizes very distinctly the design of God in appointing some sermon, or meeting, or friend, to be the instrument of his conversion. Sometimes a trifling incident occurs, or a reflection spontaneously springs up in his mind, leading him suddenly to change his course and become religious, in which he discovers a remarkable interposition of the Holy Spirit. He has great facility in discerning the mysterious influences of the Spirit upon his heart; all of which is a work of mere religious fancy, or a suggestion of Satan.

Unrecognizable forms also a marked contrast with *unacknowledged* regeneration. The false professor is not reluctant to acknowledge himself a Christian. He has no inward struggle in regard to coming out from the world, and publicly professing the name of Christ. So far as propriety and modesty will allow, he is forward to do it. He is ready even to go beyond the word of the Lord, as did Saul, when he saved Agag and the best of the sheep and oxen for sacrifice. It is a source of pleasure to him to be called a Christian. His self-righteousness leads him to esteem it as a matter of right and just credit to himself. If this is questioned, he argues his own cause. His language is, "Lord, when saw I thee an hungered, and did not feed thee; or thirsty, and did not give thee drink?" "Have I not prophesied in thy name, and in thy name done many wonderful works?" He is even particular in regard to being acknowledged as a Christian; is anxious to be respected as such; thinks he is deserving of credit on the account, and desires to have his proper rank accorded to him. He is sensitive to being slighted, and will not bear rebuke.

Oftentimes the false professor breaks away from worldly pleasures and associates, and represents it as a great sacrifice and a serious struggle; whereas it is merely a matter of pride and honor, such as that which prompts a man of wealth to wish it known that he is rich. He desires it to be understood that he has made a great sacrifice and struggle, in order to be esteemed a heroic Christian, and one of high attainments, forgetting "that obedience is better than sacrifice," and that "the sacrifices of God are a broken spirit." The relation which such persons give of their experience is really an account of what good things they have done, and not what God has done for them. These manifestations, however, vary according to the disposition. If the individual is naturally modest and sincere, he is still forward to profess himself a Christian; but his object is to strengthen his hope as well as increase his security, — to which, he feels, that claiming publicly to be a Christian, and having his claim admitted, will greatly contribute. He declares himself to have been converted, and then implicitly asks of others if they do not indulge the same opinion; so that by the mouth of many witnesses it may be established.

The false professor manifests this forwardness to profess himself a Christian in various ways. He proclaims it in his pretensions to strict honesty in his dealings with men; in his benevolence and kindness to the poor; in abstaining from all immoral practices and irreligious society; in his advocacy of every system of benevolence and the cause of religion. He is ready to take his position with respect to these things at all times and in all places, — his supreme motive being to make himself appear to be, and so increase the probability that he is, a Christian. A proclamation is made of this in the matter and manner as well as in the forwardness of his public prayers and exhortations.

This same forwardness to be acknowledged as a Christian appears in the view he takes, and wishes to have taken of his experience. He interprets all the symptoms in his case favorably. By his practice, and his strong desire to have them so understood, he has become really well skilled in turning them all to good account. The tendency of all his feelings is in a plausible manner to make good his case. Nor would he hesitate, as in the case of the New Testament Pharisee, to disparage the experience of other poor Christians to make his appear the more excellent. Though ignorant of it, this motive lies concealed behind all his utterances. It prompts him to insist that he is very greatly changed; that he has been very deeply convicted of sin; has great love for Christ, and enjoys prayer very much at all times. If doubt is expressed as to any feature of his experience, he has an explanation for the seeming deficiency, which appears to him satisfactory. He ascribes it to some unfavorable circumstance attending the relation of it. He thinks he was not understood; believes if he were to relate his exercises again he would make them clear. He manifests great fear that it will not be understood so favorably as it ought to be.

The deceived professor may at times have internal fear that all is not right, but he declines to acknowledge it. He seeks to explain away, or suppress it; and probably, for the most part, succeeds. If he acknowledges his doubts, he does it to confirm the apparent genuineness of his experience, while he is sure to have them very soon removed. His ordinary statement is, that he has no doubts; he *knows* he is a Christian. The statement is made rather to produce confidence than give expression to it, as in the case of Micah, when he said, "Now *know* I that the Lord will do me good, seeing I have a Levite to my priest." His uniform attitude is that of self-defence. He professes a desire to know his true condition, but is unwilling ultimately to acknowledge it to be otherwise than hopeful.

The same disposition to claim being a Christian is manifested in his self-examination, which he institutes rather to prove than ascertain the honesty of his profession. He conceives that the fact of his examining himself will be a favorable symptom; and he designs that the result of it shall be favorable also, since he so conducts it as to secure that end.

We shall next exhibit some of the aspects of unrecognizable regeneration by comparing it with a recognized, or true and healthy regeneration. Of this it is the counterfeit. A spurious religious experience has all the apparent features of the genuine. This is because all the individual's education, sympathies, and desires are in behalf of a change in the proper form. There is, ordinarily, a false mental process, which runs parallel with that involved in a genuine work. All the steps of the one are simulated in the other. There is a simulated conviction of sin, distress and burden of soul, prayer, faith, loss of burden, view of Christ, peace, joy, love for Christ and for Christians, and Christian enjoyments. The individual thinks he is thoroughly convicted; thinks his sins are all forgiven; enjoys prayer very much, and, for the most part, at all times; loves Christ very much; his hope is strong and confident; he has great faith; repents of all his sins; has no doubts and fears, or seasons of darkness and gloom, *except such as all Christians have.* There is also outward reformation, corresponding in form to that which exists in the true Christian. The world is given up; immoral practices are abandoned. There is zeal in religion, in causes of benevolence, and activity in every good word and work.

All these features may not be simulated in every case, as they are not found in every case of the genuine. As in the genuine, there will be in a given number of examples a varied combination of these features, so in the false, there will be a combination correspondingly varied; and in a parallel series all the features of the one are quite sure to be exhausted in the other.

The degree of the strength, suddenness, and violence of the exercises is also simulated, since this is dependent more upon the natural temperament than upon the Spirit's influence,—a gracious work being in perfect harmony with the natural constitution, not altering the original mould in which it is cast. As in true regeneration there is every degree of these, so it is in the false. The work sometimes appears to be sudden, deep, and violent; at other times, gradual, less deep, and silent. Sometimes the change is accompanied with great outward reformation, zeal, and activity; and, again, it is externally quite unobservable, and the individual is retiring and inactive.

The apparent permanence of the change is also well simulated. As in case of a legitimate work of grace the subsequent life appears sometimes to be steady, and uniformly devoted to the end, and sometimes changeable and spasmodic, now ardent, and now stupid and cold; at one time backsliding and lapsing into worldliness, at another reviving and growing in grace; and as the individual sometimes runs well for a time, and then apparently meets with a disastrous fall, so is it, in all these respects, with a life which is subsequent to an experience that is false. All these aspects of the truly Christian life have their counterfeits in that which is spurious.

A much larger proportion of the life that is attendant upon a genuine and healthy work of grace, is doubtless outwardly commendable, than in the case of a work which is merely assumed. But it cannot be denied that these externally more excellent aspects of the Christian life have their counterfeits, to some extent at least, as well as those that are less so. The world is full of examples illustrating the truth that self-righteousness may persevere in its outward forms, and its apparently good works, to the very end of life; and the Scriptures teach that it will even plead them at the bar of God.

We remark, finally, that unrecognizable regeneration is a counterfeit well calculated to deceive. No doubt, in many instances it is undetected by all but the Searcher of hearts. *The first relation of it generally passes current.* Better acquaintance with it produces a want of satisfaction and sympathy. This, as it continues, produces perplexity and anxiety. It is felt that there is much about it that is good, but it never quite satisfies the Christian taste. Under a more patient and discriminating study and examination, every feature of it comes to fail of exciting sympathy and satisfaction. Perplexity and anxiety are changed to sadness and pain. It proves itself to be a beautiful, well-constructed, and well-furnished house, built upon the sand.

The last point in the aspects of unrecognizable regeneration is the comparison of it with an ordinary unregenerate state. Viewed thus, it is a merely *nominal* regeneration. It presents the phenomenon of an unregenerate man attempting to wear the name of regenerate. It is the phenomenon also of one attempting to act according to his name, and not his nature. The person has undergone a religious change which has the appearance of regeneration, but he is still as truly unregenerate as if he had experienced nothing. He is therefore one who deals in names, and not in realities. He is free in the use of religious language because he is ignorant of its meaning, like a trader in books who talks fluently about their titles and tables of contents, while he knows nothing of the topics of which they treat. Hence, with the Pharisee, he makes long prayers in public places. He talks much upon religious subjects, and talks well; talks about religious experience, duties, and doctrines, in all their aspects; and the impression is that it is mere talk. What he says may be good, but there is a lack of something necessary to give it relish to the Christian heart. The preaching, prayers, and exhortations of such persons, are as hollow and false as their experience. They have the effect of mere sound. The language and sentiment are good, but they fail to affect the heart. The tones and inflections of the voice seem destitute of that peculiar tenderness, humility, and spiritual significance, which are the necessary offspring of a broken heart and a renewed spirit. The feeling of Christians respecting such persons is, that, for some reason, they do not enjoy their prayers and exhortations. They seldom speak of it, supposing the feeling to be peculiar to themselves, and the fault, perhaps, all their own; and yet they are sincerely embarrassed and perplexed.

Such persons are frequently among those commonly regarded as being very excellent Christians. They are prompt, active, and even forward in the performance of all Christian duties. They are sober, honest, sincere; but others have the feeling, that while their exhortations and prayers seem to be good, yet they have no particular unction. They are of a dry, heartless, business-like nature. They seem destitute of genuine meekness and reverence. They do not pray, but *talk* their prayers to God as they would to a man. They pray about everything in the surroundings of true piety, but never enter the Holy of holies. Christians do not like to judge and call them self-righteous, yet they cannot suppress the feeling that such persons make a merit of performing duty. At all events, they utter nothing, in prayer or exhortation, to which Christian hearts respond. They seem to have no apprehension of spiritual things themselves, and hence they cannot talk about them in a significant or satisfying manner.

# CHAPTER II.

## CAUSES OF UNRECOGNIZABLE REGENERATION.

### SECTION I.

To some it seems quite incomprehensible that a person should come to believe that he has passed from death unto life, while having no just ground for such a belief. The mass of Christians, though they often admit and speak of the dangers of self-deception, yet seem practically to have no apprehension of any individual examples of it. It is conceived of rather as a theory than as a matter of fact. If an individual, with apparent honesty, professes to have become a Christian, others feel no disposition to question it, or ask for further evidence. They see no reason why, if a man has the appearance of honesty, his word should not be credited in this matter as well as in any other. They cannot conceive how it is possible any one should firmly and honestly believe that he has experienced true conviction of sin, that his sins have been forgiven, that he loves the Lord Jesus Christ, and has pleasure in his service, when none of these things are so.

In treating of the causes of unrecognizable regeneration, it will be remembered that the condition is one of self-deception; that is, of natural honesty but spiritual hypocrisy. We are not therefore to assign reasons why men should seek to make others believe that they have been born again, when they do not believe it themselves (such instances being comparatively rare); nor why they should believe it themselves, when there is no apparent ground for it; but we are to assign reasons why men should undergo a religious change which has so near a resemblance to a work of grace, as thoroughly to deceive both themselves and others. We shall endeavor to present, first, some of the *general* causes of unrecognizable regeneration, and then describe the manner in which these combine to produce each of its features separately.

It is here taken for granted that all will concede there are no causes adequate to produce a genuine work of grace but the Holy Spirit. Whatever result, therefore, may be produced by any or all other agencies combined, independently of the Spirit, cannot be a work of grace. It will also be assumed that whatever agencies are suited to produce a genuine work, when controlled by the Spirit, are otherwise suited to produce a counterfeit of the Spirit's work.

The first cause of a counterfeit of Christian experience — or, more properly, the ground out of which it springs — is *man's religious nature.* We mean by this his constitutional capability and tendency to recognize the existence and claims of some superior being, and consequently to perform various kinds of religious action. An impression prevails that all religious developments and phenomena in man's character must arise from the workings of the Holy Spirit. It seems unaccountable that any new movement or change in the direction of religion should occur except from this source. But this is perfectly well accounted for, in the fact that man is by nature a religious being. He has religious springs, a fountain of religious life within. His nature is composed, in great part, of strong religious forces.

This being so, it is perfectly natural that religious phenomena and developments should be constantly occurring. These forces can no more be kept pent up in man than any others. It is true that his religious nature is all perverted; but it is not on that account necessarily inactive and dead. Man is as active, religiously, as though he had never fallen. His fall perverted, but did not destroy his religious nature. Because the fountain of his religious life is bitter, the springs do not therefore cease to gurgle up, and the streams to flow. If man has a religious as well as a moral nature, we should expect to witness in him religious as well as moral phenomena and developments.

The doctrine that every new religious development must be the fruit of the Spirit, supposes that the Spirit is the creator, and not the sanctifier of our religious nature. It supposes that regeneration is not a change, but a production; that it is a being born, and not being born again; not a conversion, but a new endowment. It is as if a religious character should be engrafted upon a brutal nature. The Spirit's work, however, is not to create, but to sanctify what already exists. It is not to produce religious affections, but to change their quality. Some of the mightiest movements in the earth have sprung from religious sources unsanctified by the Spirit. The world is full of worship, independently of the Holy Spirit. The sun, moon, and stars, fish, birds, beasts, and every creature, have been the objects of it. How unwarrantable, therefore, to regard every religious movement and phenomenon in man as the work of regeneration. This is but one of the many religious phenomena attendant upon the character of such a being as he.

It may be objected that, though religious movements and developments may be otherwise accounted for, yet all religious *changes* must be ascribed to the interposition of the Holy Spirit. Analogy, however, will teach that this is by no means a legitimate conclusion. Whence spring the changes constantly occurring in man's mental and physical constitution? Are they not unaccountable, except as the ever-varying product of internal forces, now combined in one proportion, and now in another, thus constituting the mind of man self-capable, like all other living existences, of undergoing an almost endless permutation? Whence come the varied aspects of a plant, or the ever-changing expressions of the human face, but from a corresponding combination of the living forces within?

So it is with the ever-changing aspects of man's religious character, springing from the varied combinations of the forces of his religious being. Man, neither religiously nor morally, is like an engine propelled upon one single track, from which he cannot depart, except by some overpowering external force. His movements are characterized by all the variations of a living creature, impelled by the force of a multiplicity of muscles, bones, and limbs, united in every possible combination. If he has a religious as well as a moral nature, then he must be capable of religious as well as moral changes. He may occupy varying attitudes of disposition towards his Maker, as well as towards his fellow-men. He may undergo transitions from one religious state to another, and no one of them be a return to favor with God. Hence the extreme unsafety of pronouncing every change of religious character to be the peculiar change wrought by the Spirit. Man's naturally religious constitution presents a ground out of which there may arise many counterfeits of the Spirit's work.

Nor is there necessity for such a conclusion, in case of

examples which bear a general resemblance to the Spirit's work. It would not be strange if the resultant action of the religious forces in man, variedly combined, and frequently changing, should occasionally assume, among its other forms, a very near resemblance to a genuine work of grace. It would be nothing remarkable if these changes should sometimes be sudden, in the line of good, and permanent for a long period, even for life. Forces in the air, which have been for a time latent, but not inactive, often manifest their resultant action in a sudden and marked manner. Man's mental and moral powers often remain latent, but not dormant, for a long period, and then, by a sudden and striking outburst, exhibit the aggregate resultant effects of their long-continued action. So it is with his religious forces, without any interposition of the Holy Spirit. The social and lively daughter of wealth and comfort suddenly removes herself from the fond excitement of a busy world and the society of loving friends, into the solitary, life-long seclusion of the convent, to the grief of doting hearts, and the astonishment of all observers. If the internal religious forces may suddenly produce such a change of heart and life as that, would it be strange if they should sometimes assume the appearance of a striking work of grace, and impel to an abandonment of the world, and even of father and mother, and lead to a profession of the religion of Christ, in his visible church!

We inquire, next, what external influences there are, aside from the Holy Spirit, which combine to promote religious developments in man, and mould them into the outward form of a work of grace. Of those which *promote* such developments are the influences of *natural religion.* These are abundantly adequate to produce religious phenomena to no small extent. The monitions of the natural conscience teach man, in some part, that he is a sinner. When he does wrong, they cause disquiet, and incite a desire for the return of peace. All the works of God tend to impress man with a sense of the Creator's wisdom, goodness, and power. All his providential dealings with his creatures also teach that he is angry with sin, and lead them to stand in awe of its just retributions.

Man being thus possessed of an internal religious susceptibility, and located in a scene exhibiting on every hand the attributes of Deity, cannot fail to manifest even marked religious phenomena. His natural conscience, the displays of divine skill in his own being and in the outer world in which he lives, and the mutual adaptation between them, all combine to kindle on the altar of his heart the fires of worship towards some superior being.

Of those influences which tend both to promote religious developments, and mould them into the external form of a work of grace, the first and most effective is that of *religious education.* At the present time, almost as extensive means are employed for giving to the youth of our land a good religious as a good literary education. The utmost pains are taken not only to acquaint them with the doctrines of the Bible, but also to impress upon their minds the necessity of an experience of those doctrines. All our youth who are nurtured under truly Christian instruction, necessarily grow up into an educated belief of the necessity of undergoing a certain prescribed and marked change of feeling, called the "new birth," in order to escape the wrath and secure the favor of Almighty God.

And not only are they instructed in the *necessity* of a work of regeneration, but in all the steps and features of the work. An educated knowledge of an initial experience is of necessity ordinarily obtained prior to a vital knowledge of it. The process to be passed through is all marked out beforehand. So far, therefore, as the combination and arrangement of the exercises is concerned, there is little difficulty. Acquaintance with their usual arrangement would most naturally cause them to assume a similar one.

But how is it that, by the subject of a spurious conversion, the natural religious phenomena are intensified and wrought into what he confidently supposes to be spiritual exercises? Concerning this, we remark that an unconverted person's ideal of the new birth, though it may be correct in form, is necessarily false in spirit. The natural man can no more *conceive* of the essential spirit of a work of grace without the Spirit's aid, than he can experience it thus. And such a change as his education alone enables him to conceive, it may not be presumptuous to suppose it will enable him to experience. Besides, a change which conforms to the individual's ideal, and which he confidently believes to be the work of the Spirit, is quite likely to deceive others, as well as himself, as to its genuineness.

There are also certain principles of man's religious nature which combine with his education to promote religious exercises, and also to mould them into a proper outward form. The first of these is that of *imitation.* Man is as much a creature of imitation religiously, as in any other respect. He can scarcely prevent himself from imitating the experience of others, especially that which he venerates on account of its superiority. The person who has been educated under truly Christian influences, thus regards the experience of those who have been born of the Spirit. It constitutes the pattern after which he would gladly be moulded; and on account of his reverence for it, by a natural bent of his mind, almost before he is aware, he copies it. His own experience naturally becomes conformed to that which he so highly esteems in others, just as persons unconsciously fall into imitation of the habits of thinking and acting of those whom they regard as their superiors.

When controlled by the Holy Spirit, this principle subserves a gracious result, but otherwise a counterfeit. The Christian, in seeking to induce a spiritual state in others, naturally and properly presents to them a pattern of the same, in his own feelings, for their imitation. In this manner he most successfully describes to them this condition, and secures the advantage of their imitation in inducing it. If the Holy Spirit put his seal upon the work, it is genuine; if not, it is an imitation only.

The next principle is the *power of sympathy.* When employed by the Holy Spirit, this contributes greatly to true conversion, but otherwise to false. It is the direct effect of sympathy, both to call forth our feelings, and to mould them into the form of those which enlist it. The work of the Spirit in changing the heart, is well calculated to enlist sympathy. It produces a change of the affections, by which they are made to go out, not only after God, but after man. Christians, in pointing out the way of salvation, naturally relate to others their own experience, in order to awaken their sympathy with a work of grace, and so incline them toward it. These are proper means. If we would be successful in leading men to repentance, we must ourselves have the spirit of repentance. So of all the Christian graces. But if the Spirit do not employ these means, the result will be the work of man, and not of God. Sympathy with a work of grace will be taken for the work itself. The sympathy, it is true, will be spurious, but no more so than the individual's *conception* of the Spirit's work. Hence he will not hesitate to accept the sympathy for the work.

Another principle contributing to the same result is that of *desire* and *expectancy*. These also, when directed by the Spirit, promote true conversion; but without it, false. Almost every individual who is soundly instructed in religious things, becomes desirous of being made the subject of a change of heart. The uncertainty of life, and the dread of final punishment, render the experience of this change a matter of the deepest anxiety. Strong desire to be changed predisposes the mind towards it. It actually relaxes its fixedness, and inclines it towards some kind of transition.

This is promoted by the instruction which the individual has received, that he must *seek* for a change of heart, and at the same time must yield himself up to being changed by the Holy Spirit. He therefore strives first to change himself, then to resign himself to being changed. He seeks to be in a changeable frame; and the consequence is, that change of some kind must ensue. If the Holy Spirit control the event, his experience will be a gracious one; if not, an imitation.

If one is not under the influence of the Spirit when he determines to seek to become a Christian, he is likely to be confident of success, since he has no apprehension of the greatness of the change. As the process advances, expectancy of a change is created. Distress or relief, or joy or sorrow, expected, soon comes — the material for them being furnished abundantly in man's religious nature; but they will be a copy only, the material being unmoulded by the Holy Spirit.

Not unfrequently, also, the *imagination* performs an active part. This occurs where there is a high degree of mental excitement. When the individual fails to experience even his false ideal of a gracious work, the intensity of his mental excitement becomes increased. In such a state, the imagination can easily supply the deficiency. Having once passed from the region of the actual into the ideal, there is no longer any difficulty. The imagination can create love or hatred, joy or sorrow, assurance or doubt, faith or unbelief, happiness or unhappiness, intensity or moderation of feeling, as the natural desires may dictate, or the case require. This imaginary process, however, is not presented as a common, but an extreme one, to which recourse is had when others fail; though in ordinary instances of a spurious work, it may perform a more or less important part.

## False Graces.

We proceed now to show how these several causes combine to produce each of the features of unrecognizable regeneration.

### FALSE CONVICTION OF SIN.

Every person who has been religiously educated, knows that he is a sinner. He has been taught the moral distinctions between right and wrong. Under the influence of religious training, his natural conscience admonishes him that he has been guilty of many things which were not right in the sight of God or man. He desires now to become a Christian. His first endeavor, therefore, is to realize his sinfulness. He reviews his life, and succeeds in bringing before his mind many actions and habits which he has always felt to be wrong. By his desire to conceive himself a sinner, he comes to look upon these things as being more heinous than ever before. These sins are such as every one is naturally aware that he is guilty of. They consist of open, well-known sins, such as profanity, lying, disobedience to parents, and violation of the Sabbath. Or, if he can recall none of these outbreaking, positive sins, he brings up his sins of omission. He reflects that he has never performed religious duties, as he ought. He has done nothing to promote the cause of Christ. He perhaps thinks he has not loved God so much as he ought to have loved him, or he has not been so grateful to him for his goodness as he should have been.

Children are apt to make their convictions consist in disobedience to parents. They even weep over it, and think they were very great sinners on this account, while God is not in all their thoughts. When asked if they do not think that disobeying their parents was a sin against God, they answer in the affirmative; but offence against their parents is uppermost, and hence the conviction is only natural. Openly wicked men are likely to make their convictions relate to such sins as profanity, lying, intemperance, and Sabbath-breaking. They think they are great sinners because of these things. But this needs no spiritual illumination. If these are the leading features of their convictions, as was the case with Micah, who had stolen eleven hundred shekels of silver from his mother, then they are false. Nor is it strange that a man should be led, without spiritual influence, to stop in his career, at almost any time, and think of these things, conceive them to be very wicked, and desire to reform.

In this way the subject of a false experience is able to gather up much from his past life which he knows is not right. He is not smitten and bowed down, under a consciousness of guilt; but he seeks to make himself out as guilty as possible. He is not startled at the disclosure of his awful corruption within, trembling lest greater, and still greater depths of pollution will every moment be opened to his view; but he is obliged to search, and examine his heart and life, through and through, and interpret all his thoughts and acts in the most unfavorable light possible, probably more so than he thinks they really deserve, in order to establish in his mind a conviction of sin and guilt, which will warrant his regarding it as a tolerably fair ground-work of an initial experience. He has to labor to obtain *his* sense of sin, while true conviction is poured in upon the soul, like a flood. Oftentimes, indeed, the subject of a true work of grace does seek to be convicted of sin. This conviction, however, is not felt to be the fruit of his seeking, but it seems to come in upon him of its own accord. There is scarcely any connection in his mind between his self-examination and his sense of sin.

The subject of a merely assumed work of grace is flattered, gratified, and encouraged at every new view of sin which he obtains; while the subject of a true one is ashamed, terrified, and disheartened at every new view which he receives. The one seeks after conviction, believes he obtains it, and is well satisfied with his attainments, because he has searched so thoroughly; the other seeks after it, but his seeking fails, when conviction seems to come upon him of its own accord. The result is, that the one thinks he has seen all his sins, and been thoroughly convicted; the other thinks he has seen only a part, believing he has sinfulness not yet disclosed. The thorough conviction of the one is satisfying and gratifying to him, while the partial conviction of the other is painful and mortifying. The one is convicted of superficial sins which appear, the other of depths of iniquity which do not appear.

It is easy to perceive how any one who has been educated at all religiously may come to see that he is a sinner, without spiritual enlightenment. The natural conscience, depraved and imperfect as it is, teaches every man this fact. If now a man *desires* to conceive himself a sinner, in order to become a Christian, it is very easy for him to intensify this natural conviction. He may even conceive himself to have been a great sinner against God. He reflects that God has done a great deal for him, while he has not really done much for God.

Such a conviction is superficial and spurious, because the Holy Spirit has had no agency in producing it. It is not spontaneous, but labored. It resides in the intellect, and not in the heart. It is a conclusion, and not a conviction. The individual is obliged to make an effort to feel badly, and then does not very well succeed.

Sometimes this false conviction assumes another form in the person's mind. He has been taught that one under true conviction commonly feels a heavy burden resting upon him. Hence he seeks to bring a burden upon himself, which is always easy to be accomplished. It may be a counterfeit of the true burden, produced in the way explained, made up of external misdoings and religious short-comings; or it may be a substitute for it, composed altogether of other materials. It may be a burden of dissatisfaction with the world, of disappointment in its enterprises; of poverty or affliction in the loss of friends, or the loss of health. It may be a burden of worldly sorrow, occasioned by the betrayal of friendship, or the misery of unhappy earthly alliances, or of mere fatigue from constant toiling up the rugged path of life, comforted by no earthly enjoyment, and sustained by no hope of a better life to come. These are composed of the consequences rather than the consciousness and guilt of sin. Such burdens are easily brought upon the mind and heart, without the Spirit's aid: indeed, it is difficult to keep them off. The effects of transgression are constantly pressing upon us, on every hand. They are prevented from penetrating men's souls, and settling down upon their hearts, by putting on a panoply of worldly care, business, and pleasure. Let this panoply be broken by failure or disappointment, let the energies be relaxed and the mind cease to be diverted from its own reflection, and the bitter consequences of sin will rush in upon the soul like a flood.

In a season of religious awakening, therefore, when the mind is arrested from absorption in worldly pursuits and pleasures, to a contemplation of the end thereof, it can but be oppressed with a heavy burden of grief, anxiety, and sorrow. Having no knowledge of any other than that which is made up of the consequences of sin, the individual readily adopts this as the true burden requisite to a work of regeneration. If deep distress can be produced, in view, not of sin itself, but of its unhappy consequences, it is likely to be regarded as the distress desired.

Such distress is far more easily acquired than that which arises from genuine guilt. The consequences of sin have a thousand various forms, while real guilt has but one. Guilt is fastened upon the conscience, while the consequences of sin are sensibly felt in every part. The latter are naturally realized in the external man; the former is wrought in the heart by the Holy Spirit.

## FALSE REPENTANCE.

The principal idea of repentance is that of sorrow for sin. This is a Christian grace which one easily comes to suppose he has in exercise without the Spirit's influence. The Bible recognizes a sorrow of the *world*, to produce which does not require the agency of the Holy Spirit. This worldly, or natural sorrow, is mere regret, and is quite likely to ensue upon natural conviction. A person of sufficient religious tendency to lead him to reflect upon certain open sins, such as disobedience to parents, profanity, lying, and Sabbath-breaking, in such a manner as to excite spurious conviction, could hardly fail also to exercise spurious repentance. A consideration of the consequences of these things is sufficient cause to produce it without the Holy Spirit. A person of respectable morality must, upon reflection, regret indulgence in such sins, while every one who has had any religious education feels it to be highly proper that he should be sorry for all his sins, and, according to the strength of his natural convictions, he will be likely to exercise natural sorrow. This, occurring in immediate connection with what is supposed to be genuine conviction, will most naturally be taken for genuine repentance. Repentance being also a retiring grace, and not of so marked and positive a nature as conviction of sin, or joy of forgiveness, is with less difficulty feigned. Not consisting so much in a mental struggle, but being rather a state of mind consequent upon sense of sin and humiliation, its existence may with less apparent inconsistency be assumed, without any corresponding mental exercise. Moreover, if it is considered that the disposition of a person under false conviction is thoroughly self-righteous, the step to spurious repentance becomes inevitable. The unenlightened man thinks too well of himself not to believe that he is truly sorry for his sins.

## FALSE SENSE OF FORGIVENESS.

It is surprising upon what insufficient grounds a person who is spiritually unenlightened comes to be confident that his sins are all forgiven. The sense of forgiveness is so refined a Christian grace that it is exceedingly difficult to be counterfeited. The general tendency of the subject of unrecognizable regeneration seems to be to take it for granted that sin is forgiven, rather than to acquire a spurious sense of forgiveness. If asked why he thinks his sins are forgiven, he can assign no reason; but he thinks they *are all* forgiven. There seems to be somewhat of self-will about it. He is determined to think they are forgiven. He is so blind and self-righteous that he can see no reason why it should not be so. He is sure he has repented of them all, and he believes they are all forgiven.

Sometimes this belief of his being forgiven may be traced to some announcement which he conceives has been made to him to that effect, in the form of a passage of Scripture, or otherwise.

When conviction has assumed the form of a burden resting on the heart, then the belief that sin is forgiven is referred to a sudden and remarkable loss or removal of the burden. This takes place on this wise: The individual has been taught the necessity of a felt burden of sin as a feature in regeneration. He has also properly enough been taught the necessity of the removal of the burden, and, perhaps, as to the manner of its removal. Strong desire and expectancy, aided by man's natural power to mould himself into the form of his desires, are the chief agencies which produced the spurious burden, and now they will be adequate to remove it. Relief felt to be sternly necessary, and anxiously expected, soon comes. And when it comes, it is as spurious as was the burden which gave occasion for it.

In many instances the process of obtaining relief is in this manner: There is a burden on the soul; there is trouble, yet not on account of sin, but only its unhappy consequences, in the form of embarrassment, or some kind of affliction. It is not a burden which has been produced by the Spirit, and hence has no vital grasp upon the sinner's being. Relief is desired. It is earnestly sought, and confidently expected. It is desired and sought not only for its own sake, but also as a sign that the sinner has passed from death unto life. Desire for relief, and effort to obtain it, soon become irksome. The sinner wishes the struggle were over. Delay is painful. Desire to experience relief becomes modified into desire to feel that it is already obtained. He thinks he has sought sufficiently long; thinks it is high time relief had come; believes he has done all that is required, and sees no reason why he should not be relieved. He tries to feel relieved; examines to see if he does not feel so; thinks he does feel better, and is relieved. He hopes he is not deceived; prays that he may not be, and believes he is not. Thus, by the play of spurious exercises, he removes his spurious burden, and rests upon a spurious belief that his sins are all forgiven.

In other instances the exercises are more violent. The imagination plays a more active part. The individual conceives that the change is to be a very vivid and striking one. He is impelled by some very powerful, selfish motive to a most earnest seeking to realize his ideal of being born again. He brings all the religious appliances he can command to bear upon his feelings, in order to raise them to the highest possible pitch of intensity. The process is continued till human nature can endure it no longer. The relief which is obtained is merely the reäction of exhausted nature. In the morbid and unhealthy excitement to which the mind is subjected, it experiences very vivid impressions, sees great lights, and receives almost miraculous revelations.

In some instances the mind undergoes a shock for which it is impossible to account, but having none of the aspects of a gracious work, though the subject of it regards it as most convincing evidence that he is born again. This occurs where undue means are used to excite the religious susceptibilities and passions. Reäction of some kind must ensue; and since the person is deeply penetrated with a quite correct idea of the external form of a work of grace, the reäction almost necessarily assumes that form.

Sometimes the removal of the burden is on this wise: The person has been imbued with the idea that he must *pray* for its removal, and must believe that his prayer is heard and he accepted. Thus by the merely natural force of a praying attitude of mind, he actually prays away his anxiety and distress; and the removal of it is then confirmed by his erroneous idea that it is his duty to believe that his sin is forgiven and he accepted.

In treating of the formation and removal of the conviction and burden of sin in unrecognizable regeneration, we have thus far proceeded upon the supposition that the conviction and burden are false, created and removed according to natural principles, the influences of the Holy Spirit being not at all connected with the process. The doctrine is, that the same means which the Holy Spirit appropriates and makes subservient to a genuine work of grace, are, without the Spirit, suited to the production of a spurious work. The means which the sinner is to use to lead him to become a true Christian, and which promise to do so if he secure the interposition of the Holy Spirit, are, without His influences, likely to lead to self-deception.

The question, however, may arise, whether genuine conviction may not be produced by the Spirit, but removed by natural means. To this we reply, that it is difficult to determine the presence of the Spirit in connection with any given religious exercises, or the use of any particular natural means, since He appropriates these in perfect harmony with the natural principles which regulate them. Inasmuch as spiritual operations do not stand out from natural exercises and means, either in manner or degree, so as to be distinct from them, no criterion is furnished by which to judge of their presence; or, at least, for judging when the natural powers first begin to be affected by the Spirit's influence, though in more advanced stages of a spiritual work their presence might not be questioned. The Holy Spirit may strongly operate upon man when his natural powers are in a high degree of activity; or He may do so but slightly, the intensity arising chiefly from natural causes. Or, if the natural powers are in a moderate degree of activity, this may be ascribable chiefly to the Holy Spirit, and but slightly to natural causes. Hence a person may be in very great distress, and have but slight genuine conviction of sin; or he may have less distress, with deeper true conviction.

To some, facts *seem* to teach that a genuine conviction of sin, and burden on account of it, are sometimes induced by the Spirit, and then removed in a natural way. In such cases, *if they really exist*, the removal of conviction, or of the burden, by natural means, is taken for forgiveness. The Spirit is grieved away, and his departure taken for peace with God. The error is that which is commonly called mistaking conviction for conversion, which is comparatively rare. The more common form of error is, that the conviction is natural, and is removed by natural means.

### FALSE FAITH.

A counterfeit exercise of *faith* is also most naturally and easily acquired. The conception of it, arising from religious education merely, is, necessarily, exceedingly inadequate and superficial. It is, of all the Christian graces, least understood by the most experienced, and most readily supposed to be understood by the inexperienced. The natural element of human character in which this spiritual product is received, is a vessel so well suited to contain the heavenly treasure, that the container is quite likely to be mistaken for the thing contained. A merely intellectual belief is adopted as true faith.

Sometimes the inquiring sinner, by means of his religious education, conceives that the work of regeneration consists chiefly in the acquirement of faith. The necessity of deep conviction of sin, struggle with it, and removal of it, have no particular prominence in his mind. He has been taught that regeneration is often gradual, and consists chiefly in the *gradual* acquirement of faith. He is simply to believe in Jesus Christ, that He is able and willing to save, and that God is willing to hear his prayer and forgive his sins. In proportion as he has this belief, he is a Christian.

This is very easily obtained. All persons who have been educated in an evangelical manner do naturally believe this, without any spiritual influence. With the Jews, in the time of Christ, it was not so. In general, no Jew believed that Jesus was the Christ, even intellectually, but by the Holy Ghost. He would not do it unless his heart was broken and humbled by divine grace. But now it is otherwise. That Jesus Christ was the Son of God, that he has power to save, and is willing to save, is readily believed by virtue of religious education alone. To believe it is perfectly respectable. It involves no breaking of heart, no humbling of pride. It requires, moreover, no effort to believe it. It is a fact so well established, that persons rightly educated in religious things cannot resist it. All the individual has to do, therefore, as he supposes, is to seek to realize this fact more than he has done heretofore, in a simply intellectual manner; and that will be faith. By an effort of the will he strives, from day to day, to work himself more fully into this believing state of mind; and when he has attained to a tolerable degree of it, he calls himself a Christian. This type of unrecognizable regeneration is not very uncommon.

At other times the spurious exercise of faith comes in this way: The person has gained what he believes to be a tolerably good conviction and repentance, and he thinks that all he now needs is more faith; he must simply believe that God is ready and willing to receive him, without requiring any further change in his feelings — upon the supposition that he has already sufficient sense of sin, penitence, and humility. If he can believe that, it will be faith. His desire that it should be so, enables him without difficulty to cherish this belief. Or, at other times, the person's conception of faith is, that it consists of a belief that God *does* hear him, and his sin is forgiven. He is taught that unbelief is sinful, and hence thinks it is sinful for him to doubt his acceptance with God. Such a faith as this is easily acquired, especially where the desire is so strong to believe what the person thinks he ought to believe.

We remark, finally, that faith is so refined a Christian grace, that the unenlightened person is most commonly rather obliged to imagine, or take it for granted, that he has it, without possessing anything definite enough to be called a counterfeit.

## FALSE HOPE.

The hope which is acquired in unrecognizable regeneration, is also a natural product. The ground out of which this counterfeit grace arises, is the natural religious hopefulness common to mankind. Into this natural endowment Christian hope is engrafted. Originally the natural stock was good. Man hoped in God. Now he hopes in himself. Hence this sin-induced and falsely-directed hope must be broken off, and a scion of grace inserted. Man must be brought to despair of himself, and hope in Christ. In unrecognizable regeneration, this natural hope, instead of being broken off and grafted, is, by a religious education, and other influences, nurtured into maturity. The counterfeits of a sense of sin, repentance, sense of forgiveness, and faith, lying about its roots, warm and stimulate it into an undue development.

It is surprising how quickly this germ begins to shoot forth from the natural soil of the heart, — how little stimulus is needed to cause it to sprout and grow. In many cases it scarcely feels the warmth of even spurious religious exercise before its growth commences; and when this takes place, nothing checks it. No sooner does it begin to be nurtured by the other false graces, than it outgrows and throws back upon them its baneful shade, which, in turn, excites them also to a more weak and unhealthy growth.

Sometimes this natural and counterfeit hope does not appear among the other features of unrecognizable regeneration until they have become developed into their full proportions; when, being unable to suppress its pent-up forces longer, it bursts forth among them, and becomes the dominant feature in the counterfeit of the Christian character. In other instances, this Upas-tree of false hope springs up among other religious exercises which would give every promise of coming to a gracious maturity, were it not for the weakening, life-destroying shade which it casts upon them. When once hope begins to arise prematurely, it is quite certain to cause all otherwise hopeful struggles to become abortive of genuine results. It saps the life-blood of all true earnestness, destroys dependence on God, arrests the slaying work of the law, and prevents the soul from sinking down into renunciation and despair of self, where alone Christ will interpose and save.

In this way, in multitudes of cases, a progressive and promising experience is arrested and defeated of its blessed results, just as the law-work seemed about to give way to grace and faith in Christ. In all instances where once the feeling of hope, if it be false, has gained the ascendency, it becomes the queen-passion in the soul. It rules and moulds all the rest. All the other feelings must assume a form corresponding to the individual's false conception that he has a hope in Christ.

Oftentimes man's natural hopefulness, and its tendency to a premature and unspiritual development, is promoted by the idea with which the person has become imbued, that the main object in becoming a Christian is to get a hope. This is the first and last thing to be sought for, the sum total of the entire process. The natural feeling of hope, common to every man, that he shall at last, in some way, be saved, under the pressure of religious awakening, is easily quickened and developed into unusual strength. Then, guided by religious instruction, it simply defines the way in which it expects salvation, as being through Jesus Christ, and at once assumes the title of a Christian Hope.

There is also a superficial haste in which everything is done, characteristic of our time and country, which imparts its influence to religious things. A feeling exists that religious undertakings, revivals of religion, and even the conversion of an individual soul, must be prosecuted with great despatch. There is impatience with the delay which God may deem it necessary to employ, for purposes best known to himself, in order to accomplish his work of grace. The seeker after God is imbued with this feeling of haste, especially to begin to entertain hope. The point is illustrated in the interrogation of a lad, professedly seeking Christ, who asked if it was thought he could become a Christian in a week. The necessary result of such influence upon the natural feeling of hope, unslain by the law, is soon witnessed in a state of unrecognizable regeneration.

### FALSE LOVE FOR CHRIST.

The acquirement of a counterfeit *love for Christ* is also easily accounted for upon natural principles, and as the result of a religious education. When Christ was on earth, he was despised, both from political and religious considerations. He was esteemed as a root out of dry ground, on account of the external aspect of his advent among men, as well as his real character. Men contemned the idea of being saved through a despised Nazarene. Individual and national pride forbade it. But now it is otherwise. The external character of Christ, the manner of his advent, the plan by which he proposes to save, are, so far as their judgments and intellectual tastes are concerned, perfectly acceptable to all who are soundly educated in religious things. There is the same reluctance and pride of heart with reference to being saved by *grace*, now as then; but intellectually, *Christ* is honored. The original national and personal odium attached to his name has passed away, and given place to universal respect and esteem. The Jews who despised Christ are themselves despised, on that very account, by those who are as much averse at heart to being saved by grace as were they. All persons who have had a proper religious education are ready to profess a willingness, and even desire, to be saved by Christ. Their prepossessions, their intellectual tastes and judgments are all in favor of it. Nothing is in the way but an inherent self-righteousness, which, notwithstanding an intellectual sense of its propriety, yet absolutely rejects salvation by grace. Though the Jews are equally averse with ourselves to being saved by *grace*, yet we are not equally averse with them to being saved by *Christ*. If they must be saved by grace, they would rather any other than Christ would be their Saviour; but we would rather Christ than any other should be ours.

It is, therefore, easy to see how much more readily love for Christ may now be counterfeited, than in the Saviour's time. Then there was little danger. Everything stood opposed to it. Now everything is in its favor. To profess it involves no sacrifice, and is perfectly acceptable to men's intellectual prepossessions, judgments, and tastes. In consequence of an *intellectual* belief in Christ, and admiration of his character and way of salvation, almost all unconverted men suppose that, to some extent, they love him. They cannot conceive of themselves as being so wicked as to do otherwise. Hence, where the other Christian graces of conviction, repentance, and faith, are supposed to exist, a false love for Christ most naturally follows. Perfect assent to his character and plan of salvation, are taken for love. They are glad Christ has died, especially if by his death they think they shall be saved, — all of which may evidently be upon a selfish and self-righteous basis, while sin unlamented remains concealed in the recesses of the soul.

It is obvious, also, how such persons come to conceive that they love Christ *very much.* If a merely intellectual assent to and delight in his character and work is perfect, and is taken for love, they would conceive of that love as being perfect. This feeling that they love Christ very much, is promoted also by their knowledge that they ought to love him very much, as well as by their selfish desire to reap the attendant benefits.

Gratitude to Christ is intimately connected with love, and is counterfeited in a similar manner. The sinner reflects upon what Christ has done. He has also a natural sympathy with his sufferings. Then he conceives that he has done and suffered all for him, and can but feel a gratitude for it. But he has no true spiritual apprehension of the sufferings of Christ, or of his sin which occasioned them; and hence his gratitude, however great, must be unspiritual and false.

A counterfeit of love to God is also acquired in a similar manner, without the Spirit's aid. When any one reflects how much God has done for him, he can but feel a kind of gratitude. Almost all unconverted men suppose that on this account they really love Him. If, therefore, they come to believe that they possess the other features of a work of grace, they will not consider this to be wanting.

### FALSE HAPPINESS.

*Happiness* in religious things immediately consequent upon a change, is supposed to be a decided mark and fruit of grace. It has been stated that the subject of a spurious conversion represents himself as being uniformly very happy. He does not see why he should be so happy, if it is not because he has been converted. But there is adequate cause for great happiness in the confident *belief* that one is born again. It does not matter that such is not the fact. The unwavering belief that one has just passed from death unto life, that he has escaped the wrath to come, and been made an heir of immortal blessedness, in the company of saints and angels; that all his sin has been forgiven, and that the favor of God is to be uniformly enjoyed henceforth, must of itself produce very great happiness. Suppose some unhappy, unfortunate, and neglected child of earth comes to believe that he has suddenly been made an heir to an ample fortune, under circumstances promising all the earthly comfort heart could wish, — would it not, for a time at least, necessarily make him happy, even though there were no reality in it? How much more must it be so with him who supposes he has reason to believe that he has been made an heir to everlasting mansions in the skies, though there were no *reality* in that?

If such persons are asked what makes them happy, they are likely to answer that it is because they believe their sins have been forgiven, or because they think they have found the Saviour. They answer as if their happiness arose from simply an intellectual belief that they have become Christians. And this is its source — the *belief* that they are Christians, not their being such; the belief that sin is forgiven, not forgiveness.

This is a spurious happiness, most naturally mistaken for the genuine. The true Christian may take pleasure in reflecting upon the fact that he has been born again; but this is not the prime source of his happiness. He cannot so easily explain its origin. His happiness is a peace that passeth understanding. His rejoicing because he has become a Christian, is, at best, secondary. But with the false Christian it is primary. It is all the joy he has; and since he conceives himself to be a Christian, he supposes it to be Christian happiness.

We have represented the false Christian's happiness as produced by his belief that he has become a Christian. Sometimes, however, this order is reversed. He believes he is a Christian because he is happy, and then his belief and happiness promote each other. In this case, the individual originates his happiness, by a direct effort. He has learned that when persons are converted they become suddenly happy. He seeks, therefore, to feel happy, as before he had sought to feel unhappy. He expects to feel *suddenly* happy; tries to feel so; examines, to see if he does not; perhaps is asked if he does not; thinks he does, and as he thinketh so he is. Or, if anything is lacking, his imagination supplies the deficiency.

This spurious happiness is occasionally promoted, in the beginning, by a feeling of gratification with the thought of having got through with the difficult work of becoming a Christian. The process has been looked upon as trying to pride, to self-denial, and to the whole natural man. When, therefore, it is over, the individual is glad, as he would be upon the completion of any difficult undertaking. He would scorn the idea of being influenced by such a feeling, and probably could not be made to recognize it in himself, notwithstanding obvious manifestations of its existence.

The false professor represents himself as being *perfectly* happy, because he experiences all the happiness of which he has any conception. He is *uniformly* so, because his happiness is not so elevated and refined as to suffer from the grossness and materiality of earth. It rests, moreover, upon his simple belief that he is a Christian, which, on account of his spiritual blindness, is not subject to variation, arising from views of personal unworthiness, sinfulness, and fruitless strugglings after a better life. Everything goes smoothly with him, because he is ignorant of every source of alarm.

The production of a fictitious happiness in performing the various external duties of religion, is easily accounted for. It has been stated that the false professor claims to enjoy prayer very much, and, for the most part, at all times. This is because he believes it does him good to pray, and secures the favor of God. On account of his entire self-righteousness and spiritual blindness, the self-deceived professor thinks his prayers are perfectly acceptable and pleasing to God. His common and special blessings, he imagines, come in answer to prayer. This is enough to make any mortal love to pray. The idea that the Ruler of the universe regards him with so much approbation as to confer upon him blessings on so easy and familiar terms, must induce a self-complacence which can but be truly gratifying to the unrenewed man. If he thinks, as he does, that he can go to God and obtain blessings, as he would from any earthly friend, overlooking the necessity of contrition of heart and humiliation, having no conception of the infinite holiness of God, and of his own vileness in His sight, then it will be an exercise which he can but delight to perform. He will take pleasure in committing his worldly business every day to God, and spreading before Him his daily wants, if he can believe that by this means his business is prospered, and his daily wants are supplied.

To the unenlightened professor, this false enjoyment of prayer seems very great, or even perfect, because it is the full realization of all that he has power to conceive, in the performance of this duty; but to the true Christian it would be as tasteless as would have been the husks to the prodigal, after having feasted upon the fatted calf.

The false professor enjoys prayer *equally well at all times*, because his prayer is not dependent upon spiritual influence, and hence he can successfully offer it at one time as well as another. Nor is he, on account of his self-righteousness, ever oppressed with a sense of his unworthiness to pray, or to have his prayers heard and answered.

Occasionally it is understood by the false professor that the true Christian does not enjoy prayer at all times alike, and that this is a peculiarity of the Christian state. He therefore expects this peculiarity to exist in his own case, and desires it as an evidence in his favor. In this state of mind he easily discovers a slight variation in his enjoyment, such as every man finds in performing his daily labor arising from the modified condition of the various springs and forces of human nature, but having no spiritual connection whatever.

This natural variation of enjoyment in prayer is, however, a weak simulation of that which is peculiar to the true Christian. If the individual were impressed with the idea that the Christian's enjoyment is uniform, then he would not recognize this natural variation, but would speak of his enjoyment as being uniform also.

A fictitious happiness in performing other Christian duties, such as attendance upon public and social worship, Christian benevolence, and labor for unconverted men, is accounted for in a similar manner. The basis of it is satisfaction with one's self for having performed these duties, combined with the feeling that God approves it, and that it will be productive of personal weal and safety. The individual *cultivates* a pleasure in doing these things. He tries to enjoy them, and to *believe* he does, as an evidence that he is a Christian. He shuts himself off from other enjoyments, and is resolved to have here all he has anywhere. Such a course will produce pleasure in these things, as it would in anything else; but it must be, at the best, spurious. It will be a pleasure, not in the doing of these duties, but in the *consideration* that they are done. For the *doing* of them the unrenewed man has no Christian relish. His natural conscience approves him for seeking his happiness in this direction, and his unquickened conscience does not condemn him for seeking it in a false and unspiritual manner.

These causes are adequate, also, to produce *uniform* pleasure in religious duties. Enjoyment which arises directly out of the *spirit* with which duty is performed, may and is quite likely to vary. But that which arises from reflecting that duty is done, does not vary. The one is a life which is tender, dependent upon being nurtured, and liable to be impaired; the other is a hard, unyielding fact, which cannot suffer.

## FALSE "GOOD WORKS."

The sentiment prevails that if a professor of religion maintains a good external walk, and is religiously zealous and active, it must necessarily be the product of a renewed heart. This is especially so if his activity and good works are of long continuance. But when it is remembered how much more ready and willing men are to be saved by works than by grace, and what apparently excellent effects the working power of legal righteousness has wrought in the world, it will be felt that outward works can no longer be relied upon as an infallible sign of grace.

We do not deny that men shall be known by their fruits, but insist that the fruits must be discriminated. The Christian is not to be known by legal fruits, nor the legalist by Christian fruits. The fruits of legalism are as plainly recognized in the Scripture as those of grace. The good works of the New Testament Pharisee were, outwardly, of a most excellent character. They were even more abundant than the works of the publican, and, for aught we know, as long-continued. The house which the foolish man built was a legal work, and it was as well finished and furnished in every respect as was the house of the wise man. The two could not, probably, be distinguished, except by digging down, and ascertaining that the foundation of the one was in the sand, and the other on the rock. So it is with the structures of legalism and of grace. They both appear well, and answer an equally good purpose, in all the ordinary circumstances of life, until the last great storms come, which shall try every man's work of what sort it is.

The works of legalism will necessarily assume the form of spiritual works, according as they are moulded by an evangelical education. The spirit of legalism can as well put on the forms of meekness, humility, penitence, unworthiness, renunciation of self, faith, and reliance on Christ, as any other. There may be a legal spirit in keeping the law of grace, as well as the law of works. A man may be prompted by self-righteous motives in obeying Christ, as well as in obeying Moses, or reason, or Mohammed, or the Pope, or any other master.

The spurious good works of unrecognizable regeneration will be more clearly accounted for, if we consider what are one or two of the elemental forces of legalism which impel to such works. First, it may be observed that it is in perfect accordance with man's natural constitution, that he should attempt to please God by his good works. He was created and endowed for this very thing, but by sin he has disqualified himself for it. Nevertheless, the same natural constitution still remains. When aroused to seeking the favor of God, the natural impulse of his whole being is, to do it by good works, as he always ought to have done, and always would do, but for sin. The result, when he is awakened by any other power than the Holy Spirit, is a vitiated system of good works. When the Holy Spirit awakens, he also enlightens and humbles the soul into the method of grace; but no other power at the same time enlightens and humbles. Hence, when awakened by any other, by whatever religious creed he may be guided, he goes forward in the line of works, despising the method of grace because of its humility, and exalting the legal on account of his pride and blindness to its vitiated nature.

Another motive-power which impels to legal works, having a resemblance to the works of grace, and which especially incites to perseverance in them, is the fact that the individual has no other ground of trust. He has never yet rested his foot on the Rock. He has never dared to venture himself on Christ, and hence clings instinctively to his legal righteousness. He does it, too, with the perseverance of a man who feels that it is his only safety. If he fall from his legality, he has nothing else to save him. He may at times feel that this is giving way, but, like a drowning man, he will cling to it as long as a plank remains. If his education and creed are evangelical in their character, his legalism will be evangelical in its form.

## FALSE DOUBTS.

The subject of a false religious experience sometimes understands that Christians are, at times, subject to doubts and fears lest they may have been deceived, which are regarded rather as signs that they are not deceived. The false professor, therefore, likes to have some doubts himself, and even expects them. He does allow himself to doubt for a brief period, in order to strengthen his hope; but he does not really doubt, after all. His manner of speaking of his doubts, discloses their counterfeit nature. When asked if he has them, his answer is, "Yes; I suppose all Christians do." This is the reason he doubts, — simply because all Christians do. His doubts are therefore superficial and weak. They are as weak, compared with real Christian doubts, as are his sense of sin, faith and hope, when compared with those which are genuine. They are, therefore, quite as easily accounted for on natural principles, as are those. His hope being created by himself, he can easily for a time suspend it. This suspension of hope is doubt, and it is doubt of no greater depth than the hope whose suspension creates it. The false professor has no power to experience doubts like those of the true Christian. His conceptions of religion are all shallow, and his doubts and fears are equally so. He has no religion which he did not himself acquire, independently of the Holy Spirit. And he has no conception of the existence of any which he has not power to acquire at pleasure. Hence his doubts and fears cannot be very strong or alarming. He is pervaded with the feeling that, if he is deceived, he could easily seek again, and, doubtless, the second time he should be successful.

The *removal* of the Christian's doubts, also, is as readily counterfeited in unrecognizable regeneration as the production of them. The individual having produced them by the exertion of his own will, has power in the same way to remove them. His language respecting the matter is, that he prays, and they quickly go away. But his prayer is only the exertion of his own will. 'T is true that the force which he uses to remove his doubts is a feeble thing; but the thing to be removed is feeble also. It would be inadequate to remove a Christian doubt. *This* penetrates the very foundations of the soul, and requires the force of prayer which reaches the ear of God, and no slight or momentary application of that. He does not entertain his doubts as anything serious, nor does he suffer them to remain so long as to gain a grasp upon his being which he could not relax.

We have thus far spoken of a class of doubts in unrecognizable regeneration which are nearly imaginary. In some cases, however, there seems to be, for a time, a real, honest doubt on the part of the individual whether he has been made the subject of a work of grace. This has more substance than that just spoken of, but less sensibility and vitality, and, consequently, less painfulness, than the true Christian's doubts. It is based more upon the reason and judgment than either. The subject of such doubts, by reflecting upon what he has experienced, fears, in a moment when his better judgment prevails, and almost concludes, that it is nothing real after all. This is a simulation of what the Christian sometimes experiences; but it is a simulation only. It does not, like his doubts, penetrate his whole being through and through with alarm. With the Christian it is a sort of suspension of his life, and produces a kind of death-agony. In the other case it is a mere conclusion of reason, an exercise of the judgment. But, in view of this conclusion, there is no vital suffering. The soul, not having been quickened into life, has no susceptibility of death-pains. There is no spiritual view of the heinousness of sin, or of God's anger, or the pain of final separation from God. There is the same basis of indifference, in view of the possibility of being in an impenitent state, as exists in a condition of unawakened and unacknowledged impenitency. Such persons have sometimes been persuaded to give up their hopes entirely, without any more pain in view of their condition than if they had never cherished hope.

This class of doubts are removed by a like superficial and counterfeit process. Sometimes they lead to a kind of self-examination, which is as false and unspiritual as are the doubts which occasion it, and is in perfect keeping with all the other features and exercises of the assumed Christian character. The subject of a spurious conversion has no spiritual light to take into the dark chambers of his soul, and hence he has no means of conducting a true work of self-examination. A false examination, of course, results favorably to himself; or, at least, he interprets its results thus. He does not understand that the fact of his discovering nothing vile in himself, nothing contrary to what a Christian ought to be, is a sign that he has no spiritual light, rather than that he has no sin, and should be interpreted against him; but, having searched as thoroughly as he has power to search, and finding nothing in himself, his doubts and fears are at once dispelled, and are also prevented from intruding upon his peace in time to come.

There is another kind of doubts belonging to this state, which are on this wise. There seems to be a kind of substratum of doubtfulness in the person's feelings, upon which rests a superstructure of great confidence, being the reverse of the true Christian's feelings, which have a foundation of immovable reliance with a superstructure of doubtfulness. This substratum of doubtfulness expresses itself in this way: "I don't *know* as I am a Christian, but I think I am." The expression may have been called out by want of encouragement, or an expression of distrust on the part of others. The individual utters doubt for the purpose of furnishing occasion to establish his position more firmly, in others' minds and in his own. Suspicion from without existing that the structure of his hopes may be ill-founded, he jostles it, first on this side and then on that, in order to prop and brace it up more firmly.

In the previous discussions we have contemplated a merely assumed work of grace as resulting from a religious education which is correct, the falsity of the work arising from the fact that the Holy Spirit was not connected with it. In such a case, since the education is correct, the work is not only false, but well counterfeited. In some cases, however, of partially erroneous instruction, a kind of change occurs which passes for a work of grace, but has hardly enough of the appearance of it to be called a counterfeit. An illustration or two must be mentioned.

Sometimes an inquirer is taught that he can give his heart to God at one time as well as at another; or that he can do it at any given time, if he will only make the effort. He is told, in a religious meeting, that he can become a Christian before leaving the house, or before again closing his eyes in sleep, and is exhorted to do so. The result is, that, after having sought for a time without success, he determines to bring the matter to a final issue. He resolves that he will not eat, or he will not sleep, or he will bow down in prayer and will not rise, until he has found relief. Such a course is quite likely, ere long, to bring relief. If the individual is not under the influence of the Holy Spirit, the imagination will come to the rescue, and induce a supposed relief before he has become reduced to any very extreme suffering of body or mind.

Another similar method of spurious conversion is as follows: The person has been taught that his becoming a Christian is to consist chiefly in his coming to a decided resolution that he will henceforth give up the world, break off his sins, and serve the Lord. His change of heart is to consist in his solemnly determining to be no more a worldling, seeking after the pleasures and riches of earth, but to abandon these, and live a truly Christian life. He is to make up his mind in a deliberate manner, to deny himself, to cast off his pride, and devote himself to true religion.

Such a work is easily performed. The individual reflects that it is a very important and necessary thing to become a Christian. He always meant to do so at some time, but could never fully make up his mind to give his attention to it until the present. *Now*, he thinks it is his duty. Some affliction, or disappointment, or religious awakening, or an apprehension of the termination of life ere long, leads him at once to adopt such a course. Without any breaking of heart or deep emotion, he comes out, deliberately and coolly, from the world, breaks off from his useless or vicious pleasures, and professes to be on the Lord's side. He feels determined to persevere and see the end of the Christian race. His natural conscience approves the change, his spiritual blindness does not detect the error, and so he actually takes a self-righteous pleasure and satisfaction in the course he has chosen, believing this pleasure to be the enjoyment of true religion.

## § II. — False Treatment.

We have thus far treated of man's naturally religious character, and a religious education, as sources of a counterfeit of regeneration. The principle adopted is, that without a naturally religious constitution, man would be capable of experiencing neither a true nor a false conversion; and that without a religious education to some extent, he is not *likely* to experience either. And, moreover, that education which gives most promise of a truly gracious result, if it be appropriated by the Holy Spirit, is most likely to produce a counterfeit of it, if the Spirit is not bestowed; and the more perfect the education, the more perfect will be the counterfeit.

We inquire now what connection religious *treatment* has with the subject under consideration. And here it may be remarked that a perfect religious treatment cannot, as in the case of a correct education, be conceived of as contributing to a false conversion. This may, however, be the case with the best religious treatment that can be received from the wisest and best of Christian men. Such treatment, through want of perfect spiritual insight, may be ill adapted to the end desired. By a slight want of fitness in some word of counsel or exhortation, the feelings of the seeker after God may be turned into a channel which shall lead to an unspiritual issue. That treatment which to human wisdom may seem best suited to a particular case, may, under the Divine eye, be seen to be quite the reverse. This being so, it is evident that much of the common, but well-intended treatment to which inquirers are necessarily subjected, must not only in some cases frustrate the end sought, but in many others lead to an issue which is false.

Perhaps no kind of false treatment is more general at the present time, and more likely to lead to spurious conversion, than that of urging inquirers to embrace the gospel, to the neglect of an endeavor to secure conviction of sin. Constantly to urge and press it upon men to embrace the gospel, in such terms as "to come to Christ," "to give their hearts to God," "to believe in Jesus," "to accept of a Saviour," before they have any real sense of sin or of their need of a Saviour, must often result in a spurious work. Such treatment, so far as it has any effect, forestalls the foundation-work of regeneration.

It may be said that these exhortations are intended to

embrace conviction of sin and being slain by the law. If so, then it is objected that they do not make the impression intended. Men are strongly inclined to pass over, in the easiest manner possible, their sin against God, and seek to become reconciled to him without a recognition of it. When, therefore, God is represented to the sinner as merciful only, and the sum of regeneration is exhibited as consisting in simply "coming to Christ," "believing in Jesus," "giving the heart to God," and "accepting the Saviour," he is quite likely to ignore the fact that he is a sinner, and that God is angry with him for it. There must be a direct declaration of that truth, in the most positive terms; otherwise he will regard God's mercy simply as goodness. He will look upon Christ, not as an atoning Saviour, but only as a kind and sympathizing friend.

Or, again, it may be objected that these are scriptural exhortations, and that we have the sanction of divine authority for their use. To this we answer that no objection is made to the use of these exhortations, in a proper manner, and under appropriate circumstances. Neither Scripture invitations nor precepts are to be indiscriminately employed. The objection lies against urging persons to accept of a Saviour before they feel any need of a Saviour, which is powerless, as it would be to invite men to drink when they are not thirsty, or eat when they are not hungry. Christ said, "Come unto me all ye that *labor* and are *heavy laden*, and I will give you *rest*." But the exhortation is not to those who do not labor and are not heavy laden. Such could not rest if they came. "The *law* is our schoolmaster to bring us unto Christ." The objection lies against Christians attempting to take the work of the law into their own hands, against their inviting the sinner at once to Christ, without first directing him to the law, to be instructed thereby, and convinced of his need.

Christ should be exhibited agonizing on the cross, to *prove* that men have need of a Saviour, and to cause them to realize it. Conviction of sin may be sought by means of the law or the gospel, either or both, as in any given case may be deemed most effectual. But is it not in vain to urge men to *come* to Christ, to accept of him as a Saviour, till this end is gained? He himself declares that he came not to call the righteous — those who think themselves righteous — but sinners to repentance. The reason men do not come to Christ is not so much because they are not enough *invited*, as it is because the invitations, even of Christ himself, are powerless upon them, since they do not feel their need. When men see that they are sinners, that they have not only violated the law, but trodden under foot the Son of God, and that there is no way of escape for their guilty souls but through Jesus Christ, they will, almost instinctively, like the blind man, cry to him for mercy. They can hardly be *kept* from embracing him. They will, at most, need to be pointed to him, with the exhortation, "Behold the Lamb of God!"

The treatment which is regarded as liable to produce a false effect seems to be based upon the supposition that men *naturally* feel that they are in a lost condition, especially if they have been religiously instructed. Hence they are urged to come at once to Christ, and trust in him; and the only conception they have, or can have, of the exhortation, is, that they are to come and live for Christ, promote his cause, and trust in him for blessing; whereas they should feel that they are in no condition to enter his service till they have first repented of their sin. They cannot come to him as their master, until they have first come to him as their atoning Saviour. He will not receive their service till they have been washed in his blood.

Objection does not lie against employing these exhortations in public address, if they are not used out of due proportion, when compared with instruction and exhortation pertaining to the law and sin. Nor does it lie against their application to an anxious sinner, personally, if the law has already done its work in his heart, although in such a condition there will seldom be occasion for the exhortation. But to invite the sinner to trust at once in Christ, and accept of a Saviour, when the commandment has not yet come and revived his sin, must either produce no effect upon him, or a spurious one.

It has been shown that circumstances, essentially affecting the use of exhortations to believe and trust in Christ, have materially changed since these invitations were employed by him and his immediate disciples. The Jews, as a people, did not believe in Christ *intellectually.* They were bitterly opposed to acknowledging him as their Saviour, for a variety of reasons, aside from their natural disposition to trust in their own righteousness, and their unwillingness to be saved by grace. At the present time it is not so. Men do believe in Jesus Christ intellectually. Intellectually, they are perfectly willing to trust in him. The only hinderance to their acceptance of him is their natural self-righteousness, and consequent want of a felt necessity of having *any* Saviour. To exhort men to believe in Jesus and come to Christ, therefore, has not the same power now as when these exhortations were originally employed, since it does not now, as then, constitute the outward consideration over which the heart of the sinner breaks. Then a merely intellectual acknowledgment that Jesus was the Messiah, was an unmistakable sign of faith. It was certain proof that the law had done its work, and that the heart of the sinner was broken on account of sin. Then an intellectual belief in Christ, and willingness to accept him, came only after conviction of sin; but now it goes before, and that, too, very far.[1]

It clearly follows, therefore, that to exhort men to come directly to Christ, to trust wholly in him, just as they are, and accept of him as their Saviour, where there is no conviction of sin, is well calculated, so far as it has any effect, to cause a merely intellectual belief and trust in Christ as a friend, to take the place of conviction of sin, and a hearty embrace of Christ as an atoning Saviour and glorious Redeemer.

Man's primary relation is toward God as his Creator, Lawgiver, and Benefactor, while his relation to Christ as his Redeemer and Saviour is secondary and intermediate. Repentance is to be exercised toward God, and faith toward our Lord Jesus Christ. At the present time, man's relation to God as the Lawgiver is greatly neglected. Christ is urged upon the sinner as a Mediator between himself and God, before he realizes that himself and God are at variance, or that there is any need of mediation between them. Acceptance of Christ, therefore, becomes forced and unnatural, whereas it should be spontaneous and earnest. This arises from the liability of the public mind, in religious things as well as in others, to become unduly swayed in one direction, and so lose a well-balanced view and practice of the entire scheme of grace. The evil, moreover, perpetuates itself. The greater the momen-

[1] If there were exceptions to these statements, they were doubtless rare.

tum in a given direction becomes, the greater it is liable to become, until it expends itself, and a violent reäction ensues.

It should be added, in confirmation of the above, that while an acknowledgment of faith in Jesus Christ furnished the ultimate test of the conversion of a Jew, yet the Scriptures enforce the duty of repentance as abundantly as they do that of faith; and when they occur in connection, repentance takes the precedence. "John the Baptist came preaching in the wilderness of Judea, and saying, Repent ye, for the kingdom of heaven is at hand." "From that time Jesus began to preach, and to say, Repent, for the kingdom of heaven is at hand." "And he called unto him the twelve, and they went out and preached that men should repent." "Then Peter said unto them, Repent and be baptized for the remission of sins." "God commandeth all men everywhere to repent." "Jesus came into Galilee preaching the gospel of the kingdom of God, and saying, Repent ye, and believe the gospel." Paul, also, declares that he "taught publicly, and from house to house, testifying both to the Jews and also to the Greeks, *repentance toward God*, and faith toward our Lord Jesus Christ."

Another mode of treatment which contributes very strongly to produce a counterfeit of a work of grace, is that arising from the sentiment that all persons who are seeking to become Christians must be *uniformly encouraged* in their efforts. No discouraging aspect of the subject must ever be presented to their minds, lest they should be disheartened, and their efforts relaxed. To talk to inquirers of God's purposes, of sovereign grace, of human inability and utter dependence on the Holy Spirit, is but to cripple their courage, and defeat their salvation. Many Christians fear to have inquirers told that "No man can come unto Christ except the Father draw him," and that "it is God that worketh in them, both to will and to do," lest they shall feel their weakness and dependence, and so abandon their endeavors to come to Christ.

Such treatment, applied uniformly and indiscriminately to every stage of religious inquiry, is, in all but a few exceptional cases, likely to result in a spurious conversion. It does indeed greatly increase the number of nominal Christians, and as greatly prevent the increase of genuine ones. "No man *can* come unto Christ except the Father draw him." There is no encouragement for the sinner, whatever, unless God, of his own free and sovereign grace, have mercy on his soul. To realize these truths is the fundamental part of a work of grace. The sinner must be reduced to absolute despair of all his own efforts, before he will flee to Christ. The process involves a state of extreme discouragement and hopelessness. The sinner must see that every other resource and refuge is gone, before he will fall at the foot of the cross for mercy. He must be brought actually to taste of death, before salvation can become most sweet to his soul. It is thus that "the righteous are scarcely saved," and only thus that a Saviour becomes most precious.

Carefully to suppress, therefore, every word of alarm to the sinner, and constantly hold up before him a hopeful prospect of success in his efforts, is to use the direct means to defeat the end in view. The seeker after God who is in a state of hopefulness that he shall soon realize the object of his search, is yet in a very unhopeful condition. He has not begun to appreciate the danger to which he is exposed, nor the dreadful wrath of God toward him on account of sin. To encourage such hopefulness, is to ignore the sinner's sin, the holiness and justice of God, and the sovereignty of the Holy Spirit.

To effect a reconciliation between God and the sinner, is the most difficult work ever undertaken, even by God himself. It is that in view of which every impenitent soul has infinite reason to tremble and be afraid. To exhibit it to impenitent, unenlightened, and unawakened men, as a matter in regard to which they have every reason to be hopeful and encouraged, and to seek to induce them to enter upon the work of securing their salvation, by representing that it may be accomplished with ease, is the direct means of leading them to a false conception and a correspondingly false experience of a work of grace. A man's efforts to effect any undertaking will be energetic and earnest, according to his conception of its greatness and difficulty. It is not natural to expend much energy, over and above what the end to be accomplished demands. So an individual's experience of a work of grace will be likely to be deep and thorough, according to his conception of the greatness of the work to be wrought. If its difficulties are all ignored, if his conception of reconciliation with God is that there is no difficult adjustment to be effected between a rebel subject and an offended Jehovah, but that God is already reconciled, and it is only requisite that he should resolve to forsake his sin, and live for God, which he may do at any time, then his reconciliation will be likely to be entirely spurious. He will be utterly unprepared for a work that is genuine and thorough.

Man's natural conception of what it is to become a Christian is altogether superficial. He is, naturally, too hopeful, and too much encouraged in regard to it. He says to the Saviour, "Go thy way for this time; when I have a convenient season I will call for thee." The idea that he will attend to it at a convenient season, implies that he conceives it to be so easy to become a Christian, that it is not necessary to regard particularly the Lord's will or the Lord's time. He may attend to it at any time most convenient to himself. To encourage this disposition, therefore, when it should be broken up, and the feeling induced that the soul is in great danger, that God is angry, and that it is fearful to tamper with his mercy and justice, is the direct course for promoting a work that is false.

Here it may be asked, If no encouragement is held out to men to seek to become Christians, who will make any effort? Must not Christ be set forth as a Saviour ready "to save to the uttermost, all who will come unto God by him?" It must be understood that the treatment objected to is not that of encouraging men to seek to become Christians, but it is that of endeavoring to produce an encouraged and hopeful state of mind in impenitent and unenlightened persons who are inclined to seek religion. They should be encouraged to seek for such a view of themselves as would be exceedingly discouraging to them, and as would reduce them to a state of utter hopelessness. They should be taught that when they have attained to this, they may be encouraged that a work of grace is in progress. No man is ever converted while in an encouraged and hopeful state of mind. Christ is accepted by the sinner only in the last extreme of conscious peril. He is saved as a *brand* from the everlasting burnings.

Another kind of treatment which tends to promote spurious conversion, consists in the effort to induce men to become Christians for the sake of the *happiness* which the Christian life affords. No objection lies against instructing unconverted persons that the Christian life has a peace that passeth understanding. This should be impressively set before them. But to represent this life as one of unmingled happiness, and to endeavor to induce them to become Christians by virtue of the implied motive of enjoying this happiness, has the tendency to supplant a genuine experience by one that is false.

In the first place, such a statement regarding the Christian life is not true; and we are not warranted in employing an untruth to persuade men to become Christians, however well adapted to the end it may seem. The Word of God, and all experience, teach that in this life the Christian shall have tribulations; that he shall be persecuted for righteousness' sake; and that, like his Master, he shall be "a man of sorrows, and acquainted with grief." He may, like Paul, glory in all these things; yet not for their sake, but on account of the discipline they minister to a higher end. "If ye be persecuted for righteousness' sake, happy are ye;" yet not on account of the persecution, but the end it serves. There is a joy in true religion which the world do not know; and there is a sorrow in it which they do not, and cannot know, until enlightened by the Holy Ghost.

To acquaint unconverted men with this truth as it is, and allow it to have its legitimate effect upon them, is important and salutary. But to present unvarying happiness on earth as the grand inducement for becoming Christians, is utterly powerless to effect a true Christian experience. How can such a motive conduce to enlighten man as to his guilty nature, and lead him to repentance and faith in a crucified Redeemer? It would seem, sometimes, as if it were supposed that the great, magnetic power of the cross lay just here. Some Christians are thoroughly penetrated with the sentiment that nothing but the pleasures of religion must be exhibited to unconverted men, lest they should be discouraged from seeking it. There must be no dull notes in their songs. If they have sorrows, they must be carefully suppressed,—as if true religion could not commend *itself*, but, to be attractive, must be only partially known.

It is admitted that such an aspect of religion is inviting; but it is evidently inadequate to lead to anything more than a spurious result. It may incite to reformation of the outward life, upon a self-righteous basis; but it has no adaptedness to awaken a sense of guilt, or produce repentance or humiliation. It may lead men to seek for an increase of the same kind of happiness they already possess, arising from satisfaction with themselves; but it will not lead them to abandon this, and seek for a happiness which is diverse, arising from brokenness of heart before God, and undeserved forgiveness of sin, through a gracious Redeemer. Such a mode of treatment, therefore, of unconverted men, must be not simply ineffectual, but deleterious.

Similar in their spirit, and equally liable to produce spurious conversions, are the means sometimes employed for creating and promoting revivals of religion. We refer to those which are of a politic rather than a spiritual nature; such, for example, as an endeavor to create a revival by producing an expectation that a revival is about to occur, and then endeavoring to promote it by representing the work as very great, and greatly increasing. Objection lies not against making a truthful statement of facts, and allowing it to have its legitimate effect, but against insulting God's sovereignty, and ignoring man's dependence, by resorting to means of a worldly nature to accomplish a spiritual end. Doubtless such means may be overruled to the real conversion of some souls, though adapted to produce conversion that is spurious.

It hardly needs to be said that of a like character is the practice of urging persons who may be inclined to seek religion to perform certain external acts, which imply a committal of themselves as seekers after God, a subduing of pride, and a willingness to do whatever may be requisite for becoming Christians. Objection lies not against the practice itself, but against an improper mode of employing it, especially against great urgency and frequency in its use. Wisely employed, it may be of benefit; unwisely, of great injury. A peculiar attitude of mind often exists among religious inquirers, upon which it may be serviceable to bring to bear some tests of their willingness to commit themselves as having entered upon the work of seeking their salvation, or of their willingness to submit to any terms the gospel may impose, involving whatever sacrifice of pride or aught else. But if the inquirer is not in this particular frame, then the performing of such acts is likely to be harmful rather than beneficial. Frequent and strong urgency to commit themselves, may indeed be overruled to a salutary end; but it is calculated to produce the opposite.

In the first place, this urgency involves and conveys the impression that these acts have some efficiency, or that they are an essential part of true conversion. Having repeatedly performed them, the inquirer conceives of himself as having gone through with a certain part of the process of becoming a Christian. Or, he thinks that his willingness to perform these acts is a proof of his being a real, earnest, and sincere seeker after God; that his pride is humbled, and that he is fully willing to submit to the terms of salvation; whereas in these outward acts there is no test of these inward feelings, unless the inquirer is precisely in the frame of mind suited to being tested by the particular means employed.

The young man in the gospel would, doubtless, have freely submitted to the act of rising for prayers, or taking the anxious seats, or any other test except the one the Saviour employed; and his submitting to these would have greatly strengthened his false hope that he was a Christian. As with the test applied to this young man, these external acts should serve to expose to the inquirer the point of unwillingness in him to become a Christian. Hence *refusing* to submit to these tests, often has a better effect than compliance with them. Performing these acts may either be mistaken by the inquirer for the inward feeling, or regarded as signs that the feeling is in advance of what it really is. Or submission to these requirements may even be taken by the individual for submission to the terms of salvation.

### § III. — Deceitfulness of Sin.

The discussion has hitherto pertained to those external influences which operate as the causes of a counterfeit experience of religion. There are two other causes contributing to this result, which must not pass unnoticed. They are the real animus, or rather the virus, the poison of all the others. These are the deceitfulness of sin, and Satanic influence. Without these to infuse their influence into them, the other causes would have no power to produce the disastrous results which have been described. It is by these that good means are made to promote a bad end.

Doubtless the most prominent and fatal characteristic of sin is its power thoroughly to deceive both the subject of it and unsuspecting and undiscerning observers. He who is deceived by sin, is entirely unaware of the fact. To be deceived, one must be confident that he is not deceived. This confidence sin has the power to produce and sustain. It perfectly disarms the individual of all ability to detect the deception he is under. It is willing to adjust itself to any creed whatever; it will make any professions, and any confessions, if it may only retain possession of the heart. It is willing the individual should make any declarations he please regarding his views of sin. He may declare his hatred of it, his non-possession of it, or his determination to war against it. It is not the highest aim of sin to cause its presence and its works to be seen and acknowledged. It is willing, if necessary, to live and reign in the heart, and receive no credit. It is more anxious about deeds than professions. It cares more for the spirit than for the outward works. It is so anxious to retain possession of the soul, that it will readily consent to leave the matter of credit to be adjusted at that tribunal where "every secret thing shall be brought into judgment, whether it be good or whether it be evil." So far as may be, it doubtless loves to have open triumph in this world. It desires to make the ranks of its professed votaries appear as formidable as possible, for the sake of its greater sway. But where the restraints of a religious education, or desire to escape the consequences of sin and secure the rewards of holiness, prevents, it is quite ready to yield the advantages of an outward profession, for the purpose of retaining to itself the citadel of the heart. It will, for the sake of a better protection, even lend its influence to produce a good external living.

The fact that sin possesses such a characteristic, is not sufficiently regarded. The supposition too commonly prevails that

> "Sin has (*not*) a thousand treacherous arts
> To practise on the mind;"—

that it has no disposition to conceal itself, and that it so hates holiness as never to put on even the garb thereof. It is supposed that the sinfulness of the heart always exhibits its true colors, and in this respect discovers a praiseworthy honesty. Hence if a man with apparent sincerity professes to have found the Saviour, it is thought it should not be questioned. One must know his own feelings, and he can have no motive to deceive. If he honestly believes and declares that he loves the Saviour, or that he enjoys prayer in the true spirit, to doubt the statement, and seek for other evidence, is uncharitable and unkind. But if it is remembered that the heart, by reason of sin, is deceitful above all things, and that, in consequence, a person who is not enlightened by the Holy Spirit is ignorant of himself, the propriety of such a course becomes apparent. A man's honest opinion of himself cannot be trusted. He becomes the subject of a work which he does not know is feigned.

The sentiment is also sometimes expressed, that though it might not be safe to trust the statements of the young and ignorant respecting themselves, yet it is otherwise in regard to persons of intelligence and known integrity. This, however, is utterly false to the premises in the case. Is he less likely to be deceived by sin, who has been under its dominion for forty years, than he who has been so for only ten? Or, it is said that the man of forty has a more mature judgment, and better understands his own feelings.

So, we answer, has a man of forty, who is blind, a more mature judgment than a child of ten who is also blind. But has he, in consequence, any better knowledge of colors than the child? Mental cultivation has not the slightest power to open blind eyes, or give spiritual perception. Sin has ample ability to deceive the most intelligent and mature, as well as the young and ignorant; indeed, in them it finds a larger material into which to transfuse its baneful poison, and so produce a deception deeper and stronger, and far less easy to be broken up. Hence the liability that a man of intelligence and strength of character will be deceived by sin, is at least equally strong with that which exists in the case of a child, or a person of limited intelligence. The more mental development and religious knowledge the individual possesses, the more ample means sin has for producing a counterfeit work, which shall be most likely to deceive. The materials being abundantly furnished, the inducement is strong for the sinner to attempt to erect a structure himself, with which to cover his houseless head.

### § IV. — Satanic Influence.

The last cause of which we shall treat as contributing to a merely supposed work of grace, is that of *Satanic influence.* Here we have to contemplate the personal agency of Satan himself, exerting a direct influence upon the minds of men in any and every possible way, in order to prevent them from becoming the true followers of Jesus Christ. He is "the prince of the power of the air, the spirit that now worketh in the children of disobedience." His influence is the opposite to that of the Holy Spirit, — the one being for evil, the other for good. The Holy

Spirit is the mightier agency; but the inferiority of the Evil Spirit is compensated, in part, by the fact that his operations are in accordance with the natural tendencies of the heart, while those of the Holy Spirit are against them. They form a parallel, too, in that these personal agencies themselves are invisible. "The wind bloweth where it listeth, and thou hearest the sound thereof, but canst not tell whence it cometh and whither it goeth; so is every one that is born of the Spirit," *or destroyed by the works of the Devil.* The Evil One, like the Holy Spirit, operates upon the mind, in perfect harmony with its free moral agency, so much so as to prevent all suspicion, on the part of the individual, that he is influenced from any external source. Like the Holy Spirit, he has an accurate knowledge of the human mind, the motives by which man is wont to be actuated, and is thoroughly acquainted with the secret avenues to the inmost recesses of his heart. He is well acquainted, also, with the plan of salvation, and all the features of an experimental work of grace.

But, unlike the Holy Spirit, the preëminent attribute of the Evil One is to deceive. He is a liar, and the father of lies, and especially of such lies as have the most resemblance to the truth. It is his particular province to deceive and blind the mind, as it is that of the Holy Spirit to undeceive and enlighten. He loves to see men resting upon false hopes of heaven, and loves to use his influence to produce them. He is the fabricator of spurious conversion, as the Holy Spirit is of genuine. He uses the same materials to construct his false work that the Holy Spirit does for the true, and, by a most artful counterfeit, he moulds them into the same external form. The Holy Spirit has a peculiar power to enlighten and convince the soul as to the genuineness of his work, and the Evil Spirit has a peculiar power to deceive the soul as to the genuineness of his. When men are being persuaded to seek for true religion, Satan knows too well how to thrust into their possession an artful counterfeit, if he cannot entice them into open sin. He loves to induce false hopes of being saved in the gospel way, because of the almost certain barrier they form against future genuine experience.

# CHAPTER III.

## RESULTS OF UNRECOGNIZABLE REGENERATION.

The results of being left to experience a false conversion, are inexpressibly sad. That chiefly to be lamented is the almost insuperable barrier it forms against an experience that is genuine. We can conceive of nothing which stands so directly in the way of a true work of grace, as a counterfeit of it; and the more perfect the counterfeit, the more efficient an obstacle it becomes. A false experience based upon sound doctrine, is most of all to be avoided. No change of sentiment can be expected to produce an improved condition. Hence a false professor of true religion is in a more dangerous case than a true professor of false religion.

It would seem as if the outward performance of Christian duties would, in process of time, lead to a vital acquaintance with them; but neither observation nor a sound philosophy confirms such a supposition. How rare an occurrence is it to see a person become truly converted, after having been introduced into the visible church of Christ! If the tendency of performing the outward duties of religion is to lead to conversion, such occurrences ought to be frequent in the churches, or else the membership is far more free from false professors than has ever been supposed. At all events, if the profession of religion tends to conversion, we should expect more conversions in the churches, or fewer exclusions from them. Facts, however, prove that neither the performance of the outward duties of religion, nor the restraints of a Christian profession, nor the discipline of the churches, has comparatively the least tendency to induce a vital knowledge of the truth where it has never before existed.

Who ever heard of church discipline being instrumental in the conversion of a wayward member? It has often been instrumental in the return of a backslider, or the repentance and reformation of a disciple that had wandered; but where the life has evinced that the person had never tasted the grace of God, the general effect of discipline has been to drive such from the visible fold. Those who have been led by this means to repentance and reformation, have seldom regarded this as their original conversion. Judas was driven to his own place, while Peter repented; but neither was converted after being received into the apostleship. Nor has the reflex influence of having performed, for a time, the outward duties of religion in the visible church, enjoyed its instructions and associations, and received its discipline, been referred to as the means, under God, of the individual's conversion at a subsequent period.

It is not the design of the cultivation attendant upon a Christian profession to produce a new and vital change in the heart, but to nurture that which is supposed to have taken place already. Nor can we expect that the Holy Spirit will interpose to bless the sacred influences of an outward profession of religion to the conversion of a deceived professor. If it were so, then Judas ought to have been converted, instead of hanging himself. The Holy Spirit operates upon the minds of men in harmony with natural laws. He never violates a true mental philosophy. We have no right to expect that he will employ that which is naturally suited to develop character, for the purpose of producing a radical change in the same. The individual who is deceived, whether he has publicly professed religion or not, naturally and necessarily, from the position he occupies, uses all the means of grace, not for the purpose of radically changing his character, but to improve it. Hence it is simply presumption for him to expect a vital change. It is not uncommon to find persons who have recently ventured to believe they have become Christians, using such language as this: "I mean to perform all my duties, and if I am not a Christian, I hope I shall become one." This is a vain hope. The performing of external duties does not make one a Christian. No man is in a position to do the duties of a Christian until he has become reconciled to an offended God. To attempt to perform them without repentance is assuming the changeableness of Jehovah; and no one can hope that that assumption will be blessed to his conversion. To direct a person therefore, who is seeking to become a Christian, to go forward and do his duties, leaving the question as to whether he has been converted, is dangerous in the extreme, in case such a one has not already passed the crisis of a gracious work.

Another obstacle in the way of the conversion of a false professor, is, that he has formed in his mind an idea of what the Christian graces and spirit are. It is an idea which he has cherished long, and hence it has become thoroughly imbedded into his mental constitution. From the want of spiritual enlightenment, no deficiency in his views has been discovered. His confidence is therefore unwavering and unbounded. He thinks he perfectly understands his feelings as they are and ought to be. To become truly converted, he must be stripped of these false conceptions. His confidence in his own views must be destroyed. It matters not how much nor how long he may have studied, and read, and heard, and compared, and seen, and weighed. If the Holy Spirit has not enlightened his soul, then he knows nothing yet as he ought to know. Before he becomes a Christian he must realize this. His knowledge must be reduced to the zero point. He must be brought, like a little child in absolute darkness, to beg for light. But this is difficult. These natural and false conceptions have become indurated into a long cherished and established creed. He has been in the habit of exercising a kind of repentance, faith, love, joy, and hope, and has regarded them as truly Christian exercises. He has been accustomed to enjoy prayer, and has firmly believed it to be real spiritual enjoyment; whereas, in spirit, none of these have the semblance of a truly Christian character. He has not the slightest conception of the possibility of an experience of these things lying beyond his own. To undergo such an extreme change, therefore, in his views, becomes, humanly speaking, a moral impossibility. He has, indeed, no inclination to seek for such a change. He performs all duties, therefore, receives all instruction, and makes all research to confirm the course he has chosen.

The deceived professor has been accustomed, also, to a false *exercise* of the Christian graces. This is likewise an obstacle in the way of an exercise that is genuine.

In the first place, the feeling that one is very *far* from having in exercise the Christian graces, is one of the most favorable mental states for acquiring them. There needs to be a cultivated habit, on the part of unconverted men, of believing that they are by nature utterly destitute of everything that has even the semblance of the fruits of the Spirit, in order to ensure the greatest promise of future blessing. This should not be merely a passing feeling, but an abiding conviction, which has grown with the growth, and become an essential part of the mental constitution.

He who has been in the habit, for any length of time, of believing himself to be a Christian, is in the opposite of this condition. He has been accustomed to believe that he has had the Christian graces in exercise. Or, if he comes to the conclusion that he has been mistaken in regard to the nature of his exercises, he still retains the feeling that he has made a somewhat near approach to true religion. A man who has had in his possession counterfeit money, which he believed to be good, has a different feeling from one who has never owned even a counterfeit dollar in his life. He still retains, for a time, the worthless material about him, and does not feel so poor in possession of it, though convinced of its worthlessness, as he would without it.

It is even so with him who has for a time been in possession of a counterfeit religion. In the nature of the case, it is impossible for him to realize his destitution as otherwise he would. That which has the close appearance of real money, or true religion, serves to create and sustain the impression that it is such; and, in the case of religion, by so much is the earnestness in seeking for that which is genuine impaired. To be deeply and vitally earnest in seeking, the sinner must be dispossessed of the feeling that he has ever made the slightest approach to a spiritual condition. Under ordinary circumstances, this is difficult. It is even more difficult than the work of conversion proper. In the case before us it is especially so. It is more difficult to become disabused of old habits of thought and feeling, than to acquire new ones.

The individual, for example, has been in the habitual exercise of a kind of prayer, repentance, faith, and love, which are thoroughly spurious. To divest himself of the habit induced by these exercises is, humanly speaking, a matter of almost utter impossibility,—which stands in the way of a vital religious experience. If an original, literary education is imperfect or false, it is fatal to a finished and perfect scholarship thereafter. Analogous are the effects of a false religious experience. It were far better for a person never to have had any conceptions of the Christian graces, or any religious exercises, than such as are false.

The natural *pride* of the heart is also opposed to the abandonment of one's opinions and exercises, especially if they have been cherished long. The *truly* regenerate person may have sufficient humility to confess to an error in religious experience, but it can hardly be expected of one whose natural pride is yet unsubdued. Such persons often declare their willingness and desire to see and confess their error, if they are in error; but they have not the slightest conception that such is the case, or they would not be so ready to make this declaration. Indeed, they are resolved to shut their eyes against it. Their pride stimulates them to cling to their profession, when it has once been made, in the face of the most appalling danger.

It is also a *disappointment* to an individual to abandon what he has believed to be a good preparation for death and a glorious immortality. It is a disappointment which he dreads to incur, and feels he cannot endure. Besides, an instinctive feeling of *unsafety* is connected with it. The person says: "If I abandon this, I have nothing to cling to. My hope is then entirely gone." The actual sentiment of his heart is, though he would not like to acknowledge it, that a false hope is better than none.

The deceived professor also being unenlightened, and hence incapable of perceiving any imperfection in his hope, cannot feel that he *ought* to abandon it. Ordinarily, persons in this state conceive that to do so would be exceedingly wrong. The true Christian often thinks it wrong to cherish his hope while so much cause exists for its abandonment; but the false professor thinks it would be wrong to abandon his while so much cause exists for cherishing it. He looks upon the integrity of his life, the correctness of his example, and his promptness and strictness in the performance of religious duties, and ascribes them to the efficiency of his hope. He believes that he has great love for Christ, enjoyment of prayer, desire to do good, and ascribes these to the same source. To abandon a hope, therefore, which is productive of so much good, he thinks would be a great moral wrong.

The question may arise here whether false professors of religion do, ordinarily, thus continue to cherish hope, and maintain an outward conformity to the requirements of their profession; or whether, in process of time, from the want of a true relish for religious things, they do not lose their zeal, lapse into worldliness, and so conclude they have been deceived; or, still again, whether they do not, ere long, fall into some open violation of their profession, become subject to excommunication, and in this way arrive at the same conclusion of self-deception? Undoubtedly many do thus lapse into worldliness, and lose their religious zeal; and many more fall into open sin, and lose their connection with the visible church. What proportion of all who suffer exclusion are false professors, or what proportion of false professors suffer exclusion, we cannot say. It is, however, to be regretted that so many, who give no evidence of true piety, are left to persevere so long in maintaining an outward conformity to the requirements of their profession upon a self-righteous basis. Facts will sustain the statement, also, that those who fall from their profession seldom conclude, in consequence of it, that they were deceived; or if they do, they seldom or never afterwards become truly converted.

Undoubtedly the collected history of those who, from want of a true relish for spiritual things, have lapsed into worldliness and lost their profession, would show that their course has been as follows: Either they have become careless and indifferent about their religion until the approach of death, when their old hope has been recovered from the rubbish in which it had been buried long, for the purpose of sustaining them in the dying hour, and easing them off as comfortably as possible into a dreadful eternity; or else, in some time of affliction or religious awakening, they have been led to resume their profession upon the original basis, and retain it until eternity has revealed to them its real nature. The history of those, too, who have lost their profession by open violation, would show that they have, in consequence, either acquired a profound disgust for religion and distrust of its reality, which has continued to the end of life, or, except in the rare instances of confession and reformation, they have justified themselves, decried the decision which condemned them, and so determined to continue until the final judgment which shall settle all. In neither of these classes has there been an abandonment of the original ground of hope, and a new and genuine experience of vital religion. Hence it may be stated, as a general rule, that false professors of religion live and die resting for salvation upon no other than the basis of a false profession.

This leads us to speak finally of the mental *attitude* of

hope, in a deceived professor, as being an almost insuperable barrier against genuine experience. Facts show that hope once cherished for any length of time, whether true or false, is seldom abandoned. An intelligent Christian deacon, upon a sick-bed, in reply to a remark that it was hoped he was enjoying the comforts of religion, once said: "If I am not prepared to die, it is too late; I shall probably rest upon the hope of my youth. It is difficult to abandon a hope that has been cherished so long." The remark is full of truth, and is as pertinent to a false hope as to one that is genuine. Men seldom pull down a pleasant and comfortable dwelling, simply because its foundation is in the sand.

The mental habitude of hoping is directly averse to those states of mind which are most favorable to regeneration. It is a state from which it is exceedingly difficult for the individual to free himself, and one whose effects it is impossible for him wholly to remove, even when convinced that his hope is spurious, and must be abandoned. The mind cannot restore itself to the position in which it would have been if it had never occupied the attitude of hope. It cannot, so to speak, *un-hope* itself, and assume the condition of one lost. When, through the persuasion of others, or conviction of its worthlessness, the hope of the individual is given up, as is sometimes done, it fails to be accompanied with that deep sense of alarm which is experienced by the awakened sinner. He does not realize his utter helplessness and dependence on the sovereign power of God in such a manner as to subserve a work of grace. What he has done already, he has done in his own strength, and he feels that by greater exertion he could do still more.

It would seem as if an individual, having exerted himself to the best of his ability, and supposed he had succeeded, on discovering that his success was false, would distrust his own strength, and cast himself upon God for help. This is doubtless often the case, with one who does not go so far as to entertain hope; but when that position has been attained, and occupied for a time, it is believed that such a result seldom follows. The language of the individual is more likely to be, "I have done the best I could, and if my hope is not good, I cannot help it; I am not to blame." Instead of being led to cry to God for mercy, because of the insufficiency of his own efforts, he is rather disposed to self-justification, in consequence of having done the best he could. Since he can do no more, he is determined now to throw the responsibility of his salvation on God. In this mental attitude, his original hope revives. It is nurtured by a recollection of what he has done. He cannot resign himself fully to the conviction that all his prayers, and works, and professions, in the exercise of which he thought he enjoyed so much, will be utterly lost, and go for nothing. Instead of being penetrated with a sense of his awful guilt in having rendered to God nothing but a solemn mockery, and having worshipped and served him solely from selfish and self-righteous motives, his self-justifying spirit gains the ascendency, and prompts him to fall back upon what he has done, and risk the event.

In some instances, by the persuasion of faithful Christian counsellors, persons who have been left to entertain false hopes of salvation, conclude, with little reluctance, to abandon them, and resolve to seek God anew. Even then the prospect is equally dark and unpromising. A repeated effort is almost sure to end in a second spurious result. The mind and heart are more likely to resume their former course than they were to adopt it at the first. The individual, instead of feeling his helplessness and ignorance of all spiritual things, and crying to God to teach him and give him strength, renews his undertaking to become a Christian, by exercises of the same character with those which had before subserved his self-deception.

He has been accustomed, for example, to the exercise of prayer. In his endeavor to seek God anew, he resorts to the same kind of prayer with that to which he had long been accustomed, but which had produced only a spurious religion. He is far less likely to feel that he cannot pray, — that he does not know how to pray, but must be taught of God, and be so broken down under the weight of the feeling, as, out of the depths of his despair, to implore for mercy, — than he would have been if he had never accustomed himself to a kind of prayer which he believed to be good. The same is true with his attempt to realize all the Christian graces, repentance, faith, love. Instead of regarding these old exercises as useless and worthless, and seeking for others quite diverse, he attempts so to repair and improve the old as to render them acceptable with God.

The false professor, who concludes that he has been deceived, frequently thinks he has discovered wherein his error lay. He sees where he made his mistake, and now resolves to correct it. In such a case, according to human view, it is impossible to discover the slightest ray of hope. The belief that he understands his error, and that he sees how he can rectify it, is one of the most discouraging features of the case. If he felt that he had been groping in the dark, while he knew it not; that he was blind; that godliness was a mystery infinitely beyond his comprehension, and that he had sinned in presuming to understand it; if he felt that he knew nothing about himself, or the way of life, but was shut up in darkness and despair, not knowing whither to turn for light or help, but ready to be forever lost, — there would be some encouragement of a speedy relief. Such is not commonly the case with one who is seeking to revise and correct a spurious hope. He thinks he has discovered his error, and tries to avoid it only to fall into another equally fatal and deceptive.

In view of these results of a spurious conversion, it will be felt that the prospect which lies before one who has been deceived is exceedingly unpromising and forbidding. And this we believe to be the truth. It is the feeling which we have sought in these remarks to produce, and that for two reasons. The first is, that a greater fear of such a result may be awakened in the minds of unconverted men, and of Christians who have the guidance of them, as the best safeguard against it. The second is, that those who are occupying such a position may be deeply alarmed at the almost necessarily fatal consequences attendant upon their state, as the best means of being rescued from it. And yet we can discover *here* scarcely a ray of hope, since those who have most cause for it are least likely to be alarmed. Even this consideration, the hopelessness of their condition, will be unlikely to move them. Their confidence and their blindness constitute a barrier against the inlet of all light upon their state. *We* see no way of escape from the finally fatal effects of being left to experience a spurious conversion, if hope is indulged for any considerable period. Jonathan Edwards has remarked that the condition of a deceived professor is next to that of those who have committed the unpardonable sin. The nature of its workings, so far as we have witnessed and can comprehend them, combine with facts to sustain the belief that a false hope is one of the snares of the devil, in which the souls of men are taken captive by him at his will. It is Satan's life-boat, in which he gives, to as many souls as he can persuade to betake themselves to it, a pleasant and sunny voyage down the current of time, safe from its shoals and quicksands, to the gates of endless death. The only relief we can find in the midst of these considerations, for those who are self-deceived, is, that "*with God all things are possible.*" Where there shines not a ray of human hope, God's help can come. Whoever has been deceived, will be saved, if saved at all, by a special and unusual act of sovereign grace. He will be among those exceeding few, who constitute the rare exceptions to the rule of God's universal dealings with men.

# CHAPTER IV.

## REMEDY OF UNRECOGNIZABLE REGENERATION.

From what has been said in regard to the results of false conversion, it will be evident that but little can be added upon this final part of the subject. The remedy of a state of self-deception is to be looked for only in an extraordinary interposition of Him with whom all things are possible. Our wisdom fails, therefore, to point out a mode of treatment best suited to bring unconverted professing Christians to a knowledge of the truth. And yet it does not follow that Christians have no duty to discharge towards them. If the only hope for them is in an extraordinary divine interposition, surpassing the reach of human understanding, and if there is here the slightest ground of hope, evidently one great duty of Christians is earnest supplication to God in their behalf. They are eminently suitable subjects of prayer, which is appointed to be employed especially where all human wisdom and help have come to nought.

This class of unconverted men demand also Christian *sympathy*. Their condition calls for a sympathy, or at least a pity, which they cannot appreciate, and of which they feel no need. The true Christian, who rightly apprehends their condition, must be deeply affected in view of it. He will have no disposition to denounce or condemn; but his soul will yearn with compassion over them.

Nothing is better calculated to induce the profoundest humility before God, and a sense of gratitude for divine illumination, than a just apprehension of the spiritually benighted condition of a self-deceived professor of religion. In this state of humility and gratitude, the Christian will be moved with the deepest sympathy for his brother, whom God, "who giveth not account of any of his matters," hath not seen fit to enlighten. A view of real midnight darkness, in contrast with a supposed noonday brightness, must sorely pain the heart of any Christian who has the slightest appreciation of the value of spiritual light. This sympathy and pain are greatly increased, too, when he learns that all his efforts to dispel the fatal illusion seem destined to utter failure. If the Christian is ever grateful for his own experience of divine grace, and longs to witness the same in another, it will be in such a connection as this.

In addition to the manifest duty of prayer and sympathy, we suggest whether it is not also the duty of the Christian, however painful it may be, if he has reason to feel that a fellow-man, with whom he must stand ere long at the bar of God, is thus fatally deceived by sin and Satan, faithfully and kindly to warn him of the dreadful danger to which he is exposed, leaving the result with Him whose rightful province it is, after all we can do, to "have mercy on whom He will have mercy." Can the Christian stand acquitted at the bar of God, without having performed this duty?

If, to human view, no remedy can be found for such a state, when it has been induced, the question will arise, Are there no means of preventing it? For this purpose, the cultivation of a more thorough acquaintance with the operations of the Holy Spirit in regeneration, in distinction from the workings of man's religious nature, as excited by other causes, seems to us to be of the utmost importance. Human instrumentality appears to be of no avail to remedy a spurious conversion, except in its earliest stages, before a state of false hope has become fairly settled. The work of God's spirit upon the soul ordinarily carries with it its own credentials. When God performs a work of grace in the heart, it gives, at an early period and throughout, to one who is conversant with the Spirit's operations, a peculiar promise of a happy result. It is a promise, of which a work carried on by the individual himself is destitute. It is impossible that a person should seek to become a Christian in the same manner without as with the Spirit's aid. We have shown that he may produce a counterfeit of the Spirit's work which is very likely to deceive. It will, however, at most, have the form without the power.

The character of false religious experience, even before it has come to maturity, should be understood as thoroughly as possible by those who have the guidance of inquiring souls, and the remedy applied at an early stage of its progress. The first rising of the natural hope of the person, if he has had no sense of his lost condition, should be arrested. He should be distinctly shown that he does not yet realize his condition, and that he is in imminent danger of finally losing his soul, if he allows himself to rest upon his present foundation. Even the feeling of *hopefulness* that he is making progress, should be promptly checked. The inquirer should be taught that if he realized his lost condition to any adequate degree, instead of feeling hopeful, he would be almost in the agony of despair, till rescued by sovereign grace.

The means employed to check the rising of a spurious

hope must be positive and decided. Simple caution, or a mere suggestion to the person that there is danger of being deceived, and that he should carefully examine himself, will not suffice. This might be sufficient in case he were not deceived; but otherwise, it will be of no avail. Not being enlightened and softened, he will not seriously lay to heart a mere suggestion. Or, if it should lead him to self-examination, it would be so superficial as only to confirm him in his false position. He must not be left to examine and decide as to his condition for himself. He has no ability to make a true self-examination. He must be *shown* that his exercises come far short of being truly gracious. Nor is it enough that he should conclude, merely upon the decision of another, that he is deceived. He must, if possible, be led to see for himself that all he has done is only the acting of his sinful and deceptive heart, and must go for nothing. Every source of reliance must be removed from his mind, so that, of his own accord, he shall abandon all semblance of hope.

It must, after all, be remembered, as an unchangeable truth, before which both the Christian and the sinner must bow, that nothing can be done to change a spurious to a genuine conversion, without the interposition of God's Almighty Spirit. Such a change can no more be effected by human instrumentality than a genuine work of grace can be commenced and carried on thus, in the heart of the most abandoned sinner. Supplication must be made for the Spirit's aid, with complete submission to his rightful sovereignty in renewing the hearts of men.

Thus we have said what little we can in regard to the remedy of a spurious conversion. It will be felt that even before a false hope has come to maturity, the prospect of effecting a happy change is exceedingly small. The reason a false work is going on, or has been completed, is, that the Holy Spirit is not connected with the means employed. This is a deficiency which man cannot remedy. The most he can do may be to break up or arrest a work that is spurious, and leave the person with no hope, instead of one that is false,—a condition much to be preferred. And yet facts seem to teach that this can seldom be effectually accomplished. A false conversion is the fabrication of the Evil One, whose wiles are quite sure to foil the wisdom of man. A spurious hope, though entertained with apparently much greater confidence, is yet often more readily abandoned than one that is genuine; but the abandonment of it is commonly as false and insincere as the hope itself. Ordinarily, it seems to be given up rather to produce a show of honesty than from any honest purpose, since it is so certain to revive at a subsequent period, and again deceive its possessor,—the whole being merely a deceit of Satan, the more perfectly to beguile the soul which he has in charge. It is natural for both Christians and the deceived person himself to take it for granted that if the latter has abandoned one hope and obtained another, the second must necessarily be genuine; especially if, as is commonly the case, it professes to be quite unlike the first,—the principle being forgotten that while an article which is genuine can be but one, its counterfeits may be many. The Great Deceiver of men seems to be aware of this, and hence allows the subject of a false hope to abandon it, for the purpose of thrusting into his possession another, which shall effect a more complete deception of himself and others.

These statements are founded upon careful observation of facts. They have been made to show that too great caution cannot be exercised in regard to renewing a spurious hope, or substituting another in its place. It is believed that the danger of self-deception is far greater in the second instance than the first. It must, however, be stated that the prospect here, though gloomy, is not entirely dark. Experience and observation teach that the faithful performance of duty will sometimes find, even in such circumstances as these, a present and happy reward. In some instances, though rare, the prompt arrest of a false experience, even after having for a little time passed its crisis, has been known to be followed, eventually, by a truly gracious result. Duty, therefore, is plain, while the event is with God.

# PART III.

## RECOGNIZED REGENERATION;

OR,

## FAITH AND HOPE.

# RECOGNIZED REGENERATION.

## DIVISION FIRST.

### PRELIMINARY DISCUSSION.

## CHAPTER I.

POSSIBILITY OF RECOGNITION — BY THE SUBJECT — BY OTHERS.

It has been stated in the first part of this volume that there are many professing Christians who do not know when they were converted. In the second part it has been added that there are also many who do not know that they never were converted. We remark now, that there are many professing Christians who do not *know* that they *ever* were converted. This is by far the largest class. Almost all true Christians do, at some time, have misgivings whether they are really the children of God. This is quite likely to occur in the early part of the Christian life. In some it is outgrown with advancement in knowledge and experience. With others it is only an occasional and transient feeling. With others still, it is abiding: they have a constant desire, if they are Christians, to know it more perfectly, and be able to give a reason of the hope that is in them.

This feeling has doubtless been fostered, rather than

otherwise, in the minds of Christians of this class who may have read the preceding parts of this volume. They will be embarrassed more than ever respecting their evidence of having been truly born again, and will more than ever feel the need of being instructed in regard to the Spirit's work upon the heart, and so confirmed in the hopes they have ventured to cherish. If many persons, who are truly converted, believe they are not, and many more, who are not, believe they are, the question will arise, How can any one know whether he is a Christian or not? and how can this be known with regard to others? Some may have felt that there *is* no positive knowledge upon the subject. They will say: "We do not believe any one can know certainly that he or any one else is a Christian." It is incumbent upon us, therefore, to exhibit the features and marks of a recognized and genuine work of grace, in distinction from the unrecognized and spurious, which have been described.

We shall attempt to answer these two inquiries: First, Can a regenerate person be certified of his regenerate state; and if so, how? Secondly, Can a regenerate person be certified of the regenerate state of others; and if so, how? The inquiry is not how a professing Christian may know whether he is a true Christian, nor how *any* one can know whether others are Christians. The case of a self-deceived professor has been considered, and the conclusion is, that he is not likely, in this world, to discover his condition. The inquiry pertains, therefore, to persons actually in a regenerate state. Nor do we raise the question whether unregenerate persons can be certified of the regenerate state of others, since they have no knowledge of spiritual things, and, of course, can know nothing of the regenerate character.

That these are inquiries of importance, none will deny. If any light can be thrown upon them, good will be accomplished. Some will say: "It is presumptuous to discuss these topics — God only knows the heart." We acknowledge the truthfulness and solemnity of the thought. He who pretends to know much of his own heart, or the hearts of others, evidently knows little. But should we on this account be deterred altogether from considering the subject? Because we can know little, shall we not seek to know what we can? It is idle to say that because we cannot be as gods, we will not be as men. God is willing to give all the light it is best for us to have, upon every subject; and it is best for us to seek all he is willing to give. Nor need we fear that by our research we shall find out any secrets which it is improper for us to know, or which God designs to keep to himself.

Each of the inquiries submitted is of a twofold nature. In the former, the first question is, Can a regenerate person be certified of his regenerate state? If this is answered affirmatively, the question will be, *How* can this be done? In the latter, the first question is, Can a regenerate person be certified of the regenerate state of others? If this is answered affirmatively, the question will be, How can this be done?

The reader is desired now, once for all, to remember that we are not seeking for the tests of sanctification, but of regeneration. The point is this: Is provision made, in the economy of grace, for a person in the ordinary regenerate state to know that he is a child of God? and is provision made for Christians to know the same respecting others? Besides, when we speak of *knowing*, we do not mean absolute or infallible knowledge. This belongs to

God. But is there as real a basis of human knowledge here as in any other sphere?

We shall first present some considerations to show that this must be the case. The first is, that Christians *act* as if they were certified of having been born again. They order the entire course of their lives according to this supposition. When they publicly profess the religion of Christ, they declare before God, men, and angels, their belief that they are Christians. This requires no slight conviction of its truthfulness. It matters not that it is done with fear and trembling. This only indicates that they realize the solemn import of the action. The false professor does the same without fear and trembling, because he does not appreciate the nature of the act.

Besides, Christians assume *responsibilities* which indicate a certitude of their condition. In uniting with the visible Church of Christ, they place themselves in a position calculated to forestall their becoming Christians, if they are not such already. It leads them not to seek to become changed, but to maintain the change they are supposed to have undergone. Hence they risk their salvation upon their belief that they are Christians.

God also requires Christians to act upon the supposition that they know they have been born again. He requires them publicly to profess his name and celebrate his ordinances, which he would not do without giving them the needed qualification.

Though it is not becoming in man to claim absolute knowledge in any sphere, yet the actions of Christians give the strongest indications of it possible. It would be no more legitimate to infer that the husbandman who cultivates the seed he has sown knows he shall reap a harvest, than that the Christian who cultivates the seed of divine grace in his heart knows he shall reap the fruit of everlasting life. The Christian will encounter the most serious risks that can be incurred, upon the simple strength of his belief that he is a child of God. Death itself, in the most painful form, has no power to shake it.

That regenerate persons have the means of being certified of the regenerate state of *others*, is also manifest. The existence, perpetuation, and operations of the visible churches of Christ, involve the necessity of it. If these are, in the main, composed of Christ's disciples, collected together out of the world, then it cannot be conceived by what means this should take place, unless by virtue of an ability not only to be certified of their own regeneration, but also to recognize the regenerate condition of each other. Without an ability to discover the regenerate character in others, how could Christian churches appropriate to themselves regenerate persons and at the same time debar the unregenerate? What significance would there be in the relation of Christian experiences and the examination of candidates, in order to guard against the admission of unconverted persons to the membership of the churches? The labors also of Christians are put forth, upon the supposition that they have the means of knowing whether others are in a natural or a spiritual state. They treat all men with whom they come in contact as being either in a lost condition, or as heirs of salvation.

The mission on which Christians are sent into the world necessitates a knowledge of its religious condition. Of what avail would be spiritual guides to lead men to Jesus Christ, if they can have no means of knowing whether they are already in Christ? The disciples of Christ, in carrying out the command to go and teach all nations, cannot avoid forming their judgments in regard to the religious condition of those whom they teach. They are obliged to expose the false pretensions of men, to declare to them that they are yet in their sins, and except they repent they shall all perish.

In forming their judgments, also, they are obliged to assume most weighty and solemn responsibilities. The baptism of persons professing piety, and their reception into a visible church, are expressive of the belief that they have been truly born again. It does not avail to call it a judgment of charity, or to instruct candidates that they must not regard these acts as a sanction of their hopes, but must assume the Christian name upon their own profession of faith. These are useful cautions, but they do not diminish aught of the significance of an admission into the fellowship of a Christian church. This will still be regarded, especially by the self-deceived, as confirmatory of their own belief that they are Christians. Here is a responsibility which Christ must have furnished his followers qualifications for assuming. So long as they labor for the conversion of men, they must have some means of recognizing it when it occurs.

But how is it practically? Are not Christians often as well convinced of the regenerate state of others as of anything within the limits of their knowledge? Nor is this confined to a few exceptional cases of such as are known to have attained to an unusual degree of godliness. Two Christians, hitherto strangers, fall into each other's society, and at once become as well assured of the renewal of each other by the Holy Spirit as they are of each other's moral and rational character. Each is as thoroughly satisfied of the regenerate state of the other as he is of his own, or of the reality of true religion. Unless these impressions are altogether delusive, they indicate that Christians have an ability of knowing each other. They are not left in entire uncertainty who are their real associates in this world, and who are to be so in the world to come.

It will be said that it cannot be known who are Christians, with any infallible certainty. But this does not preclude the supposition that a foundation of actual knowledge exists here as really as in any other sphere. The fact, too, that in some cases so high a degree of certainty is derived from so limited acquaintance, is evidence that there are sources of knowledge here as yet undeveloped.

These considerations lead to an affirmative answer, modified in its positiveness no farther than all subjects are as comprehended by men. Either the means of propagating experimental religion, as they have existed since the time of Christ, are upon a false basis, or there must be in its nature a ground of certitude of our own regeneration, and the regeneration of others, as real as exists in any other department of knowledge.

# CHAPTER II.

## MODE OF RECOGNITION — GENERAL PRINCIPLE STATED AND ILLUSTRATED.

### § I. — People of God peculiar — Christ peculiar — Godliness a mystery.

The questions to be considered now are, first, How can a regenerate person be certified of his regenerate state? and secondly, How can a regenerate person be certified of the regenerate state of others? It cannot be expected, however much it may be desired, that questions of such magnitude can be answered in a word. To be of any service, an answer will involve a brief review of the groundwork of experimental religion. The proposition by which we shall be guided in taking this review, is this: *The regenerate character is peculiar and distinct from all other, and by its peculiarities and distinctiveness it is to be known.* The idea designed to be conveyed by this statement is, that it is unlike all other, in being possessed of a singularity, strangeness, incomprehensibility and mysteriousness. It is not meant, however, that the people of God are an eccentric people. They are peculiar, not absolutely, but relatively. Their peculiarities are actually regularities, in perfect harmony with man's original and proper constitution; and only so far as they are peculiar, are they true to nature, — the departure from the real standard of human character being on the part of the unregenerate.

The doctrine is everywhere taught in the Bible that

the people of God are a peculiar people, distinguishable by their peculiarities from all other religionists. They have upon them a seal which marks them as the chosen of God and regenerate by the Holy Ghost. They stand out as an unworld-like, spiritual, *sui generis* people. They are a sect everywhere spoken against, on account of the strangeness and incomprehensibility, not less than the excellence of their character.

Christ himself arrested attention, and excited hatred from the world, not solely because of his holiness, or of his religious strictness and zeal, — for the Pharisees were outwardly, in most respects, as strict and zealous as he. It was, in part at least, because of the strangeness of his holy character and precepts to unenlightened men. His presence constituted a disturbing force in the world. Humanity was moved by it wherever he went. His character was a profound mystery to all who witnessed it. "The people were astonished at his doctrine." "The men marvelled, saying, What manner of man is this?" "They besought him to depart out of their coasts." Even his followers are often represented as standing in awe of his character, from the want of a perfect apprehension of it. "When the disciples saw him walking on the sea, they were troubled, saying, It is a spirit." On another occasion, it is said that, in view of a certain manifestation of himself, "they fell on their face and were sore afraid." He was at last put out of the world, in part, because men stood in a kind of superstitious awe and fear of his presence. Paul informs us that had the Jews known the hidden wisdom of his mysterious character, they would not have crucified the Lord of glory. When they did crucify him, it was performed somewhat as a matter of doubtful experiment. They looked on to see whether he would die like other men, or would save himself and come down from the cross. The men of the world were agitated and perplexed, in view of the supernaturalness of his character, up to the hour of his death; and that perplexity will never cease to the end of time.

The followers of Christ are one with him, and partake of the mysteriousness of his holy character.

The Scriptures also represent godliness, which is a characteristic of the Christian, as being to the natural man a mystery. Paul declares to Timothy, that "without controversy, great is the mystery of godliness." But it is so only to the natural apprehension. The language of the converted soul is, "Whereas I was blind, now I see." Christ said to his disciples, "Unto you it is given to know the mysteries of the kingdom of heaven, but unto them that are without, it is not given; because they seeing see not, and hearing, they hear not, neither do they understand."

Godliness, to the natural man, is a mystery, both as to its nature and existence. He has no *consciousness* of what godliness is, because he has none in him — sin having corrupted him; and he has no perception of it out of himself, since he has no spiritual sight — sin having blinded him. He cannot *conceive* of the existence of godliness, for he has never witnessed anything more nearly related to it than his own self-righteous ungodliness; and this is so good in his sight, that he perceives no occasion for any other kind of godliness. The announcement of a necessity for it is to him a stumbling-block and foolishness. To the Christian, godliness is incomprehensible, not in nature, but in extent. To the natural man it is so in both. He can no more comprehend its alphabet than he can the whole science of the Godhead.

The science of Algebra is a mystery to one unacquainted with its signs and symbols. But let these be known, and its mystery is removed, though there may be no conception of the extent of its wonderful solutions. An intelligent mind is restive upon being made to believe in its existence, while ignorant of its elemental nature. So, to the unenlightened, spiritual things are a mystery. They have no conception of their superior nature or existence, while compelled to believe in both. No wonder a moral being, thus conditioned, is restive. Christ is a root out of dry ground to the men of the world; he has no form nor comeliness; and yet a conviction of his superior character and presence disturbs them. Let, however, the unenlightened be initiated into the mere beginnings of spiritual things, and their perplexity is at once removed. They have come out of darkness into light. Profound depths lie before them unexplored; but this does not pain them as before, because the nature of these things is no more involved in mystery. Having been enlightened as to their excellent character, they are nothing disturbed by the conviction that in extent they may be infinite.

Had man never fallen, godliness would have been no more a mystery to him than natural science. He would have had the capacity, when instructed in its elements, to understand its nature. But now it is not so. He may be instructed to any extent, and still be unable to penetrate the thick darkness which encases it, because he has no qualification to discern spiritual things. In renewing the heart, the Holy Spirit not only produces godliness, but also a perception of its nature. The person has only the smallest beginnings of godliness; his perceptions, also, are correspondingly limited; yet they are clear as the morning light. These new moral affections and perceptions are the peculiarities which mark the regenerate character, and by which it is to be known.

### § II. — Regenerate Character not known by Religious Manifestations.

A common and natural supposition is, that the regenerate character is to be known simply by its religious manifestations, which are equally comprehensible by all. If a man is actively and zealously religious, especially in an evangelical direction, the impression naturally produced is that he is pious. But this is not legitimate, because man is not less really a religious being by nature than by grace, in his fallen than his unfallen condition. The fall did not destroy, but perverted, his religious constitution. Before he fell, he had tendencies to worship, which still remain. Then he was inclined to worship God, but now to worship gods, of which himself is chief. Man has always possessed a faculty to love God, to pray, to exercise faith, hope, repentance, religious zeal, and indeed all the Christian graces. Before the fall, this faculty was upright; now, perverse. His love for the Creator and the creature is corrupted by the infusion of a selfish element. The object of regeneration is not to create religious faculties, but to restore existing ones to their original and proper exercise.

Man is also as *thoroughly* a religious being now as before he fell. God made man solely to reflect honor upon himself in all his relations. Hence his religious character absorbed originally every feature of his constitution. This constitution still remains the same. Nothing has been lost, nothing added. Every act, word, thought, and feeling, still has a religious bearing. God commands that whether we eat or drink, or whatsoever we do, we do all to his glory. If we do this, we shall be entirely religious; if we fail, or act otherwise, it will be sin; and all sin has a religious connection. It is a violation of religious obligation; that is, it is perverted religion. All hypocrisy and self-righteousness are not more properly and truly false religion than selfishness, pride, covetousness, and every kind of open vice and crime. The first murder had an immediate religious connection. It was the fruit of a perverted religious constitution. The same is true of the highest crime the world ever witnessed, — the crucifixion of the Son of God. All immorality and crime are the result of man's departure from his Maker. Before he fell, he was thoroughly and properly religious; since the fall, he is thoroughly but improperly so, unless renewed by grace. Hence the regenerate character cannot be known by the *extent* of man's religious manifestations.

Man is also as *actively* religious as before he fell. The fall did not impair the energy or vitality of his religious forces. They still produce fruit, therefore, but a wild and unwholesome product. The distinction between the spiritual and the natural state pertains not to the fruitfulness, but the healthiness of the two conditions. The object of regeneration is not to produce religious activity so much as to sanctify it. This is recognized in our Saviour's words, "By their fruits ye shall know them." He reminds the disciples that there are false religious fruits, as well as true, illustrating it by representing a corrupt, equally with a good tree, as bearing fruit, but of a different quality. Hence he instructs them to beware not of persons of no religious activity, but of false religious teachers; and that they should know them not by the abundance, but the kind of their fruits. He declares that "not every one that saith Lord, Lord, shall enter into the kingdom of heaven;" that many at the last day will claim that they have prophesied and cast out devils, and done many wonderful religious works, to whom he will say, "Depart from me, ye that work iniquity!" If Paul was not as active, religiously, before as after conversion, he was more so before than many are after. He was more active in advocating false religion than most are the true. The heathen worship as abundantly as do Christian nations — the most unevangelical sects as any others. Oftentimes the rectifying of man's religious nature stimulates its action, as the grafting of a tree may increase the quantity of the fruit; but no amount of religious activity can be regarded as an unmistakable sign of grace. It has been shown that other causes of awakening exist besides the Holy Spirit, — the degree depending not always upon the power of the awakening force, but upon the individual's constitutional susceptibility.

Man may also be *in form* as *soundly* religious in his apostate as his original, in his natural as his spiritual condition. It has been shown what causes, independently of the Holy Spirit, may conduce to mould his religious activities into a proper form. In view of this, our Saviour exhorts the disciples to beware of religious teachers who were outwardly sheep, but inwardly wolves; who advocated the external exercises and forms, not of false but of true religion. He adds, also, that to many who claimed to have prophesied *in his name*, and in his name cast out devils, and done many wonderful works, he would say, at the last day, "Depart! I never knew you!" On this account, too, he declares that they should be known by the nature, not the form of their fruits.

It cannot be inferred from this that there is anything in

man's naturally religious condition that can be developed into piety. By saying that he is a religious being, we do not mean to assert that he is either sinful or holy, but that he has the capability of being either. Nor is it any objection to the statement that he is a religious being to say that he is not always religiously active. The unregenerate are not always in a state of perverse, nor the regenerate in a state of healthy activity; but both are susceptible of being awakened at any moment, and to almost any degree.

### § III. — Regeneration necessitates a Religious Constitution.

In regeneration, a new creature is begotten in man by the Holy Spirit. This implies a constitutional relation both between the natural man and the Holy Spirit, and the natural and the spiritual man. This relation is that of a religious constitution. Had this religious constitution become extinct, and not merely degenerated by sin, we could not conceive of such a reunion between man and the Spirit as would result in the birth of a new spiritual man. Hence the necessity that man, even in his fallen condition, should have a religious constitution, in order to be a subject of regeneration.

This new creature which is born in man, but begotten by the Holy Spirit, according to the Scripture, is of necessity a spiritual man, having all the faculties and elemental principles of a man, but spiritual in character, — the prototype being found in Christ, born of a woman by the Holy Spirit, and hence perfect man, though divine; the offspring, in either case, having no more nor less elements of character than the united sources which produce it. Hence the new man will possess spiritual sight, taste, hearing, judgment, as well as spiritual affections. In harmony with this, it is written, "He that hath ears to hear, let him hear;" that is, he that hath spiritual hearing, let him hear spiritual things.

The production of a new man by means of a spiritual birth, does not imply that the old man is cast away, and another formed of new materials, unaffected by sin. Regeneration is the beginning of a process of sanctification. The Spirit of God acts upon the natural powers and faculties, and restores them to their original and uncorrupted state. Man has nothing good in him, and yet every element of his nature is capable of subserving a noble end, being just suited to the purposes of sanctification and salvation. The psalmist knew how to pray, after the gospel method, even in his day: "Create in *me* a new heart, and renew a right spirit within *me*."

Or, again, regeneration may be represented as a spiritual engraftment of the natural man, — the engraftment being supposed to take place in every branch of his being.[1] An engraftment of good fruit takes place only upon a tree of like nature with itself; since the design is not radically to change the kind of its fruit, but its quality, — there being in this only an essential unlikeness. Hence there must be a constitutional relation between the natural stock and the engrafted fruit, so that the sap — the vital fluid of the former — will also flow in the latter. Apple must be engrafted upon apple, or upon a tree of kindred nature to itself. In like manner, piety must be produced in a naturally religious stock. The influences of the Spirit are

[1] The figure must not be pressed beyond the points it is designed to illustrate. The leading ones are these: It represents the constitutional relation between the natural man and the Spirit; the religious life being supplied from the natural source, while its quality is changed by the Spirit which is imparted. It represents, also, the fact that all man's faculties may and must be sanctified, while his constitutional structure remains.

given to religiously constituted beings, — as angels and men, — but not to brutal natures; the object being not to endow with a religious constitution, but to change the quality of that which exists.

Wherein, then, consists the peculiarity of the regenerate character, its strangeness, incomprehensibility, and distinction from the unregenerate? How is it that the spiritual man is a new creature, and that godliness is to the natural man a mystery? When man fell into sin, he not only lost his spiritual affections, but his spiritual perceptions. When his heart was changed from good to bad, his spiritual perception was changed, with every other faculty. Having ceased to love God, he lost sight of him in everything. When Christ came into the world, men saw no form nor comeliness in him. "In him was life, and the life was the light of men. And the light shineth in the darkness, and the darkness comprehended it not." Wickedness became so thoroughly a second nature to man, that the existence of godliness in or out of himself is a mystery.

Godliness is not a mystery to man because he is destitute of a religious nature, but because he has a religious nature which is perverted. Had he not a religious constitution, he would be entirely unaffected by spiritual things. Were it upright, he would be in sympathy with them; but since it is perverted, they appear to him strange, incomprehensible, and mysterious. So long as he comes in contact with them, he will be restive and perplexed, until he is renewed by grace, or given over to a reprobate mind.

In regeneration, man is not only restored to a state of godliness, but his perceptions of it are restored. He sees God in himself, in Christ, in everything. He is introduced into a new domain of perception and feeling, which constitutes a new life, and a seemingly new creation. He is born again into the state in which man was first created. Having been born at first in sin, he is born again in holiness.

### § IV. — Correspondence and distinction between the Old man and the New.

The doctrine that in regeneration a new man is produced, and that the new is the old sanctified in every element of his being, implies that between the spiritual and the natural man there is a perfect correspondence. If the new creature is a spiritual *man*, he must have all the faculties and elemental principles of a man. He must not only have a new heart, but new faculties throughout. None must be superadded, and none wanting. Otherwise he would be something more or less than man. Nothing can be sanctified which does not exist; and sanctification must be commenced in every principle of man's nature, or when the process is finished his restoration would be incomplete. A spiritual engraftment can take place only in a natural stock. We cannot conceive, therefore, of a spiritual feature, or grace, in the new man, which is not set in a corresponding feature of the old. The natural man also, being thoroughly religious, every feature and element of his nature must be capable of receiving a spiritual graft. Nor would he be a complete spiritual man unless each principle of his nature received a scion of grace. He would not possess even the beginnings of an entire sanctification.

This being so, we should expect to find in the regenerate and unregenerate man two distinct but parallel religiously constituted beings, each possessing faculties similar to the other, both entirely religious and more or less actively and in form correctly so, according to incidental influences; the distinction between them consisting in the fact that the one is spiritually, and the other naturally religious; or the one properly, and the other perversely so.

This expectation is fully realized. Both the unregenerate and the regenerate have a sense of the existence of a Supreme Being, to whom they must render an account. The sense of the former is parallel to that of the latter, but vitally distinct from it. The one is perverse and blinded, the other sound and healthy. In each it is the internal life-principle of the religious character, which sends out its influence to the surrounding members near and remote, giving to them its tone. Accordingly, we find a kind of worship, of prayer, of consciousness of sin, of repentance, faith, love, hope, and religious happiness, which is natural to mankind, and another exercise of these, which is spiritual. All the forms of Christian graces are exercised among unregenerate men. The heathen — the lowest grade of religionists — have their religious hopes, and joys, and repentance, and faith, and love, and good works, and prayer, and worship, and every other grace. All unevangelical religious sects have the same. Were the hearts of ungodly men, who profess to despise every kind of religion, exposed to view, it would be found that they also possess undeveloped forms of these same exercises. Let affliction of any kind overtake them, and the forms of the Christian's graces at once appear. Were the unuttered reflections of merely moral persons brought to light, they would be found to possess within them a complete system of religion. Nor are religiously educated children and youth, who seem entirely neglectful of these things, an exception. Their religious tendencies are rather suppressed than wanting. The germ of religious exercise within them is ready to burst forth, either naturally into false forms, or by the Spirit's influences into the true, as soon as the causes of suppression will permit.

If two parallel but distinct sets of religious faculties and exercises exist among men, we should expect, as a consequence, to find also two parallel but vitally distinct systems of religion in the world,—the one natural and false, the other spiritual and true. The history of mankind shows this to be the case. The heathen, the Romanists, and all unregenerate religionists, have their systems and creeds standing side by side with those of the regenerate, more or less deformed in consequence of a perverted inward spirit, yet constituting the natural stock in which to insert, in all its branches, the spiritual graft. In numerous cases these systems and creeds, by means of external cultivation, assume the exact form of the good and true, without partaking of its spirit, just as the natural is sometimes, in form, undistinguishable from the engrafted fruit. The general aspect of the case, however, is, that the natural tree which now overspreads the earth, has received only a partial engraftment in some of its remoter branches.

From principles already suggested, we should expect that the spiritual character and religion would be inexplicable and mysterious, and a consequent source of annoyance to those who are only naturally religious, but are compelled to believe in the existence and superior nature of a spiritual state. This has always been exemplified. All natural men of religious culture have been restive and perplexed, in view of the existence and superior claims of experimental religion. From the time of Nicodemus they have marvelled, and asked, "How can these things be?" They have been anxious and impatient to see the religion of the new birth yield its claims of superiority and distinctiveness, and allow their own perverse and blinded religious character to be accredited as genuine; and because it cannot do so, they conceive of it as arrogant, uncharitable, and bigoted.

The unregenerate religionist can no more conceive of a new man diverse from the natural, than could the master in Israel, in the time of Christ. The same is true of the exercise of all the spiritual graces, such as faith, love, hope, happiness, good works, and humility. In his fallen religious character, the unregenerate man has the natural stock in which these various spiritual graces are set, but they afford no conception of the distinctive nature of the spiritual graft.

These remarks have a still wider application. We have said that man is a *thoroughly* religious being. What are called the Christian graces do not comprise the Christian character. The intellectual, moral, and physical nature, though more remote from the religious centre, have a vital connection with it. These were all affected by transgression, and will be correspondingly affected by regeneration. The new man must have a new understanding pertaining to the truths of religion, and to all truths which come within the domain of his knowledge. Every truth, and every object of knowledge, in religion, in science, in art, and in nature, is affected by being viewed in a spiritual light, — and reflection upon them forms a part of man's religion.

No Christian will deny that the natural man has one kind of understanding of the truths of the Bible, and the spiritual man another. Let a person who has been highly cultivated in the knowledge of revealed truth, be enlightened by the Holy Spirit, and it will appear to him in a new and peculiar light. He will acknowledge the essential inferiority of his former understanding. He will yield, also, a new intellectual assent to them as being good and true. His former understanding and assent had sustained a vital injury by transgression, and in his restoration by grace they receive a corresponding cure. His natural apprehension of religious truths is false, blinded and perverted by sin. However cultivated, it is suited only to receive a spiritual graft.

The same remarks are applicable to all truths, and every object, in science, in nature and art. Of all these there is a natural and a spiritual apprehension. If it be not so, whence is it that to the converted soul every object in nature, and every law in science and art, is invested with a new, peculiar light? Whence comes this, if it is not a partial restoration of the original beauties of man's paradisaic abode, arising from a corresponding restoration of his intellectual apprehensions to their pristine state? The works of nature and of art can no more be viewed aright than the works of grace, except in a spiritual light. The whole domain of truth can be properly apprehended only as it is in Jesus, who is the Alpha and the Omega of all. The same distinction, less sensible, but not less vital, exists between a natural and spiritual understanding of truth, as between natural and spiritual prayer, repentance, love, and faith, — the natural in the one case being as really false as in the other.

These things to the natural man are a mystery. He can no more comprehend the existence of a spiritual apprehension of the works of nature or of grace, diverse from his natural view of them, than Nicodemus could conceive of the existence of a new spiritual man diverse from the natural. He cannot penetrate, in any direction, the dark vail which surrounds him, — no ray of light having reached him from the celestial region beyond. All unregenerate religious sects believe they perfectly understand the truths of the Bible, and are sorely annoyed by the claims of the spiritually enlightened to a distinct and superior knowledge.

The same principles are applicable, also, to the external performance of all religious duties, — outward activity, zeal, abandonment of open sin, and conformity to Bible precepts. There is a natural exercise of these things, and a spiritual. On account of remoteness from the religious centre, the distinction here is still less obvious, but not less real. A difference is to be discovered between the very forms of the natural and spiritual exercises of religion. Let the young man who has been taught from childhood to bow at the family altar while the morning and evening sacrifices are laid thereon, be truly converted, and he will confess that he never bowed there before. An observer would be impressed with the change. He is now bowed in spirit. His heart and soul are in the act. This imparts ease, freedom, spontaneity, and a natural reverence to its outward form. It is a law of nature that the external man shall be affected by the internal. The parent cannot educate his child to bow in family worship, as God by his Spirit makes him bow.

The same may be said of the public exercise of prayer, exhortation, and preaching. Suppose a deceived professor of religion, who has been accustomed to these exercises, should be enlightened, and brought to Christ; then when the words fall from his lips, you would confess you never heard him exhort or pray before. The language might be the same he had employed a thousand times, but the manner of its utterance would be altogether new. An articulation of the shibboleth would now be distinctly heard. The tones and inflections of the voice are inevitably modified by the inward spirit. Is not such a change observable in the manner of the true Christian's prayer, when he passes from a cold to a lively Christian state? And is not such a distinction perceived and felt, on the one hand joyfully, and the other painfully, between the exercises of some professing Christians and others?

It cannot be denied that there is a form of godliness that has the power, and a form that has it not. When man works out what God works in him to will and to do, then the very manner of his working will be unlike the ordinary actings of men. It is impossible that he should speak of himself as God speaks through him. Were it not so, he who preaches the gospel in his own strength would possess the same impressiveness with him who speaks as he is moved by the Holy Ghost. Illustrations of the truth might be drawn from the external aspect of all religious activity and zeal, the abandonment of open sin and turning to the paths of true religion, and external compliance with all the precepts of the gospel, showing that there is in all these things a form that is natural and one that is spiritual. It is not so much the acts which the followers of Christ perform, as the solemnity with which the very manner of performing them is invested, that gives them their peculiar power among men.

These things are also incomprehensible and mysterious to the natural man. The son of pious parents cannot conceive how it is possible for him to bow in a more humble or reverent manner at the family altar than he has been accustomed to do, until he is taught by the Holy Spirit. Then he perceives that hitherto the motion of every muscle and limb had been wholly disconsonant with the act he professed to perform. So, also, the self-deceived professor cannot conceive of a form of exhortation and prayer superior to that which he employs. But when the Holy Spirit gives him ears to hear, he discovers that every inflection and tone of his voice must have fallen in the harshest discord upon the ear of his Maker, and of every spiritual soul.

All this is in confirmation of the proposition that the regenerate character is peculiar and distinct from all other, and that by its peculiarities and distinctiveness it may be known.

Another important application of these principles may be made to man's *moral* nature. It is that there is among men a natural and spiritual honesty, benevolence, and sincerity. When man fell into sin, he fell entirely. His moral as well as intellectual nature became perverted. The new man, therefore, must have a new moral as well as intellectual character. If the heart is changed from good to bad, or the reverse, the remotest extremities of man's nature feel the influence. They are dependent for their life upon the same blood as the heart itself.

In his apostasy, the pole of man's entire being was turned away from its proper object in the heavens. His constitutional faculty for being honest and sincere with his Maker and his fellow-men, as well as that to worship and love and pray, has been turned from God to earth and self, and he has become corrupt and base. The faculty still remains, but lying prostrate in the universal ruin. No moral qualities that are true and good, are now to be found among men, but such as are sanctified by the Holy Spirit. Those that are natural are suited only to receive a spiritual engraftment, which in its growth shall be turned from self to God.

God made man to have supreme reference to Him in the exercise of all his moral faculties. He is to be honest in his dealings with men, not simply from policy or from right, but to glorify the Creator. To obey his conscience, is not enough; for this is fallen with every other faculty. He must obey his Maker. The dictates of conscience seldom reach beyond the good of man. If a person treats his fellow-men justly and right, the demands of his second and fallen nature are all fulfilled. He seems ignorant that his honesty should refer to God. Self, or, at most, self and his fellow-men, fill his vision; but God is not in all his thoughts. Or, if he thinks of God, it is from vain and selfish motives, and not to promote His glory.

Such honesty is not good. It is reasonable and proper that man, who has been made capable of it, should, in his dealings with men, seek the glory of God, whose is the supreme glory, and in all things deserves first to be regarded. But instead, he seeks, at most, the good of man. Honesty actuated by this motive, is the purest worldly men claim to possess. Even this is exceedingly rare. The highest grade of *common* honesty is based upon the dictates of a conscience which men by voluntary transgression have rendered unfit to be their supreme guide, while the ordinary grade is governed by the spirit of a mean and selfish policy. All this is an honesty which is unbecoming in such a being as man; and in the sight of God, whose glory is thus ignored, it is utterly false and corrupted. Yet it is called honesty, and men use it for worldly ends; but it is capable of subserving the glory of God only as it is susceptible of being renewed by the Spirit's influence.

Evidences that man's natural honesty and sincerity, in strictly religious connections, are perverse and false, have been made to appear in the delineation of unrecognizable regeneration. The main-spring of a false work of grace, is a determination to experience something which shall serve as a ground of hope. It matters not whether it is a work of grace, or a work of selfishness and sin. Yet the person is naturally honest, thinking he desires to be a Christian to glorify God. The good young man in the gospel exercised natural honesty when he said to the Saviour, "What lack I yet?" Nor was it a mere pretence. Satan knows how to induce dishonesty in the heart, and conceal its nature. Paul "verily thought he was doing God service in persecuting His church, and wasting it." But he was only naturally honest. He had no desire for the glory of God. How many persons, with undoubted natural honesty, believe they desire to become Christians, while God sees that their honesty has not the slightest reference to himself! and hence, like the young man in the gospel, when they approach him he sends them away sorrowful. How frequently some trifling requirement, implying, perhaps, merely a willingness to signify their desire to become Christians, exposes the fallacious nature of their feelings!

We find, therefore, an honesty and sincerity in religious things, as sound and good as any that ever enter into the transaction of worldly business, on which men risk their fortunes; but in the eye of God as hypocritical and false as sin itself. An honest, unconverted man declares he loves God, when he has no love for God in his soul; believes he enjoys prayer, when he never prayed in his life; thinks he feels he is a great sinner, when he really believes himself, for the most part, to be very good.

The conclusion is, that as there is a love, in religious things, which is not love, and repentance which is not repentance, but needs to be repented of, and hope and good works which are not such,— so there are honesty and sincerity in these things, that are not honesty and sincerity. Paul says, "If any man among you seemeth to be wise, let him become a fool that he may be wise." "When I am weak, then am I strong." So when a man is only naturally honest, he is spiritually dishonest. The experience of every Christian will bear witness, that when his heart was renewed by grace, his naturally honest desire to become a Christian, of which he had thought so much, became most hypocritical and mean in his sight.

The same remarks are applicable to religious earnestness. Every minister has been made conscious of this, both to his sorrow and his joy, among religious inquirers. Some possess a living earnestness of spirit, which inspires an instinctive assurance of ultimate success; while others toil long and hard, without affording the slightest promise of ever attaining a happy result. The reason is, that the earnestness of the one class is produced by themselves, while that of the other is wrought in them by the Holy Spirit. The former seek as God works in them to seek; the latter seek in their own strength, and hence God does nothing for them.

Every faculty of man's nature is subject to the principles which have been advanced. We have dwelt especially upon honesty and sincerity, and external and intellectual conformity to gospel precepts, because of a natural tendency to accredit these as genuine signs of grace. If a person believes the doctrines of the gospel, conforms his external life to its precepts, appears to be honest, sincere, and earnest, it is asked what more can be required. But we answer, that if he does this only in a natural manner, then infinitely more must be required. He has not yet passed from the natural to the spiritual domain.

We do not object to discovering signs of a regenerate state in one's perception of truth, or in the honesty and sincerity of one's professions, if they are of a supernatural and spiritual kind. The least discovery of a spiritual apprehension or honesty, is one of the most pleasing and convincing evidences that a person has passed from death unto life. We are no less convinced that the heart is acting, by feeling its pulsations in the remotest members, than in the beatings of the heart itself. The former will be less full and strong; but if they can be perceived, it is a happy evidence, not only of life, but somewhat of health throughout the body. So, as truly unmistakable and pleasing signs of the spiritual life exist in the discovery of a spiritual honesty, as in that of a vigorous faith in a crucified Redeemer. But no evidences of such vitality can be found in exercises which man, in his naturally religious condition, is capable of possessing. The tokens of spirituality must be of a spiritual nature.

We have dwelt at length upon the peculiarity and distinctiveness of the regenerate character, because of its importance as a preparation for answering the questions before us. It must be remembered that the point to be determined is not whether one is in a religious condition, but in which of the two religious conditions embracing all the human family, is he found. The internal life, its developments, exercises, and external fruits, which are to be examined, will all be of a religious character, while the inquiry will be whether they are of a natural or spiritual kind.

# DIVISION SECOND.

## GENERAL PRINCIPLE APPLIED TO THE RECOGNITION OF REGENERATION BY THE SUBJECT.

## CHAPTER I.

### § I.—PRELIMINARY.

IN answering the question, How can a regenerate person be certified of his regenerate state? we shall not feel obliged to show that the nature of certitude here is the same as in other departments of knowledge. Young Christians are reluctant to profess that they know they have been born again, because they think they must have a knowledge of it, as they do of a thousand facts which are ascertained by sight, or hearing, or some process of reasoning. They must know they are Christians as they know the sun rises and sets, or that the singing of birds is pleasant, or that certain kinds of food are palatable, or flowers fragrant. Or they must have the same evidence of loving the things of religion that they have of loving certain dear friends, or certain pleasures. They would then be perfectly sure they are Christians, and it would be a source of unspeakable comfort. They are unaware that in spiritual things there can be any other kind of assurance than in temporal things. They recognize it as a feature of their experience that they could not abandon their hope in Christ if they would, yet wish they had such evidence that their hope is good as they have of loving their earthly friends.

But here it must be remembered, that as there is a natural and a spiritual hope, and repentance, and prayer, and faith, so there is a certitude of acceptance with God that is natural, and one that is spiritual; and, moreover, the spiritual, like all spiritual things, is peculiar, inexplicable, and mysterious to him who possesses the natural only. The unenlightened have no conception that the Christian possesses any other kind of assurance than that which pertains to matters of a temporal nature. Christians also are liable to think it is desirable for them to be certified of their spiritual condition by natural means. But these are carnal views, and hence absurd when applied to spiritual things.

To insist that our evidence of having been born of the Spirit shall be of the same character with that pertaining to matters of sense, or to our moral and instinctive natures, is as absurd as it would be to insist upon such evidence that we are intellectual beings, as we have of our physical existence. The manner of forming conclusions must be the same in all departments of knowledge. But all grounds of evidence must be kindred to the subject to which they are applied. Natural data cannot be applied to spiritual things, any more than spiritual data to natural things. Evidence that we love spiritual things, therefore, will be distinct in its nature from evidence that we love our earthly pleasures or earthly friends. The method of arriving at conclusions will be the same in either case; but the data will be distinct, being on the one hand in the natural, and on the other, in the spiritual domain. Besides, our natural affections are corrupt and false; and how can they mirror forth the spiritual, which are good and true? Natural love for the pleasures of the world may reflect natural love for the pleasures of religion, but it cannot reflect the spiritual, otherwise the natural man might have some apprehension of spiritual things. It is unreasonable, therefore, and unwise, for the Christian to desire to be certified of his regeneration by such evidence as pertains to things of a temporal nature. Such evidence would be incompatible with the nature of the Christian life. He who is so good as to change our hearts, is good enough to give us evidence of it best suited to the demands of the case. He has not given such as we should have chosen, or as the Christian often wishes he had given. This is not strange. He did not change our hearts as we should have chosen; nor will he hereafter deal with us as we shall choose. He is so kind as not to consult our blindness and folly in regard to any feature of his gracious work. But we may be assured that what he has ordained is infinitely better suited to our wants than anything we could have conceived. God has caused sufficient reasons to be discoverable to our minds, to show the superiority of the Christian's evidences to natural evidences, and enough to make us grateful that he has consulted his wisdom, and not our folly, in choosing a mode of certifying us of our spiritual condition. Some of these reasons will be pointed out, as we proceed to describe the manner in which the Christian becomes assured of his regenerate state.

Before entering directly upon this, a position not unfrequently assumed must be considered. It is that the whole question, whether one is a Christian, must be reduced to the simple test of hearty obedience to the will of God. A person must put to himself these honest questions, and by them his case must stand or fall: "Am I conformed, in heart and life, to the will of God? Is it my sincere pleasure, my meat and drink, to obey his requirements? Am I conscious that my whole heart and soul do spontaneously and habitually go out after God and heavenly things?"

These are confessedly important questions. But do they serve as a test of one's regenerate state? May a person feel that according as he can answer them affirmatively, his case is decided? Here we confess to finding difficulty; since, if a person is self-deceived, he will invariably answer them in the affirmative; but if not, in the negative. How many true Christians are prepared to say that they feel they are in heart and life conformed to the will of God? — that it is their highest pleasure, their meat and drink, to obey his requirements; and that their whole heart and soul do spontaneously and habitually go out after God and heavenly things? If the point to be settled were how a person who is in a state of great Christian advancement may have evidence of it, these tests might be relevant. Yet, even then, they would be pertinent to exceptional, rather than ordinary cases. The law of growth in grace is, that the more the Christian advances, the more sinful he appears to himself to be, — not because he is more so — he may be less — but because he beholds his sinfulness in a clearer light, in stronger contrast with Christ and holiness. Love for Christ, the Scriptures teach, is in proportion to forgiveness; and this is in proportion to repentance and sense of sin. Knowledge that one is advancing, is not so much a matter of consciousness as of inference. All Christian experience will sustain this view. Jonathan Edwards speaks in the strongest terms of the depths of iniquity in his heart, while having the most rapturous views of Christ. The most advanced and devoted Christians, after a life of eminent usefulness, feel that they are, after all, unprofitable servants, even hell-deserving sinners, expecting to be saved only through sovereign grace in Jesus Christ.

Moreover, it is submitted that Christians do not, *as a matter of fact*, rest mainly upon a consciousness of possessing a spirit of obedience to the will of God, as the ultimate ground of their hope. They see no excellence in their outward conduct or inward feeling adequate to serve as a ground of belief that they have passed from death unto life. On the other hand, it appears to them passing strange that they should live as they do, if they are really new creatures. Their language is, that if they had nothing to depend upon but what they see in their hearts and lives, they should despair. This is the honest conviction of those who exhibit lives of commendable conformity to the will of Christ. It is also represented by our Saviour as being the Christian's feeling at the judgment-day. When the righteous are welcomed into the kingdom prepared for them from the foundation of the world, on the ground of what they had done for Christ, they express surprise, saying, "Lord, *when* saw we thee an hungered, and fed thee; or thirsty, and gave thee drink?" They scan their lives in the light of the judgment, but find nothing in them to serve as a basis of such a welcome from their Lord.

It may be remarked also, as an objection to this mode of the Christian's certifying himself of his regenerate state, that it is such as unconverted persons conceive to be the proper one, and such as they suppose every Christian employs. If this is the full explanation of the believer's hope, then unconverted men can comprehend it.

The same course of remark would be applicable to another class of questions, such as these: "Do I exercise repentance for all my sins? Do I love the Lord Jesus Christ as my Saviour, renounce all self-dependence, and trust solely in him for my salvation? Have I real humility, self-denial, and faith in Christ?" The result of applying these tests will be the same as before. Christians of a well-proportioned development cannot answer these questions in the affirmative with a confidence sufficient to convince them of the genuineness of their hope, especially those who feel most need of being confirmed in regard to it. Their language will be, "I am conscious of great short-comings in these respects. I know I do not repent of sin as I ought. I fear I do rely upon myself, and do not trust solely in Christ. I am not humble and self-denying, and fear I have no genuine faith." The rule will be, the better the Christian's state, the more likely he will be to return a negative answer; while the false professor will by these tests be decidedly encouraged. All genuine experience will show that, as a matter of fact, the Christian does not primarily base his conviction that he is a child of God upon a consciousness of performing these duties in a suitable manner. And, besides, this kind of evidence is no more incomprehensible to the natural man, soundly instructed in religious things, than that before described.

It may be urged, that notwithstanding the Christian's sense of his short-comings in these respects, yet he has also a sense of some degree of attainment: he may have a well-proportioned consciousness both of his spirituality and carnality. That this is possible, we cannot deny. Yet it must be confessed, that it is the tendency of a sense of sin to impair the believer's views of his spiritual advancement, and so cause his short-comings to occupy proportionately too large a place in his mind. Admitting that he may have a well-balanced view of all his exercises, it is evident that a hope resting upon it must be, at the best, exceedingly unstable, vibrating constantly between its positive and negative poles, and liable to settle finally upon the one or the other; and hence be inadequate constantly to support the Christian in his trials and toils.

The more intelligent may plead that regeneration does not depend upon the question whether all or any considerable portion of the affections are in accordance with the requirements of the law or the precepts of the gospel, but whether one has any spiritual desires whatever — upon the supposition that the slightest spirituality is an indubitable sign of a gracious state. It must be admitted that this is legitimate; and it would seem that any regenerate person, adopting such a view, might find sufficient ground in his experience to warrant the conclusion that he is born of God. But the objection to so regarding this is, that experience does not sanction it. What Christian rests his hope of heaven upon such a basis, however legitimate he may conceive it to be? Universal experience will sustain the statement, that the primary source of the believer's evidence of his new creation is not even the consideration that he is conscious of very great delight in obeying the will of God. He may look upon this as a matter of comfort and encouragement; but that it is by no means the sustaining power of his hope, is evident, since when he becomes doubtful, and is led to examine himself, he dashes the cup of his high enjoyments to the ground, and demands an evidence of his acceptance with God which lies deeper in his being. And when he obtains a restoration of his evidence and peace, it comes not from his recollection of having once possessed very high religious enjoyments.

The false professor will so revive his hope and peace, but not the true.

The believer's certitude of his being a child of God, is grounded, primarily and essentially, upon no process of reasoning or inference, however labored and complex, or obvious and simple. Multitudes of Christians, utterly incapable of constructing or applying the simplest process of reasoning to their experience, are as well assured of their adoption into the family of God, as those who are able to analyze all their mental phenomena in the most logical and critical manner. They have never even heard of such processes of reasoning, and yet will walk unflinchingly to the stake or the block, on the simple strength of their belief that they are born of God.

It is evident that no process of reasoning, or of inference, however conclusive, would be adequate to sustain in the believer's mind a sense of his spiritual sonship to the Almighty. If he had the consciousness that *all* his affections and aspirations were of a spiritual nature, and of being in the liveliest exercise of all the Christian graces, an inference drawn from this consideration would not be equivalent to the support he now enjoys independently of it, and even in spite of many inferences furnished by his experience, which are of an unfavorable nature. The truth is undeniable, that the Christian's hope has a hidden spring which is moved by no facts of his personal history.

## CHAPTER II.

### SPIRITUAL CONSCIOUSNESS THE PRIMARY SOURCE OF EVIDENCE.

We are now manifestly compelled to retire from all external and natural grounds, to ascertain the primary and essential source of the Christian's certitude of his gracious state. To attempt to rest the believer's hope upon a basis perfectly comprehensible to the natural understanding, would be to despoil our religion of its most excellent glory, — to drag it down from its exalted position, and lay it in the dust. "We must walk by faith, and not by sight." Demonstrations of a logical and inferential nature may be resorted to, as sources of collateral and secondary aid ; but if the reader's hope is a true one, he must retire, for the primary and vital evidence of his acceptance with God, into the Holy of holies of his regenerated nature, — the threshold which no feet are ever permitted to tread but such as are shod with the preparation of the gospel of peace.

In attempting to answer the question, How can a regenerate person be certified of his regenerate state? this inquiry naturally presents itself. If the Christian has a new spiritual existence corresponding in all its principles and faculties to the old and natural one, why should he not be certified of the one in the same manner as of the other? Why should not the new man, since he is as truly a *man*, be assured of his spiritual being in the same manner in which the old is assured of his natural existence? We do not inquire why evidence in both cases should not rest upon the same *grounds.* It has been remarked, that it is impossible to draw spiritual inferences from natural data. But the spiritual data being given, why should not the process be a natural and rational one, since spiritual things, though peculiar and incomprehensible to the natural understanding, yet never go counter, but are always true to nature and pure reason?

Scriptural examples and all Christian experience will show that these interrogations indicate the proper answer to the question before us. Suppose a person is asked how he knows that he has a rational and moral existence, or that he possesses a living soul, what would he reply? After hesitating and endeavoring in vain to give a reason, he would simply answer, with emphasis, "I *know* I have a living soul." At the first thought, it seems to him that he could give a thousand reasons for believing in his natural existence. They press upon him on every hand. The very atmosphere in which he moves, and the air he breathes, are impregnated with them. And yet, when they are called for, though he knows enough exist, he is embarrassed, since he fails to define even one; but his embarrassment does not weaken his confidence, for out of it he exclaims, "I *know* I have an existence." At first, he conceives of the question as gratuitous, and the proposer impertinent; but when he has reflected, and learned to reason upon the subject, he finds he can construct numerous arguments in favor of his belief. These are not, however, its primary source; nor do they materially strengthen it. That which clamors out, "I *know* I exist," without waiting for the reasons, but supersedes all occasion to think of them until called for, is that abiding *consciousness* of his rational and moral existence with which God has endowed him, and which he has made to be an essential part of every living soul.

Parallel to this is the Christian's certitude of his new spiritual existence. The primary and essential source of it is no other than the living spiritual *consciousness* of the new man. Every process of reasoning or inference is external and auxiliary to, or at most corroborative of, this inward sense. This is the principle of life in the new man which vitalizes all that is exterior to it. The reasoning process is produced by cultivation, while the spiritual consciousness is independent of it. It is matured by exercise and growth, but is dependent for its existence upon nothing but its own vitality, which comes direct from God. This is essential to the believer's hope — all else is incidental. This would be adequate without aught else, but all else would be inadequate without this.

All Christian experience will respond to the truthfulness of this position. When the believer is asked for a reason of the hope that is in him, he is at the first embarrassed, not knowing precisely how to reply. He never felt occasion to define his reasons. He is confident that enough exist. His inmost soul is full of them, and they seem to be struggling, in vain, to find expression at every pore of his being. But, in the midst of his embarrassment, his Christian consciousness replies, in that unpretending style of utterance which is peculiar to the new man, but indicative of a deep certitude of the fact: "I don't know that I can give the *reasons*, but I hope, I trust I am a child of God." If arguments are brought against him which he cannot meet, he still remains unmoved, and replies again, with an humble, composed, and trusting spirit which astonishes all boldness and violence of opposition, "I trust, notwithstanding, I am a child of God."

Nor is this contradictory to, but in perfect harmony with, Peter's exhortation to believers, to be ready always to give an answer to every man that asketh a *reason* of the hope that is in them. If the primary basis of the Christian's hope were a process of reasoning, he could not have a hope without having also a reason for it. But this being only a secondary source, added to the original by cultivation, the apostle knew that Christians might often be found having good hopes, without being able to render a reason for them, and consequently be unprepared to withstand the gainsayers. Hence the importance that they should be possessed not only of a consciousness with which to satisfy themselves, but also of arguments with which to convince others, — the spiritual consciousness and enlightened reason being in harmony.

The position that the primary source of the believer's confidence that he is born of God consists in a spiritual consciousness, may be illustrated by reference to the manner in which it originates. When a person begins to cherish hope that he is a new creature, he does not derive it from any process of inference or reasoning, or from certain facts in his history or phenomena of his heart and life. He does not, at the first, conclude that he must have been regenerated because he has so great love for Christ, or so great happiness, or so deep repentance. These may constitute good grounds for believing that he is a Christian, but they are not the grounds of *his* belief. The sinner, in regeneration, passes through a process which others may observe as bearing evidence that he is being made a subject of grace, but not himself. He has neither leisure nor ability to reflect upon the change, or make observations concerning it. Yet in the midst of it the feeling of hope springs up, either gradually or suddenly, but always spontaneously.

Oftentimes persons do come forward and declare a belief of having just been converted, presenting, perhaps, reasons for it; but it is done in a manner so cool and self-complacent, as to render the supposition that they have just been humbled before an offended God, and received pardon at his hands, incongruous and absurd. True regeneration commonly discloses itself to attentive observers before the subject of it has sufficiently regained his reflection and observation, or even before his consciousness has become sufficiently strong to prompt him to announce it. When cases of the opposite nature occur, the announcement is pervaded with such earnestness and high mental fervor as to show that the person is not in a reasoning or reflecting mood, but that he is in a high state of abiding consciousness of having passed from darkness into light, not produced nor sustained by himself, but by some supernatural power.

These remarks must be understood as applying to the very beginning of the Christian life, else they will be misconstrued. It will be said that it is common for the young convert, of his own accord, to go about at once, telling his neighbors and friends the joys he experiences, and inviting them to the same rich gospel feast. These, it is admitted, are likely to be the first outward exercises of the Christian; but he will not commonly perform them at the very first. A little space will ordinarily elapse after the spiritual birth, before the consciousness of a spiritual existence shall have become sufficiently developed and strengthened to utter itself. This may be a space of hours only, or of days or weeks; or, as in the exceptional case of unrecognized regeneration, it may be a series of years.

The spiritual birth is parallel to the natural. The infant requires a little space for its consciousness of existence to become sufficiently developed to prompt it to announce itself as having come into the arena of rational and moral being, thus giving signs of it to others before it proclaims it itself. Besides, it lives on for a long period, and often to the full age of man, upon the simple ground of consciousness, before it adduces a reason or draws an inference in support of it. The argumentative process is never adopted except by cultivation. Nor is it absolutely needed. The consciousness is found to be adequate to all the practical purposes of an existence. So it is with the spiritual man. He comes into existence an infant. His spiritual consciousness being at first weak, and developed only gradually, he gives signs to others of his new creation, before he proclaims it himself.[1] The reasoning process is added subsequently, by cultivation. If cultivation is never received, he lives and dies on the strength of his spiritual consciousness alone, which is not an uncommon occurrence.

The point under consideration, rightly apprehended, will be of service to Christians in examining their religious experience. In judging of themselves, however, by the position here laid down, their exercises must be properly understood, else the correctness of the position will be denied, or the genuineness of their conversion distrusted. It is not uncommon nor surprising for even highly cultivated Christians to misapprehend their initial experience. Their views of it, formed perhaps in youth, and under the

[1] Many examples, which seem to be exceptions to this remark, are cases of unrecognized regeneration. See part I. page 56.

light of little personal instruction, naturally grow with their growth to perfect maturity, and become settled convictions.

Perhaps nothing pertaining to the Christian's experience is more liable to be misapprehended than the point at which regeneration has taken place. It is difficult to conceive of it as occurring before we obtain evidence of it, — just as it is difficult to realize that the sun actually descends below the horizon before it seems to do so. The observer, in order to receive an exact impression as to the time of the sun's setting, must make a slight allowance for the refraction of the rays of light, whereby the evidence of its descent below the horizon is obtained only subsequently to the occurrence. So the Christian, in looking back to his spiritual illumination, must ordinarily allow for the refraction of the rays of spiritual light, whereby the actual occurrence of regeneration is made to be prior to the apparent. As in the case of the natural day, the effect is to lengthen its apparent duration beyond the actual; so, conversely, in the case of the Christian's spiritual day, the effect is to lengthen the actual beyond the apparent.

That the primary and essential source of the believer's evidence consists of a spiritual consciousness, is also confirmed by scriptural examples, so far as they bear upon the subject. The conviction of persons that they have been born again is often represented under the outward figure of obtaining sight. The belief that one has received sight is based, at least at the first, solely upon consciousness. The blind man who received sight at the Saviour's hands through the anointing of clay and washing at the Pool of Siloam, when interrogated as to the means by which his eyes were opened, — whether by a sinful or holy agency, — declared his ignorance and disregard of all that, saying:

"Whether he be a sinner or no, I know not.[1] One thing I know: whereas I was blind, now I see." He gave no reason for believing he could see. It was a matter of simple consciousness, and hence of the utmost confidence. This outward figure represents the spiritual truth; and it is just to regard the manner in which the individual is convinced of having received natural sight as indicating the manner of his being convinced of his new birth. As natural sight is one of those things which make a person feel that he has a natural existence, so spiritual sight is one of those which make the Christian feel that he has a spiritual existence, and that without the slightest reasoning or reflection.

In the conversion of Paul, also, the only ground of his evidence that he had passed from death unto life presented to us, is the fact that he received sight. When the scales fell from his eyes, which was a matter of consciousness, he did not wait to convince himself by any process of reasoning that he had been renewed by the Holy Ghost, but arose and was baptized. The woman, also, who was cured of the bloody issue,[2] is represented simply as having felt in her body that she was healed of that plague. And when interrogated in regard to it by the Saviour's look, it is said that, *knowing* what had been done in her, and in no other way than by feeling it, she came and fell down before him and told him all the truth.

The position under consideration is in harmony with the doctrine that in regeneration there is produced a new spiritual man, and also with the idea that the new man is an engraftment of the old. If the new creature is a spiritual man, having a full set of faculties corresponding to those

[1] John ix. 25. [2] Mark v. 25.

of the natural man, and a complement of all his elemental principles and powers, he must, among them, have a spiritual consciousness of spiritual existence corresponding to his natural consciousness of natural existence. Were he wanting in so important an element, it would destroy his identity. Or, if the new man is an engraftment of the old, it being necessary that the old should be engrafted in every branch of his being, then the natural consciousness must be spiritually engrafted. Another view of regeneration is, that by it the person becomes one with Jesus Christ. This being so, there must be a consciousness of this oneness between Christ and his disciples on the part of them both. If they are so united to him as actually to become one and the same with him, or if he is formed in them, the first legitimate effect would be a mutual consciousness of the union.

This spiritual consciousness of being a new creature is equivalent to that mysterious inworking in the soul of the believer, by the Holy Spirit, of a direct assurance that he is born of God, which is meant by the witness of the Spirit, when Paul says, "The Spirit itself beareth witness with our spirit that we are the children of God;" also when John declares that "He that believeth on the Son of God hath the witness in himself." When it is said that the Spirit beareth witness with the spirit of the believer, a source of evidence is indicated which is by no means grounded upon any process of reasoning or inference. Nor can the witnessing of God's Spirit with ours be understood as an *announcement* to us that we are born again. He is said to witness or testify, not *to* but *with* our spirits. His operations are in such perfect harmony with the operations of our minds, that His witnessing *with* our spirits becomes the witnessing *of* our spirits. When it is said, also, "He that believeth on the Son of God hath the witness *in himself*," it is meant that he has the witness in his own spirit, which is a matter of consciousness.

In harmony with the above, the apostle Peter calls the hope of the Christian a lively or living hope, unto which he has been begotten, or which he has come in possession of by the new birth. His hope is not obtained by reflection upon what has transpired in his history; but it is something which is an essential part of his new being. It is that inward life-principle which causes him to feel that he is a child of God; *i. e.*, his consciousness of his spiritual existence.

# CHAPTER III.

## SUPERIORITY OF SPIRITUAL CONSCIOUSNESS.

At this point regret may have arisen in the mind of the reader that the primary source of the believer's evidence is not of a more tangible and definable nature; and on this account he may be led to undervalue this kind of evidence. We are quite inclined to over-estimate things that are palpable, and address themselves to the outward senses, and undervalue those that are more ethereal, and find their way, with their health-giving influences, to our very being of being, through its ten thousand minute and hidden avenues. We may be thankful that we have such excellent powers of body, mind, and heart, placing us a little lower than the angels in the grade of being, and yet scarce ever think of our occasion of gratitude for that living, natural consciousness of being what we are, which supersedes the necessity of working out a knowledge of our existence from outward data, whenever we might desire to create or renew a conviction of it. So, too, it is natural for the Christian to be thankful for outward and sensible data, from which to draw conclusions in favor of his regeneration, while he scarcely thinks of his obligation of thankfulness for the witness of the Spirit, that living consciousness which constantly dwells in his inmost being, and produces in him the effect which he would otherwise endeavor in vain to produce in himself.

A better appreciation of this kind of evidence of the

believer's regenerate state, would doubtless adjust his naturally erroneous thankfulness. It is profitable for the natural man to exercise himself in framing arguments to prove that he is a rational and moral being; but, were he dependent solely upon this means of realizing it, how embarrassing would be his condition! For aught we know, he might go about among his fellow-men, not considering what manner of creature he is, except as he should stop to demonstrate it from some data by the way. So far as we can tell, the conviction thus produced would be so superficial and weak as to need a renewal, day by day and hour by hour, in order to be perpetual. Otherwise he might be left to assume to himself, in the intervals, the character of a rational and moral being, or any other which might chance to address itself to his active imagination. Whether this be so or not, it is obvious that any demonstrative or inferential kind of evidence would be wholly inadequate to the wants of such a being as man. The duties which God has devolved upon him in this world are such, and so numerous, as to require that he should have a living consciousness of his proper existence, which no effort or attention of his will be needed to create and sustain.

Parallel to this is the condition of the Christian. It is profitable for him to examine the phenomena of his heart and life, to see whether he be in the faith; but, were he dependent upon this means exclusively, how inadequate would he be to perform the duties of a Christian! If he must stop at every step of his way to examine his evidences and renew his convictions of his regenerate condition, how ill-qualified would he be to pass through the varied scenes of persecution, trial, and suffering, incident to the Christian life! If he must be constantly building up his own hope, how can he effectually labor for others?

When deep affliction overwhelms him, and he needs the consolations of religion, how could he repair to a logical or inferential process to confirm his confidence in a better life to come, for the purpose of raising him above the ills and sorrows of the life that is?

Most obviously the Christian stands in absolute need of just such a source and kind of evidence as that furnished by a lively, upspringing hope, which he is not obliged to labor to sustain, but which sustains him while he labors, — a hope self-adjusting, possessing least vigor when vigor is least needed, and quickened into unusual energy by unusual exigency.

It may be objected that the spiritual consciousness does not have that definiteness and plainness that belong to inferences and arguments drawn from the phenomena of one's outward and inward history, and in this important respect is inferior to these. This being admitted, it does not follow that it has not even a higher degree of certifying power. It is a life-principle, not needing to be comprehended in order to exert its influence. It is not definable, because it is so ethereal and pervasive, infusing its sustaining and convincing efficacy into all the faculties and elements of the soul, while the reasoning process affects the judgment only. What argument could be constructed to prove that we are moral and intellectual beings, possessing a tithe of the convincing force of that living consciousness which abides with us from day to day, throughout our life, and is the prime mover of all our actions? And yet many arguments might be constructed, having greater plainness and definiteness, and consequently a seemingly greater degree of certifying power.

So it is spiritually. Arguments and inferences may be drawn from the changes we have experienced in heart and life, to prove that we are God's children, far more definite and comprehensible than the spiritual consciousness, yet having in effect no comparison with its all-pervasive, convincing, and sustaining power, which is implied in every act the Christian performs, and enables him to perform any act that the self-sacrificing nature of his religion requires. The measure of certitude arising from any source, must not be judged of by its definiteness or pointedness, but by the extent, uniformity, and effectiveness of its influences. It is not necessary that the Christian should be sensible of the precise points of contact of the evidence which supports him with his spiritual being. Like the body floating in water, he may be buoyed up by evidences whose kindly influences sustain him in every part, while they are sensibly felt in none.

It may be objected, again, that the spiritual consciousness does not produce the same degree of certitude that is produced by the natural consciousness; that it wavers, and is not steady and firm, like the natural. In regard to this, it must be remembered that the spiritual consciousness is peculiar, mysterious, and inexplicable to the natural understanding; and so far as the Christian exercises a natural judgment in regard to it, his views will be erroneous. This he is more or less in the habit of doing. Hence his views of his spiritual condition are impaired by his remaining unsanctified apprehensions, and he has, so far, an imperfect view of what spiritual consciousness he does possess.

The exercise of the Christian's natural judgment, moreover, impairs his spiritual consciousness, while his spiritual judgment does not impair, but, if possible, confirms the natural. The spiritual state presupposes the natural, on which it is engrafted; but the natural does not presuppose the spiritual. If a man is conscious of having been born again by the Spirit of God, it gives him an overwhelming sense of the fact that he is by nature a rational and moral being. But the reverse is not true. Hence the spiritual consciousness must not only have equal strength with the natural, to gain equal credit, but somewhat more, in order to overcome the disadvantage of its position.

In the case of the natural man, also, no *arguments* can be raised against his consciousness of possessing a rational and moral existence; and hence it has no obstacles to overcome, but must simply sustain itself. The Christian, however, is constantly finding arguments against the supposition of his being a new creature in Christ. He feels unworthy. The blessing is too great. It cannot be that he is heir to the joys of heaven. His life is not conformed to the hypothesis of his having been born of the Spirit. His short-comings are a heavy weight against it. These obstacles his spiritual consciousness must overcome. It must struggle up in their midst, and still bear witness to the believer that, notwithstanding the arguments against him, he is a child of God.

A hope that is adequate to all this, must possess no small degree of certitude and strength. The power of any agency must be judged of, not alone by the positive effect it accomplishes, but also by the hinderances to be overcome. To produce in a fallen, corrupted being like man, only partially sanctified by the Holy Spirit, an abiding consciousness of his union with Christ and sonship to God, is not only a great work in itself, but is accomplished under the most unfavorable circumstances conceivable. Yet the believer's spiritual consciousness achieves this for him. It constitutes a basis on which he performs the most trying acts, and endures the keenest sufferings of mind and body that ever fall to the lot of man.

It is said, moreover, that the believer's hope wavers; that it is not steady and firm, like man's consciousness of his natural existence; but that it sometimes is trembling and oppressed, and sometimes buoyant with life and energy. To this it must be replied, that it is not wholly true that the natural consciousness is perfectly uniform and steady. It is a life-principle, and, like everything that has life, is subject to variation. But what matters it that the Christian's hope does suffer depression, and is not perfectly steady and uniform, if, after all, it is never found actually to give way under the greatest strain that can be put upon it? What matters the vibration of the branches, and even of the trunk of a tree, so long as its roots retain for centuries their grasp upon the bosom of the earth? The ultimate strength of any agency is to be determined, not by its partial yielding at times, but by its final endurance of the test. All vital forces have a power to yield somewhat to outward pressure, and then, by their elastic energy, recover their wonted position. But forces that are dead, having no vital energies, are rigid and firm. They never yield, but often suddenly and unexpectedly break, when their strength is gone beyond recovery. The former represent the lively hope of the Christian. Possessing a vital, elastic, spiritual force, it is capable of partially yielding to the heavy pressure that often comes upon it, without ever breaking. It will bow down under the weight of guilt and sorrow, only to recover, and more than recover, its wonted energy. But the hope of the hypocrite is a dead hope, rigid, firm, and brittle. It never yields in this life, but will break irrecoverably in the next.

It will be said that this evidence does not, after all, amount to absolute certitude. No one can be perfectly sure that he has been born again. But why inquire whether we have absolute certitude of our regenerate state, when that which we have is found upon trial to be adequate to all the possible practical purposes of life, both in its present necessities and in its relations to the life to come? The believer is qualified by this kind of evidence to perform the most solemn duties ever devolved upon man, and that without misgiving or embarrassment. What need we inquire, therefore, for anything beyond this, which, if we possessed it, could be put to no practical use?

The last objection which we can conceive as possible to be brought against the position before us, is, that the falsely regenerate person believes he possesses the same spiritual consciousness with the true Christian. It is alleged that he feels equally well certified, and his certitude goes for nothing; hence the Christian's must also. It is admitted that this kind of evidence may be counterfeited. But this objection may be brought against all evidence. If that could be discovered in regard to which it would be impossible for a person to be deceived, then, according to human wisdom, we should have found out the great desideratum in the department of Christian evidences. This, however, will never be. It will ever be impossible for man to find out evidences of conversion which the wiles of Satan will not counterfeit.

The position that the deceived professor is as well certified of his regeneration as the real Christian, and hence that no man can safely trust to any evidence, is not admitted to be true. The false Christian *thinks* he is as well assured of his conversion as the true Christian is or can be. He may have greater confidence than the real Christian that his hope is good, and yet it may not be so good. The question is, which case furnishes the better ground of confidence? The stronger confidence may rest on the weaker ground, and the weaker on the stronger ground. The falsely regenerate person may *feel* better certified of having been born again, and yet not *be* so well certified. The point is not how he feels, but what is the fact. He may actually have a larger *amount* of certitude than the true Christian, and yet not possess so good a hope, because it may not be of so good a quality. As has been already stated, there is a certitude of acceptance with God that is natural, and one that is spiritual, the latter of which is infinitely superior to the former, — the lowest degree of the one being far above the highest degree of the other.

The falsely regenerate man may feel certified of his regeneration up to the full measure of his *demands*, both in kind and amount, while the truly regenerate may not feel thus, and at the same time the former not *be* so *well* certified as the latter. The falsely regenerate man does not demand either the same quantity or quality of certitude to satisfy him, that is demanded by the truly regenerate. He does not demand so great an amount, because he does not apprehend so great dangers. The falsely regenerate man is comparatively unenlightened as to his exposure on account of sin, and hence his demands in the way of a guarantee for safety will be small, while those of the truly regenerate will be great, according to the clearness of his views of sin and of God's displeasure; and the more enlightened and holy he is, the clearer will be his views, and the stronger the assurance of safety he will require. The falsely regenerate does not demand the same *kind* of certitude with the truly regenerate, since he has no apprehension of spiritual things. The certitude which he demands is natural, while that of the truly regenerate is spiritual. The former is satisfied with his, for he has no conception of any other; while it would fail to satisfy the true Christian, were it increased to the greatest possible extent, since he has been enlightened as to a better.

Again: the falsely regenerate person may possess all the certitude he is *capable* of possessing; he may be as well certified of having been regenerated, as it is possible for him to be in an unregenerate condition; while the truly regenerate may not be so; and at the same time the former not be or feel as well certified as the latter. It is not possible for an unregenerate person to have as good evidence that he is regenerated, as if he really were so. False evidence cannot be as good as true. Is it possible that a blind man should have as good evidence that he can see, as one who is not blind? He may, under a delusion, be perfectly confident that he can see. He may have all the evidence, and the best it is possible for him to possess while he remains blind, but it will have no comparison with that of one who can actually see. So it is spiritually.

Again: in a dream a person supposes he is in a waking state. He is confident, having all the evidence, and the best he can have until he wakes; but when he wakes, he comes in possession of an evidence essentially superior. While in dream, he believed he was awake; but now he *knows* it. It is the product of a living consciousness. He knows it is not a delusion or a dream. In like manner, the falsely regenerate man dreams he is awake. He is perfectly confident, having all and the best evidence of it he can have while in the falsely regenerate state. He cannot know that he is dreaming, spiritually, until the dream is dispelled. Sometimes an individual dreams he is dreaming; but that is just as much a dream as the dream itself. It is a part of it. So the falsely regenerate man sometimes has a conception that he is deluded; but that conception is as much a delusion as the delusion itself. It is indeed a conception of the truth, but a false conception. The individual, in dreaming that he dreamed, dreamed the truth; but, after all, he only dreamed it. He did not know it. So the falsely regenerate person has a false, delusive, dreaming conception of the truth; but he does not for a moment know it.

# CHAPTER IV.

## PECULIARITIES OF THE CHRISTIAN CONSCIOUSNESS.

It appears that, in the falsely regenerate state, a false certitude of having been born again exists, which serves to the individual a purpose corresponding to that which the real spiritual consciousness serves to the truly regenerate. The false certitude as fully satisfies the deceived person, as the genuine does the real Christian. An important question will therefore arise in the mind of the reader: "Do I possess the false or the real Christian certitude of my regenerate state? Can I know which is the case?" In reply, we must call attention to the proposition adopted to guide us in the present inquiry, which is, that *the regenerate character is peculiar, distinct from all other, and by its peculiarities and distinctiveness it is to be known.* An important element of that character is the spiritual consciousness of having been born again, which is the central life-principle of that body of feelings which constitute the inward Christian character. As a part of the regenerate character, it is to be remarked that this *consciousness* is peculiar and distinct from all other, and by its peculiarities it is to be known. To aid the reader in answering the inquiries raised, we shall describe some of its peculiarities,—bearing in mind, meanwhile, that, as has been intimated before, these peculiarities are not eccentricities; that they are peculiarities only to the natural understanding, while to a spiritually enlightened reason they are legitimate and true to nature.

This is expected to be serviceable only to the regenerate man. To describe the peculiarities of the Christian consciousness to the understanding of the unenlightened, is impossible. If the reader is in the true regenerate state, he will apprehend them; if in the false, he will only believe he does. To exhibit to the latter such tests of the Christian state as will distinctly evince to him that he is deceived, will, doubtless, forever remain an impossibility. It may be said that it is more important that the self-deceived should be certified of their condition, than those who are not, of theirs; but still the more important end lies beyond our reach. And yet the fault is not in us, nor in the truth, but in their deceitful hearts.

Nor must the real Christian expect to find all his anxieties henceforth allayed by the perusal of these pages, his evidences made all palpable and plain, and himself freed from further trouble in regard to them. The false professor will doubtless gain greater confirmation of his hope by this perusal than the true. The hope of the latter constitutes a life which can be changed only as it is nurtured by the wholesome food of light and truth. The most that can be anticipated is, that if the reader is in a truly regenerate state, his Christian consciousness may be reached and stimulated to a more healthy growth, the life-principle of hope be developed, and himself be better able to recognize and trust in the proper source of his belief that he is a child of God. It is expected that all professing Christians will apply the tests, while those only who are true Christians will really recognize themselves as being such.

Any attempt to delineate the Christian consciousness must, of course, be limited and defective. We can only point out, in an imperfect manner, a few of its features, which each true believer must use to assist in delineating, as fully as possible, his own Christian consciousness to himself.

The first peculiarity of this consciousness which we shall mention, is its *indescribableness*. Every true Christian will recognize, as a peculiarity of his experience, the difficulty he has in describing the feeling which leads him to think he is a Christian, or which sustains him while he scarcely believes this to be his character. If one attempts to define it to others, he is conscious that he fails. It is exceedingly incommunicable. Words seem to have no power to bring this inward life out to light. The individual never feels satisfied with his attempts to express it. His apprehension of the feeling always extends beyond his utterance of it. Other Christians also apprehend the feelings of a fellow Christian more perfectly than he is able to set them forth. His description furnishes only an imperfect image of the spiritual man, which, by another, is completed and clothed with life and beauty. *Young* believers are embarrassed in attempting to describe the feelings they have in thinking they are Christians. They wish they could only express their feelings. Since they cannot, they conceive them to be unknown to others. And since others cannot describe them in turn, *they* fail to make the former persons realize how fully they comprehend them. All this is because they are indescribable. Speaking of the feelings does not exhaust them.

To the natural understanding this is peculiar. Unenlightened men think it strange that the Christian should not be able to describe the feeling that leads him to believe he is a child of God. They conceive that he should be able to do so. For themselves, they would not care to have a hope resting on such a basis. But when it is considered that the Christian is a new man, in

Christ Jesus, and that the new man has a consciousness of his existence corresponding to that of the natural man, it becomes reasonable that he should not be able to describe the feeling which causes him to believe in his new creation. The *natural* man cannot describe the feeling that causes him to believe in his rational and moral existence. Language will not communicate it. But the new birth, and a new spiritual existence, to the natural man are a mystery; and hence the indescribableness of the Christian's feeling, that he is a child of God, is to him peculiar and incomprehensible.

The next feature of the Christian consciousness is its *spontaneity.* We mean that so far as the believer's observation of it is concerned, it is self-produced. He is well satisfied that whatever feeling he has that he is a child of God, was not produced by his *desire* to feel so, for the sake of the freedom from anxiety it will afford. It has been shown that this desire is one of the main causes of the hope of a false professor. The true Christian, however, knows that it had no agency in producing the hope he ventures to cherish. He does not so much desire to *feel* that he is, as to *be* a Christian. He sometimes even cherishes a desire not to feel so, thinking he *ought not*, lest he should be deceived. The desire naturally runs counter to the feeling, and hence cannot produce it.

The believer's feeling that he is a Christian, is not the product of his desire for the *happiness* afforded by true religion. When he examines its origin, he is convinced that, simultaneously with the production of it, this was not the prevailing desire of his heart. His hope of acceptance with God was not created until this desire had spent itself, and given place to others of a different nature. The interval between the prevalence of this desire and the origination of his hope, was too great, and too much transpired in it, to allow any point of contact, or any communication between them, by which the latter could become the product of the former. He is conscious that this desire did not even lie about the buried seed of his Christian consciousness, and so serve to warm and quicken it into being. In the case of an assumed work of grace, the desire to be a Christian for the sake of its advantages, is a strongly productive agency. It does not, as in a true work of grace, awaken the sinner, and then subside and give place to better influences, but continues to exert its full force unabated, until its object is thought to be attained.

The Christian's consciousness of being born again is not the product of any kind of *cultivation*. He has employed no means for the direct purpose of creating or maintaining it. He employs means for maintaining the Christian life, but none for producing the belief that he is a Christian. Whatever hope he possesses, he has the satisfaction of knowing, is not the result of any effort to produce it; and hence, if it is spurious, certainly in this particular he is not in fault. He cannot account for the feeling that he is a Christian, unless it is the natural result of being such.

Nor does the Christian possess any well-defined sense that his consciousness of being born again *is* produced by the Holy Spirit. He connects *no* agency with its production. His certitude of his regeneration is a life-principle, created by the Holy Spirit, bearing witness with his spirit, and is a necessary faculty of the new man. The believer is the subject of a work of grace, without recognizing the agency. "The wind bloweth where it listeth, and thou hearest the sound thereof, but canst not tell whence it cometh and whither it goeth. So is every one that is born of the Spirit." And so is the Christian's consciousness of being a new creature, which is also born of the Spirit.

To the natural man this is strange and peculiar. His conception of the Christian hope is that it is the product of a process of reasoning, or reflection; that it is more a conclusion than a matter of feeling; a belief, rather than an inward life. He conceives that it arises in the Christian's mind, immediately and obviously, from an effort to realize his sinfulness, to exercise repentance or faith, or by a conscious effort to trust in God, or to be happy in feeling that Christ is his friend, or even by a direct endeavor to hope and believe that he is a child of God. But when it is understood that this hope is a vital consciousness of a new spiritual existence created by the Spirit, the fact that it seems spontaneous, and is produced by no human effort, becomes reasonable, and true to nature. The new man can no more produce his consciousness of his spiritual existence than the natural man can produce his consciousness of a natural existence. It is simply a necessary consequence of being a new creature in Christ. It is reasonable, also, that he should not be conscious of being brought into a new existence by the Holy Spirit, just as the natural man is wholly insensible of the divine agency in the creation of his moral and intellectual being. But the idea of a new birth, or a new creation, to the unrenewed man is all a mystery; and hence the spontaneity of the believer's hope is a mystery also.

Another peculiarity of the Christian's consciousness is its *solitariness* and *privacy*. Until a converted person becomes intimately acquainted with the peculiarities of Christian experience in general, he is likely to think his feelings in regard to being a Christian are very singular, and such as no one else ever had. He does not believe there ever was another just such person, religiously, as himself. He looks upon other all Christians as possessing a proper Christian character; while his is a solitary, peculiar case. Because of its singularity, he is reluctant to speak of it, being unwilling to make himself appear unlike all others. Sometimes he remarks, in a confidential way, that he believes he is different from everybody else, but hesitates to state the points of difference. He thinks he could not describe them so as to be understood. Or he feels ashamed to express them, because he suspects they would disclose a very wicked state of heart. Hence the peculiar feelings of the Christian, upon the most important of all questions, are almost wholly private. When he speaks of his experience, he dwells not upon these features, but upon such as are more commonly described, and are more likely to be understood and accredited as good. But were these expressed wherever they exist, they would be found to be common to the Christian character. The peculiar, solitary case of one is the peculiar, solitary case of all. All the rest look upon themselves as he looks upon himself; and they all look upon him as he looks upon them. It is as true in the spiritual as in the natural domain, that as face answereth to face in water, so does the heart of man to man. Circumstances frequently occur to illustrate this. When a disclosure of these feelings occurs, the exclamation of others is, "I did not suppose any one ever had such feelings but myself."

This is a peculiarity. The unconverted man has no idea that the Christian feels thus about his hope in Christ, and that he carries these feelings about, pent up within him, scarcely daring to express them even to a fellow

Christian. He supposes that his evidence is perfectly satisfactory and plain, and that he frankly speaks out all his inward experience. These feelings, however, are legitimate, and such as might be expected. When it is considered that the Christian is a person who is born again into a new spiritual existence, it is not strange that he should look upon himself as a solitary case among his fellow-beings, and that combined influences should cause him to refrain from disclosing his views of himself. This phenomenon has its parallel in the natural man. When a child begins to observe and reflect upon the workings of his own mind, he looks upon himself as having very singular thoughts, such as he supposes no other person ever possessed. They are so strange that he refrains from expressing them, not wishing to appear unlike others; whereas, if these thoughts were divulged, they would be found common to all thinking beings. This feeling is possessed, also, by adult persons not intimately acquainted with the mental phenomena of others. But the natural man has no conception that the Christian is a new man, occupying a new domain of existence, and consequently these feelings are mysterious.

Another peculiarity of the Christian consciousness, already alluded to, but deserving to be named in this connection, is its *elasticity;* that is, its capability of yielding to pressure, and then recovering itself. The Christian can doubt, earnestly and deeply, without any danger that his hope will really give way. It does not alarm us to see his consciousness of being a Christian bowing low before the blast. It can do so without giving him any real fear of a finally fatal result. He can tremble in every part, and yet have a feeling of ultimate safety. His hope has such recuperative energy, as to produce in us an instinctive feeling that it will recover itself, though crushed into the very dust. The believer's doubts always reäct into a more vigorous life. When they die, they decay and enrich the soil out of which springs up his lively hope. This is likewise incomprehensible to unenlightened reason, yet in harmony with the idea of the Christian's hope being primarily a living consciousness.

Another peculiarity of the Christian consciousness is *modesty* of *utterance*. There is a peculiar dialect in which consciousness of acceptance with God expresses itself, the leading feature of which is *modesty*. This seems to be an essential characteristic. If the professing Christian speaks of his possession of a hope in Christ with the same unmodified positiveness with which he speaks of other possessions, the genuineness of his hope is suspected. This is a peculiarity in the true Christian worthy to be observed. No feature of Christian hope is more nearly universal than this. The dialect is accompanied with tones and inflections of the voice which cannot be represented to the eye. Its idiomatic phrases are such as these: "It is now so long since I *thought* I became a Christian," or "since I *hope* I found the Saviour." If the Christian is interrogated as to his hope in Christ, his reply is, "I *trust* I am a Christian." "Sometimes I think I am." "If I ever was converted, it was at such a time." "I once thought I obtained a hope in Christ, but I am far from being what I ought to be." "I am very unworthy to be called a Christian;" and expressions of a similar character.

These idioms are indigenous to the soil of the renewed heart. Christians do not learn them of each other by imitation. They do not spread among them as provincialisms spread in certain sections of country; but in each instance they spring directly out of the Christian consciousness.

The style is original in each individual, being dictated by his own peculiar feeling. It cannot be an imitation, because the Christian supposes no one else feels as he does. He conceives of all others as having reason to speak with unqualified positiveness; but it is not so with himself. This style of expression is not the result of education, since, in cases of a false experience, education has no power to produce it. Deceived persons learn these idioms of the true language of Canaan by imitation, as marine phrases prevail among seamen, and provincialisms in particular provinces; and they *are* learned, and not dictated by the state of the heart. It is, for the most part, impossible to learn to speak a foreign language so that a representative of that tongue will not detect our speech as being a sibboleth, an imitation only. To utter the true shibboleth, we need to be born upon the country's soil. So, to speak the language of Canaan, we must be born of the Spirit.

When the false Christian has learned the dialect of the true believer, he often forgets to use it. He conceives of his conversion more as a matter of fact than as a living experience, and hence expresses himself in naked and unqualified terms. He does not speak vainly of it, but superficially, and even lightly, in comparison with the solemnity of the subject, as if he did not appreciate its real nature. His false consciousness utters itself in language like this: "Yes, I am a Christian. I have been a member of the church so long. Since I was converted, I have done such and such things," — accompanying the expressions with a superficialness of tone which cannot be represented to the eye.

It is evident that this modesty of expression in the true Christian is not the product of education, since this has no power materially to modify it. Converted persons may be instructed that it is wrong to doubt; that they ought to *know* they are Christians, and speak confidently; but it has little or no effect. The universal language of the renewed soul will ever be the same. Immediately when the real Christian consciousness begins to declare itself positively, a feeling from within arises and checks it. It breaks and subdues the tones and inflections of the voice into a peculiar mildness and meekness, and the expression into a modest form.

If it is uniformly the case with an individual, that when called upon to answer the question whether he is a Christian, he finds himself slightly embarrassed, being wholly unable to answer in the negative, and not wholly able to answer in the affirmative without some modification, he may remark it as one of the symptoms that his consciousness of being a Christian is genuine.

Sometimes the Christian does express himself positively and fearlessly, in such language as, "I *know* in whom I have believed." But it occurs only in extraordinary circumstances, when his consciousness is found to be adequate to the demand. Yet even then, his declaration is made in a depth, solemnity, and meekness of tone, which distinguish it from all that is not dictated by the Holy Spirit. A noticeable modesty of feeling pervades the positiveness of his utterance. The same is equally discoverable in the expressions of one who is naturally confident and bold.[1]

This characteristic of the Christian consciousness to the natural man, is peculiar, and not in accordance with his conceptions of a Christian hope. He does not see why a

[1] Many persons, who were originally cases of unrecognized regeneration, are also accustomed to express themselves confidently and positively, in consequence of the unusual experience they have had. See First Part.

person who is truly converted should not understand and speak of it as definitely and positively as of any other mental experience. If *he* were to be a Christian, he would wish to do so. Notwithstanding, this peculiarity is true to nature. Consciousness of pardon produces modesty. The criminal who receives it is unpretending. Though a soul saved from death may be confident and joyful, he will yet be modestly so. If the believer, in a healthy Christian state, is betrayed into a different expression, a recollection of the pit whence he was digged, combined with the thought that heaven is to him a gratuity, will arise and rebuke him. If he is destitute of this modesty, it is indicative that he does not realize the relations in which he is placed.

Nor does modesty, in the expression of the believer's consciousness of acceptance with God, impair its strength or positiveness. If a man of large wealth is asked whether he has property, his answer is expected to be modest in proportion to the extent of his wealth. A man of ten thousand would express himself more strongly, but far less significantly, than a millionaire. The one would be likely to reply that he had considerable property, with an air and tone indicating that he thought himself rich. He would, perhaps, name over his estates, to show how much he possessed. The other would reply that he had some property; or, he hoped he had enough to support him; or in language of similar character, accompanying his expressions with tones and inflections denoting a deeper significance than his language conveys.

In like manner, the modest declaration of the Christian's belief that he has been born again, is in perfect harmony with, and even indicates a deep certitude in his mind that he is heir to a glorious immortality. To express himself in any other manner, is felt to be exceedingly inappropriate by those who have no doubt of his piety. This is because it is unnatural for a belief of great realities to utter itself in very confident and positive terms. A man of small wealth may use stronger language than one of large, without rendering his expressions liable to savor of boasting. So a man of earthly riches may employ more confident terms, without offence, than he who is heir to everlasting mansions in the skies.

This modest tone in the Christian is true to nature, and to the demands of the case. No form of expressing his belief in his preparation for heaven could be invented by man so convincing to others, as is just that which is peculiar to the Christian, induced in him by the Holy Spirit. We know that others often declare their belief in their preparation for death much more confidently than the true Christian, but with not a tithe of the convincing power. In proportion, also, as the Christian is unmoved by the Spirit in the utterance of his hope, is its convincing power diminished, though its confident tone may be increased.

*Self-distrust* and *sense of unworthiness* are allied to modesty, and constitute an essential part of the Christian consciousness. It cannot be conceived how he can be a truly converted person, who is not constantly penetrated with this feeling. It is set forth in the twenty-fifth chapter of Matthew as the most prominent characteristic of the righteous at the judgment-day; on account of which they disclaim the good deeds the Saviour credits them with having performed, and implicitly declare that they cannot accept the undeserved welcome proffered them from their Lord. The unrenewed cannot appreciate this feeling. Their view of it is exhibited by the position they also are represented as assuming at the judgment—claiming to have done everything for Christ, while he credits them with having done nothing; regarding themselves as being worthy of eternal life, while he pronounces them "workers of iniquity," and declares that "these shall go away into everlasting punishment."

The last peculiarity we shall mention is *honesty*. This is a strongly marked characteristic. The Christian has a singular unwillingness to cherish a sense of acceptance with God, to any greater extent than will be warranted beyond all dispute. Nothing can tempt him to overstep the bounds of justice, even in the direction of his highest interests. He is so honest, that he is greatly fearful of being dishonest.

This peculiarity the unenlightened have no conception of, and no power to appreciate. At the final judgment, the righteous are represented as denying ever having done anything for their Saviour as the basis of their eternal reward, even when Christ himself had made his final decision in their favor. That was a decision which no power in heaven, on earth, or in hell, could change. On it their everlasting weal was to depend. All unsanctified reason, therefore, would ask, Was it not incurring an unjustifiable risk for them to question the Saviour's judgment, even though they might consider it as unwarranted? Suppose his opinion had been modified by their assertion, and he had concluded to take them at their word. They would then have lost the heaven they might, simply by suppressing their convictions, have inherited, and that without a word of opposition from any ransomed saint or unfallen angel, since none would wish or dare to gainsay the Saviour's decree. Yet this consideration does not affect the honesty of the real Christian consciousness—the true heart-temper of him who is born again. No circumstances can induce him to swerve in the least from his actual convictions as to his being a child of God. The prospect even of eternal life, has no power to move him from them; for he does not desire to be in heaven, except he can feel he is there on terms of the strictest honesty. It would be no heaven to him, were he obliged secretly to reflect that it would not have been his portion if he had been scrupulously honest with his Saviour, and told him all the truth.

We have presented these peculiarities of the believer's consciousness of his regenerate condition, in order that if the reader is in a truly regenerate state he may find some of them in his own experience, and his hope be nurtured and strengthened.

# CHAPTER V.

## SECONDARY SOURCE OF EVIDENCE — REASONING PROCESS.

### § I. — Preliminary.

The Christian's consciousness of possessing a new spiritual existence, has been treated as the *primary* and *essential* source of his hope. It has been remarked, that secondary and collateral to this, or even confirmatory of it, is the evidence to be derived, through a process of reasoning or of inference, from the facts of his history, or the religious changes and phenomena of his inward and outward life. The latter is the body of the believer's evidence; the former, the life-principle which vitalizes it. The one is the Christian character; the other, the consciousness which animates it. It has been shown, also, that the peculiarities by which the regenerate person is to be known, pertain not less to the Christian character than to the Christian consciousness.

Our object does not necessarily require us to present the most important features of the Christian character, but to mark those which are most noticeable and easily pointed out; or to exhibit those peculiarities by which pious and spiritual exercises are to be distinguished from the naturally religious. The present mode of determining the question before us, though it does not constitute the vital source of the believer's hope, is yet the one most likely to be employed. It is natural for Christians to examine themselves by observation, and reflection upon their feelings and lives, rather than by referring to their spiritual consciousness. The present mode, involving reflection upon things that are more outward and easily observed, has its advantages.

In describing the peculiarities of the regenerate character, we must premise the negative statement, that *it is confined to no outward form.* The work of regeneration, or the change from the naturally to the spiritually religious condition, is to be distinguished by no particular manifestations. No reliance can be placed upon the apparent suddenness or want of suddenness of the exercises, vividness or want of vividness of the impressions, decision or want of decision, or any similar circumstances or conditions. This follows, necessarily, from the doctrine that the new man is simply the old, sanctified; and that regeneration is but the beginning of a process of sanctification, involving no new endowment of faculties or elemental principles, and no diminution of those already possessed, as well as no change of natural constitution or temperament. We have no mould in which all conversions must be cast; but each will, in the nature of the case, have a mould of its own. The same essential likeness, and the same unlimited variety, will exist in conversions as in human countenances. Certain features, having a certain collocation, are essential to every human face; while two faces alike cannot be found. So it is with conversions. Unless two human minds can be found having no similar faculties, two conversions cannot occur without possessing the same essential features, in a similar order; and unless two human minds can be found in all respects precisely alike, two precisely similar conversions cannot occur. The work of the Holy Spirit has all the freedom that belongs to the subject in whom his work is performed; but it cannot transcend that freedom. It being the object of regeneration to reädjust the powers of the soul, and restore them to a state of health, the operations of the Spirit must be in accordance with the legitimate and healthy working of the mind. It will exhibit nothing contrary to nature — nothing disordered or fanciful. It will extend to the ultimate limits of human freedom, but not beyond. The work of the Spirit is not mechanical, nor is it dissolute, vagrant, and unlawful. Hence while the Spirit, in regeneration, operates more powerfully upon some than upon others, for reasons not apparent to us, the manifestations are in accordance with each peculiar temperament. They will be such as will occur under any other legitimate influence of equal efficiency. Each individual experience will be peculiar to itself, while all will possess a common likeness. Though the incidental circumstances may be endlessly varied, yet since the spirit which pervades them and gives them character is in all cases the same, the circumstances, when combined into a whole, will have a recognizable similarity.

It is natural to put confidence in brilliant, or what are called "remarkable conversions,"— such as occur under extraordinary circumstances, — and to distrust the opposite. But brilliancy and extraordinary circumstances are nothing, and the want of them is nothing. Neither should bias the judgment in either direction. If the new man is the old sanctified, every man will correspond, after conversion, as a Christian, to what he was before as a man. If he was an active and impulsive man, he will be, in the main, an active and impulsive Christian. If he was mild, inoffensive, and unenterprising as a man, he will be so, for the most part, as a Christian. If he was energetic, daring, and ambitious as a man, he will, so far as he exhibits the Christian spirit, manifest it in a similar manner. The strong points and weaknesses of the individual as a man, will be his strong points and weaknesses as a Christian; and his virtues and besetting sins as a man, will be his virtues and besetting sins as a Christian. These constitutional traits will by divine grace be stimulated to greater activity, or put under restraint, and that more or less thoroughly according to the degree of sanctification; but they will not be eradicated. If grace is at any time withheld, the individual will develop himself in the original direction.

But how is it that old things are passed away, and all things become new? In what consists that wonderful change called the new birth? Is it any objection to the doctrine of the new creation, that the new man corresponds, in his constitutional structure and peculiarities, precisely with the old? Is it any objection to the second birth, that it has a constitutional mould similar to the first? Old things are passed away, and all things become new, in that the individual is introduced into the spiritual realm, having broken away from the confines of natural things.

It must be remembered, that though the origination of this work is instantaneous, thenceforward it is progressive. A new light is shed upon old things, and yet they still remain. The individual receives a new creation; but the new is not independent of the old, being engrafted on it. The graft is at first weak and small, but is destined to grow, to absorb and convert into its own nature the vital fluid of the original stock, and become itself the tree. Yet the former will still remain, to hold the graft until the tree is transferred to another clime, and set in other soil. But so long as its roots retain their grasp upon their native soil, the original stock will show signs of life, and, unless it be pruned and checked, will throw out its branches, bearing baneful fruit. Indeed, the growth of the graft, the new life-principle, may be more or less vigorous, compared with that of the natural stock. Either may, for a time, overgrow the other, while neither shall become extinct. Though, in the case of the tree, the graft may die, yet in the spiritual engraftment it shall not be so. The healthiness of the graft may be impaired by the continued growth of the natural tree, but it is destined to survive when this shall decay and die. The new life-principle is of a superior quality, and, whatever partial injuries it may suffer, must ultimately prevail. It receives its vitality from Heaven, and has power to live over into the heavenly state, despite the uncongeniality of the old and sinful life in which it is set, and which it must convert and conform to itself.

This truth must be borne in mind, in any attempt to give a just description of the regenerate character. The Scriptures recognize as fully the remaining existence of the old man in the Christian, as they do the continued existence and ultimate victory of the new. The actual phenomena of the inward and outward life of the regenerate man, cannot be explained upon any other supposition than that he possesses a twofold character. They cannot be reconciled with the idea that he is perfectly or even mainly sinful, or mainly holy, or that the desire to. please God will uniformly be uppermost in his mind. Both scriptural examples, and Christian life as it now manifests itself, show that the remaining unsanctified element is liable at any time to gain the ascendency, and retain it for an indefinite period, how long we cannot tell. In the internal conflict of the two elements, partial defeats and victories on either side may occur. This only remains certain, that the divine life, whatever partial defeats it may suffer by the way, will in the end achieve an everlasting triumph. He is the superior runner in a race who comes up at the last and secures the goal, though he may at times have fallen behind, and seemed liable to an inglorious defeat. "He that endureth to the *end*, shall be saved." It is not essential to the superiority of the divine life in the soul that it should always make its superiority appear. That life is hid with Christ in God, and may appear to be small when compared with the worldly and carnal one, and yet have such superiority over it as in due time to sanctify the whole.

Let it not be said that this lowers the standard of Christian character. That standard is not here set up. While it is worthy of being urged by the most weighty considerations, that the holy aspirations of the Christian ought manifestly to predominate in his character at all times, yet, as a matter of fact, this may not be the case with those who are, beyond all doubt, in a regenerate state; and hence a uniform tenor of godliness in the life, either real or manifest, cannot be insisted upon as an essential sign of a regenerate condition. Should it be objected that these statements, even though true, ought not to be made, because of the *tendency* they may have to lower the standard of the Christian life, then we can only say, that if they suffer in this direction, it is hoped that this loss will be more than compensated by the end sought to be accomplished, which is, that many who are doubtful about their regenerate state, on account of conscious imperfections, may be strengthened in their hopes, and encouraged to activity and advancement in a Christian course.

In pointing out the peculiarities of the truly regenerate character, two classes of feelings are to be taken into consideration. The first are the cardinal graces of the gospel, such as repentance, love, and faith. The second are such as ordinarily accompany these graces, and are incident and peculiar to the Christian state. The former may be called the *characteristics*, the latter the *signs* of regeneration.

The common mode of judging of the Christian character is to describe the cardinal graces, and so determine whether one is in possession of them. In theory this is correct. The objection to it is that it is not sufficiently available, since no description of these graces can be given which shall be of much practical service in determining their existence. Besides, when this mode of examination is employed, it is likely to operate in the wrong direction. When the Christian has really the most evidence of his conversion, he will think he has the least; and when he really has the least, he will think he has the most. We shall endeavor to ascertain the existence of the cardinal graces, not so much by describing them, as by pointing out those peculiar feelings in which they are imbedded, — these being more easily described, and equally indicative of a Christian state.

### § II. — Peculiarities of the Regenerate Character. — Conviction of Sin.

Sense of sin is essential to an initial and continued experience of a work of grace. Without it, repentance is impossible; and repentance is an essential feature of regeneration.

This point is abundantly established, both by Scripture and reason; and yet at the present time it is greatly overlooked. Want of deep conviction is regarded by Christians of the older stamp as a marked deficiency in modern conversions, and almost a universal characteristic of the great religious awakening which has recently pervaded the land. In the latter connection, especially, it has produced unuttered grief and anxiety in the hearts of many who have considered it fatal to a work of grace. Others are puzzled in view of this new aspect of religious experience; fearing to discredit it as genuine, yet not understanding how the work of God should be so dissimilar to that of former times and their own experience. Others still have modified their views of the essential features of a work of grace. They believe that God can change the hearts of men to the love of holiness without any deep convictions of sin, and that he has been pleased to show his sovereignty in this day by carrying on his work in this manner. But this view ignores the immutable relations between God and man, and the fact that so long as these remain as they are, the mode of reconciliation between them cannot be modified.

Another position which seems to have obtained, is, that men are *naturally* convinced that they are sinners, and all they need is to be persuaded to accept of the pardon offered in the gospel. This is contrary to the truth that it is the effect of sin to blind, harden, and deaden the sinner's consciousness of its existence. Men commonly admit that they are sinners. They do not profess to be perfect. Their natural conscience tells them that they do many things that are wrong. This universal admission is coming to be accepted as genuine conviction. It is, however, the office of the *Holy Spirit* to convince the world of sin. As has been said of repentance, faith, love, hope, prayer, so it may be said that there is a natural and a spiritual conviction of sin, and that the spiritual alone is genuine and good.

Others declare that their *experience* does not correspond

with the position that conviction of sin is an essential feature in conversion. They affirm that they were first brought to love Christ by a revelation to them of his loveliness and beauty, and then were led to see how they had sinned, — their conviction being a result of their conversion, rather than a feature in it. But, in the nature of the case, it is impossible that original conversion should occur in this manner.[1] Examples of this description have been treated in connection with unrecognized regeneration. What is supposed to be conversion by such persons, is only a coming to a consciousness of their acceptance with Christ, — conviction and regeneration having taken place before, — or else they are examples of unrecognizable regeneration.

It is sometimes insisted that we must not look for so deep conviction in persons who are morally upright and religiously educated, as in the openly wicked; in children, as in sinners of a greater age. Such a position is fallacious and dangerous. True conviction will have in each individual an external mould of its own. Its clearness and depth will depend nothing upon morality or age. Conviction may not be according to the person's actual sinfulness. All men are wholly sinful, while some have a greater amount of sinfulness than others. Those who have the greatest sinfulness, have not necessarily the deepest conviction. This is in proportion to the degree of their enlightenment. Hence an individual possessing less sinfulness than another, may have deeper conviction, and yet not be so deeply convicted as his sin furnishes occasion for. The

[1] This impossibility is sufficiently manifest from this consideration. Instantly, when a person is regenerated, he becomes penitent: and it is impossible that penitence should exist without antecedent sense of sin, genuine in its kind, however various its strength or its manifestations.

sin of every man is of so deep a dye as to require the blood of atonement by Christ to remove it, which can be fully comprehended by none. There is ground, therefore, in the case of the most moral, for a conviction which shall be painful to the last degree.

God may see that it is necessary to convict one more deeply than another, in order to bring him to the requisite state of submission and humiliation; but all must have the same apprehension of sin *in kind*, in order to the same experience. Whether we have, therefore, been truly convicted, must be determined, not by the amount, or by the strength, or the vividness, or the outward manifestation, but solely by the kind or quality of conviction. There is a certain temper and spirit attached to sense of sin, which is alone essential. A child may have a natural sense of the sin of disobeying his parents, more painful than that of another who is convicted in a truly spiritual manner. So, also, a man may be more deeply distressed in a merely natural way, on account of some open crime, than another who is under true conviction of sin against God.

One mode of determining the genuineness of convictions would be to ascertain what causes have produced them, since true convictions are produced only by the Holy Spirit. We shall consider, therefore, some of the natural causes which tend to awaken conviction independently of the Spirit's influence.

The first of these is fear of punishment. A person who has committed crime, commonly remains comparatively quiet until the crime is discovered, and he brought to justice. Then, a clearer view of the consequences of his act convinces him that it was wicked. He may even turn enemy to it, because it has become an agent of evil to him, while he has no more enlightened view of its vile and guilty nature than before. So it may be with the sinner. If his awakened sense of sin is produced by the dread of future punishment only, then, however deep and strong, it cannot be genuine. Reflection upon the punishment due to sin, has no power to enlighten as to its guilty nature, though it may convince the judgment that it is an evil thing.

Another cause of awakening natural conviction, kindred to fear of punishment, is that of affliction, such as sickness, the death of a friend, the loss of property, the thwarting of one's worldly enterprises, and the blighting of earthly prospects. These consequences of sin more forcibly remind the impenitent man that he has sinned, but in themselves have no power to enlighten him as to the nature of his sin.

It will be said that these things cause men to reflect upon their sin, and in this way lead to a deeper sense of it. But reflecting upon sin cannot throw light upon its moral quality, though it may strengthen natural convictions. It is absurd to suppose that a mind blinded by sin can, by exercising itself, obtain light. Or, it will be urged that through reflection upon sin excited by affliction, the *Spirit* enlightens. It is admitted that God's ordinary, and perhaps universal method of enlightening the mind, is through its own reflection, and in accordance with its constitutional laws. In consequence of the rapidity with which the mind sometimes acts, we do not know that instances in which persons are suddenly "*struck*" under conviction are exceptions.

The question, then, is, Are the reflections in regard to sin, incited by affliction, suited to produce enlightenment? So far as *awakening* reflection is concerned, it must be confessed that their effect is favorable. Men are naturally hardened and unconcerned, and must be stirred up, in some way, to think of their condition. But the danger is that the reflections will not be of a suitable kind, or will not be exercised in a proper manner. In the death-bed sickness of the impenitent man, for example, the dreadful *consequences* of sin, which he is about to suffer, are likely to absorb the entire energies of his reflective powers. The alarm is too great for any healthy mental exercise. The individual has put off, in total indifference, all concern about the consequences of sin, until an event overtakes him which produces so *intense* concern as to unfit him to make any suitable preparation against them. It is like the effects of a sudden alarm of fire upon the quiet inmates of a dwelling, which so destroys their self-control as to prevent any prudent efforts to escape from danger. While unalarmed, they make no effort; and when the alarm comes, it is so great that their efforts are as good as none.

The *opportunity*, also, to prepare to die, on the death-bed, is ordinarily so brief that the exercises must be of a hurried nature, and hence are liable to be superficial. Concern is put off until death stands at the door. Then all is confusion. There is such haste to make ready, as to unfit the mind for the operations of the Holy Spirit upon it in harmony with its natural laws. Or, in case it becomes settled in the person's mind that he must die, but not, perhaps, immediately, then the condition is similar to one of health. He thinks that he need not be in haste, but will take opportunity to consider the subject in a proper manner. Consequently the alarm subsides, and with it the awakening, until the probability of an immediate termination of his career occurs, when he is brought into the same condition as before.

The history of what have been supposed to be conversions occurring under apprehensions of approaching death, will confirm the position that the circumstances are unsuited to a real work of grace. To ascertain the truth here, these conversions must be carefully discriminated. Many have been supposed to be truly converted under the apprehension of approaching death as an instrumentality, because they became reconciled to the event of dying. But less evidence is to be derived from this than is commonly supposed. Reconciliation to a necessity often occurs where grace is wanting. Submission to dying, when one finds he must die, is common to impenitent men. All the surroundings of a death-bed conversion are such as to demand a greater jealousy of its genuineness than that which occurs under almost any other circumstances. The motives of self-interest are likely to be so strong as to forestall the prevalence of any others. Men die, ordinarily, as they live. Seldom are there better evidences of true conviction and conversion exhibited in anticipation of death, than have already been manifested in the life.

Similar is the distress which arises from a temporal affliction, so far as the reflections it excites are calculated to lead to true conviction. Distress on account of the death of a friend, or the loss of property, or the blighting of one's earthly prospects, while it awakens the mind to reflection upon sin as the cause of these, does it only in a partial manner, while itself retains the occupancy of the main energies of the soul. This is not sufficient. The sinner's reflections upon his relation to God, and his sin against him, must be supreme. They may be very deep and strong; but, so long as others are stronger, they will be of no avail.

The reason why this distress is not well calculated to lead to true conviction, is, that it is too strong a force.

While it awakens, it retains itself the ascendency. It preoccupies too much the energies. It *should* incite to reflections upon the nature of sin, and then retire and allow these to mature. This is the design of all awakening instrumentalities. There must be a passing over of the mind of the sinner from connection with the instrumentality to himself — from reflection upon the consequences, to the guilt of sin. The death of very near friends, for example, has naturally too vital a grasp upon the mind to allow this. Distress on this account cannot relinquish and forget itself, and so become subservient to other ends. Hence the very cause which awakens reflections, prevents them from maturing. Reflections much less deep and strong than those which it causes, would doubtless mature into genuine conviction, if it would retire. The loss of property, the frustrating of one's plans, and the blighting of earthly prospects, are quite likely to produce the same result.

An instrumentality well suited to lead to genuine conviction must have less immediate alarming power, and produce less disturbance of the mental faculties. It should have sufficient power to awaken, but not enough to unbalance or sway the mind, or absorb its energies. It should incite to reflections upon the nature of sin, and then recede and allow these to mature, — like a ball which, set in motion by a blow, goes on to its destiny, while the blow retires. There must be a space, greater or less, between the action of the instrumentality and the results to which it gave the original impulse. But very deep and sore afflictions commonly follow, and even precede their results.

It is impossible for a person to be truly convicted of sin, and at the same time have distress on account of his afflictions, or a sense of the consequences of sin, or fear of punishment, or any other interest predominant in the soul, or occupying any considerable portion of its energies. If conviction is supposed to have taken place in close conjunction with any of these influences, its genuineness is to be suspected. If it occur while these are exerting their full strength, then it must be spurious. Hence the improbability of true conviction in the midst of deep afflictions, and especially in view of the near approach of death and the judgment. In the latter case, it would be impossible that alarm, and the dread of the consequences of sin, should subside and give place to true conviction, were it not that this may take place in the shortest conceivable period of time; though such sudden transitions are exceptional and rare.

Another aspect of the subject is that distress on account of the afflictions is liable to be mistaken for conviction, and compulsory reconciliation to the afflictive event for voluntary submission to God.

All genuine Christian experience will sustain the position that true conviction of sin is ordinarily referable, not to circumstances of deep and sore affliction, but to more trifling incidents, which naturally less vitally concern us, — trivial in their nature, but made by the Holy Spirit events of everlasting consequence to us. The instrumentality is a word or a letter from some friend or minister; it is some exhortation, or prayer, or the conversion of some associate or associates; or it is nothing sufficiently prominent to be recalled. It is the combined and general influence of pious parents and teachers, and the preaching of the gospel. The instrumentality is lost sight of in the reflections and convictions to which, by a healthy and not unduly exciting influence, it stimulated.

Hence it is that novel and extraordinary religious enterprises, which attract public attention and involve motives of ambition or curiosity, or combine strongly social and popular influences, are not so well suited to produce genuine conviction and conversion, as the ordinary and less pretentious means of grace. "The kingdom of God cometh not with observation," but is like leaven, working silently and unseen. Our Saviour went about doing good, especially to the outcast and wicked, cautiously avoiding public display and multitudinous gatherings, charging his disciples also repeatedly that they should make no announcement of his works. His most memorable sermon was delivered to some of his disciples, who followed him away from the multitudes, up into the mountain, where, it is said, he taught them as it were privately. The disciples went forth in a similar manner, from house to house and city to city. The great outpouring on the day of Pentecost was needed as a manifest and convincing inauguration of the Spirit's work. The strongholds of Satan in theatres and ball-rooms cannot be entered and taken by storm. Professed convictions and conversions originating in such connections, are at least to be treated with caution. Men are not converted *en masse.* The wicked and abandoned in our cities are not regenerated while influenced by a desire to be freed from the misery of their degradation, and to become respectable in society. Christians who will save the souls of such, must do it in a manner which involves personal humiliation and sacrifice, and not by movements inaugurated with public renown. The instrumentality must be less conspicuous, — the work more a matter of faith, and less of sight. The connection between the means and the end must be less obvious, in order to give place for the unseen and mysterious operations of the Divine Spirit, so that God, and not the instrumentality, may be glorified. The public preaching of the gospel is instituted to subserve the general prevalence of the truth, while, as a matter of fact, it is brought to a specific issue in individual cases by private and often unrecognized instrumentalities. The churches of Christ are to be the centres of reforming influence,—their members constantly going out, and returning, and garnering up in themselves the elected souls of men, gathered out of every condition of society.

Sometimes a strongly *selfish* motive is found in connection with circumstances of affliction, which, on account of its undue force, prevents the convictions it excites from coming to a gracious maturity. The death of a beloved child incites an impenitent parent to reflect upon his sins, and seek for their forgiveness, and to do whatever else he thinks will conduce to his preparation to meet the child in heaven. In such a case, though the parent may be led to think of his sinfulness more intensely than ever before, yet the affliction has so strong a grasp upon the natural affections, as to prevent the desire again to meet the child from subsiding, and allowing the reflections upon sin which it has awakened to develop and mature. Convictions originating thus seldom result in true conversion.

Sometimes first awakenings and convictions are referred to the conversion of a very dear friend, as a wife or child. In such a case, there is danger that the same selfish motive will prevail. A wife, to whom the husband is fondly devoted, becomes a Christian. He now feels that a separation between them has taken place, which incites him to reflection upon his sinful condition, and an endeavor to secure his salvation. Motives of this kind have such power of endurance as almost necessarily to continue their control until they effect a merely supposed work of grace, or worry out all better motives, and cause the individual to relax his efforts, and settle down into his wonted indifference.

A selfish motive, also, is commonly connected with the loss of property, when this constitutes the source of religious awakening. The individual seeks for true religion, to comfort him in the place of his departed riches. This motive is so strong, as almost necessarily to prevent genuine conviction.

Not unfrequently, religious awakening originates in the desire to become a Christian, as a requisite condition of entering the marriage relation. Prompted by this motive, the person most earnestly seeks for conviction of sin, as the fundamental part of an experience. He is perhaps anxious that his pious friend, whose prayers he receives, should be the instrument of his conversion; or even believes that if he is converted at all, it must be so; and really does not much desire to be converted, unless it can be by that particular instrumentality. In such a case, the selfish motive is so strong as to allow only a selfish result, or none at all, to follow. True conviction and conversion can never occur so long as the desire to be converted by a particular instrumentality occupies any place in the mind. They never occur through the means which the unconverted man elects. He is uniformly brought to Christ by a way that he knows not, — by a way which destroys all his own preferences, and merges them in the purposes of a sovereign God.

These positions will be sustained only by a discriminating observation of examples. Cases of apparent conversion through deep affliction, which are numerous, are really instances of unrecognized, or of merely supposed regeneration.

The position assumed does not conflict with the fact that the Bible appeals to the fear of threatened punishment, and various selfish motives, in order to bring men to the knowledge of the truth. Objection is not made against an appeal to these, in the ordinary manner, but against that *undue* appeal which is occasioned by the death-bed, and in deep and sore affliction. Convictions commonly originate in selfish motives, but not in such as are of an all-controlling nature. It is, doubtless, because of this, that while God has revealed the future punishment of the wicked as a certainty, he has also caused that the coming of the Son of man shall be as a thief in the night, — no man knowing the day nor the hour. So, also, when he appeals to selfish principles, it is in such a manner as to give them an awakening power, but not supreme control. He promises that all things shall work together for good to them that love God, but that only eventually, and it may be in a mysterious manner, involving perhaps suffering and privation. He has, doubtless, so adjusted these appeals in his word, as to produce the most salutary effect. Accordingly, the general belief in the everlasting destruction of the finally impenitent, unaccompanied by any special fear of such an *immediate* doom, has been instrumental in awakening men to genuine conviction of sin, to a far greater extent than that undue fear which is excited upon a sick and dying bed. A similar preference must also be accorded to those means of grace which are more rational and well-proportioned, as compared with those in which the terrors of the world to come are made the prevailing motive, and are brought so vividly before the mind as to be regarded in the light of an almost present reality. The effect of such a disproportionate excitement of fear, must be similar to that which occurs upon the death-bed.

It awakens convictions which it prevents from maturing; or it produces distress which is taken for, and so supplants, genuine convictions. More genuine convictions, by far, are referable to God's ordinary dealings with men, than to the special and deeply afflictive; more to the conversion of an acquaintance, or neighbor, or several acquaintances, or to the fact that many are coming to Christ, than to the conversion of one's dearest earthly friend, with whom the heart and soul are bound up for life; more to the common means of grace, than to some fearfully exciting religious occasion, or some novel and famous religious enterprise.

Deep afflictions are beneficial to the Christian. God appoints them to prove his children, and bring them nearer to himself. David said, "Before I was afflicted I went astray; but now have I kept thy word." Where divine grace has been implanted, affliction quickens it anew; but it is not calculated to originate it. God punishes unconverted men, on account of their sin, by means of affliction. He punished the old world by a flood; but neither the punishment nor the threatening of it resulted in the conviction or conversion of a single soul.

We have no promise that the Holy Spirit shall be especially granted to unconverted men upon a dying-bed, or when circumstances of deep affliction overtake them, after having neglected all favorable means and opportunities for becoming Christians. On the other hand, it was declared, in the parable of those who had been bidden to the feast, and would not come because of their worldly engagements, that not one of them should taste of the supper. Solomon exhorts that our Creator should be remembered in youth, *before* the evil days come. Also, in the first chapter of Proverbs, it is written: "Because I have called and ye refused; I have stretched out my hand, and no man regarded; but ye have set at naught all my counsel, and would none of my reproof: I also will laugh at your calamity; I will mock when your fear cometh; when your fear cometh as desolation, and your destruction cometh as a whirlwind; when distress and anguish cometh upon you. Then shall they call upon me, but I will not answer; they shall seek me early, but they shall not find me."

It may be objected that the great religious awakening of 1857–8 affords an illustration which is not in accordance with these principles, in that God has overruled the financial depression which occurred throughout the land, to the production of an equally wide-spread revival of religion; that he has caused, in numerous instances, the loss of property, and the blasting of men's earthly prospects, to result in their conversion to Himself. In answer we remark, that, so far as the revival has been in the hearts of Christians, or has contributed to bring out persons from an unrecognized to a recognized state of regeneration, these means are precisely adapted to the end. So far, also, as true conviction and conversion have resulted from a general awakening, of which the financial embarrassment may have been instrumental, and hence are only remotely ascribable to deeply-felt suffering, it is in accordance with the statements advanced. And, finally, so far as this awakening has assumed the *form* of a gracious work without the power, being deficient especially in deep conviction of sin, these causes have been precisely suited to produce it. To what extent this has been the case, must remain to be disclosed hereafter. If genuine conviction of sin, and conversion, have arisen directly out of the deep distress of men on account of having lost their property or their fortunes; if this distress has been simultaneous with genuine conviction, and has continued in its full strength up to the point of conversion; and if reconciliation to the loss of property has been coincident with actual pardon,—then it is decidedly contrary to our views of a genuine work of grace. Or if the loss of a fortune, or of property, in such a manner as deeply and sorely to afflict, has instrumentally *led* to true conviction and conversion, in any more than very rare and exceptional cases; and if men have been prompted to seek for true religion as a comforter to them in the place of their departed possessions, and have obtained it,—then this is also contrary to the positions we have taken. We are, however, unaware that anything has transpired contrary to the doctrines advanced.

Another influence should be referred to here, as connected with a seeming want of deep conviction of sin in the recent awakening. It has been stated that strongly popular and social influences are likely to produce false convictions. A truly gracious work may prevail among the people, deeply and strongly; but it never can be *popular* to be converted. God's work is submitted to only by divine constraint overcoming human reluctance. When it assumes a form acceptable to the masses, then it is popular and false, and conviction will be either spurious or wanting. It is not our object here to discuss the question whether the recent awakening has, to any extent, been of a popular nature. We have only to say, in passing, that it has not confessedly been so unpopular and objectionable to all classes of unconverted men and unevangelical religious denominations as former revivals, and as would have been expected from a work of such power as is commonly ascribed to this. And, moreover, if it has assumed this form and spirit, to a greater or less extent, this would, so far, account for the unusual absence of deep conviction which has so largely characterized it.

If convictions of sin are directly referable to strongly popular or to social influences, then they are to be examined with greater care. The fact that a whole family seems to have been converted, affords no more presumptive evidence for than against the true conversion of any individual member. The fact that some profess to become Christians, is suited to awaken reflections and convictions in others. If that profession is genuine, it is better adapted to awaken genuine convictions than false; if false, it is better adapted to awaken false convictions than genuine. Popular and social influences propagate themselves through the channels of human sympathy, and so do the influences of the Spirit.

We shall proceed now to consider the peculiarities of genuine convictions. First, we remark, their origination is *progressive.* Persons are not commonly *struck* under conviction. This is not in accordance with the ordinary workings of the human mind, in harmony with which the Spirit operates. Examples of this kind of genuine conviction are exceptional. Paul possessed an extraordinary character, and extraordinary circumstances existed which rendered it desirable that his conviction should appear to be almost miraculous. Such a character is seldom to be found, and such circumstances will never again exist. Besides, we have only an imperfect account, the mere framework of his mental exercises. This must be borne in mind, in contemplating any merely written or reported experience.

Universal Christian experience, as well as the laws of mind, teach that true convictions are, at first, weak and small, and increase in depth and strength up to the point of final relief. Variations often occur by the way; but, as a whole, the process is progressive, and its culminating point is just before relief. This is the fact, whether the individual recognizes it or not. Convictions do not pass off gradually as they come on, being removed one after another, till all are gone. *Christian's* burden grew heavier and heavier, until it fell all at once from his back. Paul says that sin revived, and he died; but not that sin revived *and subsided*, and he died. God, by enlightenment, increases the weight of the sinner's sin, until it becomes too great to bear, when he *falls* upon the mercy of Christ. The deepest conviction of sin, and the first real sweetness in prayer, are likely to stand in close connection, and in the order named.

This progressive conviction is peculiar and inexplicable to the unenlightened man, but true to nature. The natural conception of the manner in which conviction takes place, is, that the individual examines and reflects upon his various sins, one after another, and, as he does so, repents of them and puts them away; and so, by this diminishing process, they gradually grow less and less, until the last is removed,—a course which is always reversed before a gracious end is attained. The woman with the bloody issue spent all she had, and gained nothing, but rather grew worse, until she abandoned her efforts and submitted to the will of Christ.

The error in the natural conception is that it presupposes in man, by nature, a sense of sin and disposition to repent,—it being only necessary that his attention should be turned to the subject. The spiritual process presumes that man needs to be both enlightened and humbled; and when he becomes sufficiently so to exercise repentance for one sin, he will for all. The process, therefore, increases in intensity, until submission becomes complete.

Another peculiarity in the origination of genuine conviction, is a consciousness of a decided change in a person's view of his sin, after having supposed he understood it; or, a consciousness of having passed over from natural to spiritual conviction. This change is sometimes indicated by a voluntary expression of this kind: "At this time I knew I was a sinner, but did not *feel* it," — denoting a clear distinction in the person's mind between knowing and feeling.

Another mark of genuine conviction is, that the person is not conscious of the commencement, or of any steps in the progress of his conviction, — the entrance of light being imperceptible. The reason is, that the Holy Spirit engages all the powers of the sinner in the contemplation of his guilt, while light follows in the train. He has no leisure to ascertain, step by step, whether he is gaining light; so that, ere he is aware, he finds, upon his attention being arrested to it, that whereas once he was blind, now he sees. Another reason is, that the person makes no direct effort to secure illumination, it being, so far as he is concerned, spontaneous. In the natural process, the direct aim of the sinner is not so much honestly to understand his precise condition, as to obtain such an amount of knowledge that he is a sinner as is requisite to conversion. He examines, therefore, his conduct and feelings by his own unaided efforts; seeks for new views of sin; and when acquired, sets them down as so much advance in the way of gaining light; and is thus conscious both of the beginning and the progress of his conviction.

He who is under true conviction, will feel, as the process advances, that he is departing farther and farther from the kingdom of heaven. He will be more and more discouraged in regard to his ever becoming a Christian. This is peculiar. No one anticipates that while he is being brought to Christ, he shall feel that he is actually departing from him; and yet it is a legitimate result of a constantly increasing view of sin. The fact that an enlightening work is going on, could be known to him only by inference, from the increase of a sense of guilt; but that inference the sinner cannot make while the work is advancing, because the diversion would retard the work. Even if the fact were announced to him by an observer, his consciousness could not appropriate it, on account of its being fully occupied with a sense of his sin.

Another peculiarity of genuine conviction is, reluctance to confess it. He who is under true conviction, is not pleased with the fact, so as to make him forward to proclaim it. Subsequently, when his convictions are removed, he may take pleasure in giving an account of them, but not while they are resting upon him. It is then too serious a matter. His great concern will be to get free from the curse. If he feels that the piercing eye of God's wrath is upon him, his utterance will be choked. This will be as true in the case of a regenerate person as of one in the process of conviction. In proportion as he is inclined to talk freely of his sins, may he infer that he is wanting in a sense of them. A sense of sin involves conscious guilt and shame, and one will not talk of these except as duty requires it. It will be enough for him that his wickedness is known to God.

Another peculiarity of a true sense of sin is, that he who possesses it will feel that he has not so deep a sense of it as he ought to have. Many young Christians are afraid they were never converted, because they think their convictions were not so deep as they should have been. Whether they had as strong convictions as they ought to have had or not, real alarm in regard to it is a sign that the convictions they had were genuine. This is not a peculiarity of false convictions. It is true light only that makes the sinner feel that his sin is deeper and of a more aggravated nature than what has yet been exposed to his view. Many young Christians also are alarmed because they are so sensible of being sinners, thinking that on this account they cannot be Christians. They have never supposed that Christians feel sinful, and least of all that they have a sense of deeper sin than has ever come to light. They are confident that no others feel so but themselves, and hence greatly fear they are not true Christians.

This is peculiar. It is such feeling as no man naturally expects to find attendant upon the regenerate state; whereas it is habitual with the true Christian, and is a sign of regeneration. Men naturally suppose the Christian has a constantly diminishing sense of his sin, especially if he is growing in grace. They conceive if he is actually growing better, that he would feel so. But the spiritual view is the reverse. While he is actually growing better, his sense of sin is growing stronger. The better he grows, the more light he receives; and the more light he receives, the deeper he perceives to be the fountain of his iniquity.

Another peculiarity of true conviction is, that it does not pertain to particular sins, but to sinfulness in general. The person is pervaded with a sense of his guiltiness, without being able to define the reasons for it. He rather mourns over his wicked heart than the few sins which happen to escape out of it. Under true conviction, open wickedness, however great, will lose the prominence it naturally has in the mind, and almost disappear in the abyss of iniquity in the heart. After conversion, one may refer frequently to one's open sins as *signs* of great wickedness, but not as constituting it. He may speak of them more frequently than others, because they are more palpable and convenient to be named; but he will not magnify them as if they were the only sins he had ever committed. The Holy Spirit lays the axe at the root of the tree. He causes the sinner to mourn more over his sinfulness than his sins; over his disposition to sin, than his sinful acts.

Conviction of sin is very often conceived of as a burden on the heart. This conception is incidental, not essential. Nor is it necessarily a sign of true conviction. There is a natural and a spiritual burden. One of the peculiarities of the spiritual, is that it is not well defined in the individual's mind. He feels oppressed and wicked, without being able to say on what particular account. This is because his burden is not made up of his sins, but arises from a view of his wicked heart. He has no conception of the cause of his burden, because he does not at the time realize the connection between his consciousness of guilt and the weight on his soul, — the burden seeming to come upon him spontaneously.

Sometimes true conviction assumes the form simply of distress, for which the individual can assign no cause. Consciousness of guilt is the cause, but he does not connect it with the effect. He is so absorbed in a sense of his guilt, that he does not think of himself as being under conviction, and of course does not assign this as the occasion for his distress.

Sometimes objection is made to an experience on the ground that the person seemed to feel badly, and then better, but could not tell why. This *may* be a favorable symptom. It shows that whatever work existed was not the sinner's own production. It should be considered whether the cause of this symptom is great depth of conviction, or its entire absence.

True conviction, also, sometimes assumes the form of great and growing hardness of heart. The individual feels that he is *not* being convicted, but is daily becoming more insensible. The fact, however, is, that he has not an increasing hardnesss, but a growing consciousness of it, which indicates an increasing tenderness. This is one of the peculiarities of true conviction, and never exists in that which is false. The unenlightened man expects to *recognize* an increasing tenderness, which all analogy would show to be untrue to nature.

True conviction assumes, in addition to the above, a variety of other forms in the mind. Indeed, it is confined to no particular one, but takes such as arise from variety of training, mental habits, and other causes, which perhaps cannot be identified.

Finally, it may be remarked, as another peculiarity of genuine conviction, that that which exists in the regenerate state never makes the same impression upon the mind with that which occurs in regeneration, though it may be the same both in kind and degree. This seems to be the only difference between original convictions and those of subsequent occurrence. As there is no love which seems like the first love, so there are no convictions which seem like the first convictions. The cause is to be found chiefly in the fact, that all new exercises make a deeper impression upon the mind than those to which the soul has been accustomed.

A sense of sin has been treated of as an essential feature in conversion, and also of a regenerate state. The question may arise, however, whether it is a certain sign of regeneration. To this we answer, that a genuine sense of sin is by no means a feature of an unregenerate state. It is not natural for men to feel themselves verily guilty in the sight of God. All Scripture and human experience teach that man is by nature a thoroughly self-righteous being. The question, whether a person may not be truly convicted and not converted, or may not be under conviction for a series of years, has been already considered.

### REPENTANCE.

Repentance is an essential feature of a regenerate condition, and is found in no other. If it can be determined that a person has ever exercised true repentance, it is an unmistakable evidence that he has been born again. But the difficulty is to determine whether we possess this Christian grace, since it is not easy to be described. Besides, we are taught that there is a sorrow of the world that worketh death; that there is a repentance that needs to be repented of. We must therefore inquire what peculiar marks distinguish true repentance from false. We might say that true repentance is ingenuous, sincere; that it is deep and thorough. But this would not suffice. The question will still arise, Is my repentance sincere? Is it deep and thorough? And this would be as difficult to determine as the original question. It is also commonly said that true repentance is accompanied with reformation. But this does not meet the case; for if by this is meant reformation of heart, then it will be even more difficult to determine this than the exercise of repentance. Or, if mere outward reform is meant, then the difficulty is not removed, since this may occur without repentance, or accompany that which is false. We must inquire, therefore, whether any peculiar marks or states of mind are attendant upon true repentance, by which its existence may be determined.

One of the characteristics of true repentance is, that it is not altogether a process, but chiefly a mental state resulting from a process. We are said to *come* to repentance. "The Lord is not willing that any should perish, but that all should come to repentance." The sinner does not repent first of one sin, and then of another, and so go through a process of repenting. He comes to a *state* of repentance, through a process of conviction and humiliation. When he has come to true repentance for one sin, he is in a state of repentance for all sin. Repentance is therefore an *exercise*, so far as sin is presented to the mind, and a *state* of readiness to repent of all sin.

It follows from this that a person cannot exercise repentance by any deliberate determination to do so. It is not an act of the will, but a mental state which ensues spontaneously, as a result of other exercises. Hence an individual cannot resolve to enter upon the duty of repentance, as upon that of prayer. True prayer, and true repentance, are equally the gift of God; but the exercise of the one is to be gained through an effort of the will, while the other is attained by other means.

One who has exercised true repentance, therefore, is not likely to say that he feels he has repented of all his sins, as if he had gone through the process of repenting, until he had completed the work. A repentance which inclines to express itself thus is natural, and needs to be repented of. Ask the true Christian if he thinks he has repented of all his sins, and he will hesitate, hardly knowing how to reply. His answer will be partially suppressed and modified,—the reason being, that he does not conceive of the subject in such a light. He has simply been in a state of repentance, in which a partial view of his sinfulness has been before his mind, — the connection between his sins being such, that true sorrow for one is virtually sorrow for all.

Repentance being not mainly a process, but a state, does not present so many points for description as conviction of sin. One other peculiarity, however, is to be mentioned. He who has exercised true repentance is likely to feel that it has not been so deep and extensive as it ought. This is, doubtless, a uniform peculiarity, which arises from the fact that he who has been really convicted of sin is conscious that he has been so only in part; and, consequently, whenever genuine repentance has ensued upon such conviction, the person will feel that he has repented only in part. When other sin is brought to his mind, or as his views become more clear, he will still have to repent. Accordingly it is that when the sinner comes to repentance all his sins are blotted out, without his being under the painful necessity of viewing them all in their most aggravated sinfulness, which perhaps the human mind could not endure.

We remark, finally, that we shall be aided in determining the genuineness of true repentance by the genuineness of antecedent convictions. If these have been only natural, then no spiritual repentance can ensue. If convictions are spiritual, then spiritual repentance is at least likely to follow.

## SENSE OF FORGIVENESS.

If a genuine sense of forgiveness of a single sin is actually felt in the soul, it is an undoubted sign of regeneration. How, then, shall it be determined whether such a feeling has existed? This is confessedly not easy. Forgiveness is God's act, which produces no such *palpable* effect upon the sinner as to enable him to ascertain with ease just when it is performed, or whether it has been performed at all. And yet it is common for persons, under some religious exercise, to declare with confidence their belief that God has forgiven all their sins. But this is rather a sign that forgiveness has not taken place. Hence we remark, as the first peculiarity of a sense of forgiveness, that he who has experienced it will not ordinarily express it in definite and positive terms. A sense of forgiveness, conceived apart from all other exercises, is emphatically a matter of faith and trust, not marked by any sensible impressions. God has no given signal by which he always makes it known to the sinner that he is pardoned. He does not, in any direct manner, communicate to him a knowledge of the event. The presentation to the mind of passages of Scripture cannot be relied upon. They may or may not have connection with actual forgiveness. This is in its origin a matter of indistinct, undefined consciousness. A sense of forgiveness, in like manner with conviction of sin, conceived of separately from other exercises, comes upon the mind gradually and imperceptibly. We do not mean that the sinner is thus forgiven, only that a sense of forgiveness is thus obtained.

It might be expected, however, that when God pronounces the rebel pardoned, and withdraws his anger, it would, in consequence of the spiritual connection existing between man and his Maker, produce some conscious effect upon the sinner's mind. An effect is produced when forgiveness takes place between man and man, and much more may it be expected when it takes place between man and God. Such an effect *is* produced, varying according to the character of the individual, and perhaps other conditions. But it is not that, ordinarily, of a direct announcement of the fact, by any easily recognized signal.

This would be gratifying to the natural man. Some sensible sign that sin is forgiven, is often desired, and sometimes asked for, but never granted in the manner desired or sought. If the individual supposes he had a token from God to this effect, he should rather regard it as indicating his mistake. It would not meet his wants if received, and hence God does not grant it.

The first effect produced, when God forgives, is merely a state of mental quietude. Sometimes it is conceived of as actual indifference; at others, it assumes the form of a sweet peace, or positive joy. But these effects are not produced by God, or regarded by the individual as a sign that forgiveness has been granted. They are merely the legitimate consequences of pardon. They, however, necessarily arrest the sinner's attention, because of the circumstances under which they are experienced ensuing immediately upon great mental distress. When the effect assumes the form of mental quietude, then it excites suppressed curiosity to know its meaning. If it takes the form of indifference, it excites alarm. Not recognizing his spiritual state, the individual fears that, by some mysterious cause, his convictions have been supplanted by great hardness of heart and abandonment by God. If sweet peace, or positive joy ensue, these chiefly absorb his attention and reflections, — there being, perhaps, an occasional inquiry in his mind whether they may not be the result of forgiveness.

When a sense of forgiveness first arises, it consists of an indistinct or feeble consciousness of acceptance with God, combined very soon with an undefined inference to that effect, drawn from the exercises through which the person has passed. This feeling, however, does not become most prominent. The new life — the sweet peace and joy unfelt before — which the pardoned sinner now begins to experience, mainly occupy his mind, and supersede any special inquiry whether sin has been forgiven. He finds in his new life abundant satisfaction, and as much peace as he is capable of enjoying, so that he has no occasion or leisure to seek for them from the settlement of the question whether he is now a Christian, or is forgiven, or from any other source.

Thus it is, that at no stage of the process does the individual find himself inclined to state, in definite and positive terms, that he believes his sins have been all forgiven. Since he does not feel that he has fully repented, he will not feel that he has been fully forgiven. Where this does occur, it indicates that to obtain pardon as a matter of prudential interest, had been the highest aim of the individual, and that the ground of his rejoicing is the consideration that he has been pardoned, and not the quietude of mind ensuing from reconciliation with God. The spontaneous expression of the new-born soul does not indicate that a belief of having been forgiven is the primal source of his joy, as is the case with the person who is deceived. If the real convert is asked what makes him happy, he will hesitate what to answer. He has been too happy to find leisure for settling that question. The same remarks apply where the first state of mind attendant upon forgiveness is that of mental quietude, or of indifference. If it be mental quietude, there is no agitation of any question, and no positive declaration. If it is indifference, such as to cause alarm, the sinner does not believe he has been forgiven, but rather fears that he has been forsaken.

Sometimes these several states occur in succession.

First there is quietude, then a felt indifference and consequent alarm, and then, as a reäction, great peace and joy. This is, perhaps, the natural order. Sometimes these several states follow in such quick succession that the mind does not note the process, and hence the last seems to be the first. In such a case, the first manifestation of feeling, when sin is forgiven, is a sudden outburst of joy or transport. But, even then, the individual does not express a definite and positive belief that all his sin has been forgiven, as the ground of his rejoicing. The cause of this transport is a matter of faith, which he is not able to define. In his high state of mental excitement, the person may declare, especially if interrogated, that he believes his sins are forgiven; but it will be merely the outburst of his excitement, rather than a well-defined belief. This is evident from the fact, that very soon this transport is for a time changed into the deepest gloom and belief of self-deception, showing that the expressed belief of forgiveness was rather a result of the transport than the cause of it.

Another peculiarity attendant upon a true sense of forgiveness, is the absence of a full and strong exercise of the understanding. This is equally attendant upon all the initial gracious states and exercises. A sense of forgiveness, so far as the individual himself is concerned, is spontaneous. It seems to be entirely self-produced, and hence the intellect has very little to do with its creation. The cause of this is twofold: First, a sense of forgiveness, as well as all other gracious states and exercises, is produced by the Holy Spirit, which is an unseen and unobserved agency; and, secondly, a work of grace, while it affects the understanding, has its seat in the heart. This is the altar on which the fires of divine grace are kindled, and from which the smoke of its incense ascends through all the soul. The result is, that the exercises of the intellect are not prominent, full and strong, nor sharply defined. There is scarcely the least intellection in the process. The understanding is naturally brought into harmony with the gracious biases of the heart, by cultivation. This is a point of vital importance. "With the *heart* man believeth unto righteousness."

We have presented thus far the marks of a sense of forgiveness in the earliest stages of its existence; but its subsequent character does not essentially differ. Like all other exercises, it has at the first more vividness and tenderness, and, in consequence of its newness, makes a more marked impression on the mind. As it continues it becomes more settled, firm, and steady. It acquires greater depth, breadth, and strength, but becomes less acute. The contrast between it and the preëxistent state is never so noticeable as at the first. Common to all the stages of its existence is the fact that the person is not inclined to express his sense of forgiveness by saying, in definite and positive terms, that he believes his sins are all forgiven. Though he might be conscious of its being so, it would yet be expressed in partially suppressed, modified, and modest language.

We shall be aided still farther, in determining the genuineness of a sense of forgiveness, by considering the circumstances under which forgiveness originates, and its antecedent, instrumental causes. And here we remark, that true forgiveness of sin is, in its origin, closely identified with, and consequent upon, the passing off of convictions, or the removal of the burden, both of which are equivalent to the subsidence of distress on account of sin, whatever form it may assume in the mind. We speak not of *sense* of forgiveness, but of actual forgiveness. It has been shown that these are not, ordinarily, simultaneous; but that a brief state of mental quietude, or indifference and consequent alarm, are likely to intervene, — thus affording space for a sense of sin to originate in an imperceptible manner, like the space between night and morning, in which the morning dawns. The circumstances, therefore, in which the burden is removed, or convictions subside, will be those in which sin is forgiven; and the antecedent causes of the one will be the antecedent causes of the other.

We remark, first, that, so far as the individual is concerned, the removal of the burden is *spontaneous.* He does not pray for its removal, or desire it, though he does desire forgiveness, which will cause it. To all human appearance, the burden *goes* off rather against the person's will. The precise expression of his feelings is, that he has *lost* his burden. He regards its removal as a loss, and is at first alarmed and grieved on account of it.

Again: the burden is removed when the sinner is not expecting it. If he is not praying for its removal, nor desiring it, he is not likely to be looking for it. He cares little about his load. He would be willing to carry that to his grave. His anxiety is for peace with God. He is rather glad to be burdened and distressed, yea, even slain, on account of sin, because he believes he so richly deserves it. When he becomes conscious that he deserves to suffer the full penalty of sin, and is broken and humbled before the Divine justice, God ordains that he shall suffer no more, but that he shall be relieved, through the sufferings of another. In coming to this condition, his mind approaches a state of expectancy that he will forever make his bed in hell. When God, therefore, in mercy, through Jesus Christ, takes his sufferings away, and gives him quiet, he is for a brief space at a loss. He may be alarmed, and suffer again the most intense distress, until the Holy Spirit induces within him the consciousness that his sufferings have been laid on Christ, when he beholds, by faith, the Saviour, in heavenly innocence and beauty, enduring on the cross the full penalty which, through surprising, unmerited grace, had been already taken from his guilty head. Thus it is that the sinner finds himself, ere he is scarcely aware, relieved of his burden, and rejoicing in Christ, who is bearing it for him on the cross.

We remark again, that the sinner does not, at the time, understand that the burden is being removed. The idea of his having *lost* his burden involves this. When a person loses something from his possession, he does not become aware of his loss till after it occurs. So it is with the sinner. His attention is not called to the fact that his convictions or his burden are being removed, till after they are gone, when he has to look about him a little, to certify himself whether it is really so. This peculiarity arises from these causes: First, the sinner is not expecting the removal of his burden when it occurs; secondly, it is removed by the Holy Spirit, whose operations are never *sensibly* felt; and thirdly, the soul is so deeply absorbed in the antecedent causes of the removal as not to be able to recover itself to the contemplation of it till after the event has transpired. The mental exercises have acquired such a momentum as to carry the individual somewhat by the goal to which he is tending, before he is aware.

Another peculiarity is, that when the removal of the burden occurs, and the person's attention is arrested to it, he is reluctant to believe it to be the pardon of his sins. This is caused, in part, by a feeling of so great unworthiness to have his transgressions blotted out, that he cannot, for a little period, believe it possible that so glorious an event has taken place. Besides, his previous conception of a sense of forgiveness was altogether erroneous; hence, when it occurs, it is so unlike his ideal, that he discredits it until he learns to view it in its proper light.

It seems to be a common idea that the cause of the removal of the burden, and of convictions, is a conscious, intelligent looking of the sinner to Christ, when in distress, for help. Feeling that he is very sinful, and perhaps bowed down under the weight of his guilt, and being directed to trust in Christ as willing to save him, he does endeavor to cast his soul upon him, and by this means his burden or distress is removed. This is, however, a natural view of the subject, supported neither by Christian experience nor a spiritually enlightened reason. According to the testimony of all true Christians, an impressive view of Christ as a Saviour is experienced only subsequently to the removal of the burden. If its removal is followed by simply mental quietude or indifference, and consequent alarm, then the view of Christ is only subsequent to this. If the removal is followed by these states in so quick succession that transport seems to be immediate, the view of Christ will seem to be so too.

This position is sustained by a practical investigation, which shows that, in a large proportion of genuine conversions, no impressive view of Christ is experienced in any stage of the work, and, of course, in these the burden must have been removed by some other instrumental cause. And, moreover, when this view occurs, it is more a matter of spiritual consciousness than an act of the understanding. The fact that Christ had died on the cross, had resided in the understanding long before; but now it sinks down into a living consciousness in the soul, and, consequently, is less a matter of intelligence than of intense, but undefined feeling. Christ is viewed by faith, and not by sight. It is the spontaneous enjoyment of a new and heavenly life, in union with Jesus Christ. All the utterances of the new-born soul are in harmony with these positions. Yet as soon as the mental powers come again into exercise, the new life, which springs up from the heart renewed in Christ, illuminates the understanding in regard to the excellency of the plan of redemption, as it had never been before. The view of Christ which is received, in some instances, is one and the same with that new and lovely appearance which nature and the Bible and Christians assume in other instances. The one is a new view of Christ; the other is a new or Christ-like view of nature, the Bible, and Christians.

The instrumental cause of the removal of the burden, or of convictions, and, consequently, of forgiveness, is the coming of the sinner to the requisite state of submission, humiliation, and sorrow. Instantly, when this state is attained, God forgives. This occurs more frequently in prayer, yet also in every variety of circumstances. The point which completes the process is sometimes recognizable in conversion, and sometimes not. It consists of the yielding of some object hitherto tenaciously held, or the forming of some new resolution which the person had been unwilling to make. The objects to be given up are, sources of worldly pleasure, attachments, or considerations of ambition and pride — in themselves perhaps trifling, but constituting with the individual the final test. The resolutions to be made consist of a determination to perform some act involving humiliation or submission. Among the Jews in the time of Christ, the final test was likely to be an acknowledgment that Jesus was the Messiah, and willingness to be saved by him. This, however, now, is unlikely to be the test, since the name of Christ is universally respected by unconverted men. Humiliation and submission now are involved rather in a willingness to be saved by *grace* than by *Christ.*

One peculiarity attendant upon the giving up of these points and the making of these resolutions, is, that the sinner never understands beforehand what point is to be yielded, or what resolution is to be made, in order to bring relief. If he obtains relief upon the giving up of just the point which he was confident would secure it, then it is an indication that the relief is spurious. He may have a hard struggle with the object, but he will not recognize it as the final test till the struggle is over. The point of which he is tenacious is his darling sin, and, consequently, is least likely to show itself as being that which must be given up. All Christian experience testifies that the sinner is brought to Christ by a way which he knows not. He is not converted as he anticipates. But, if he could know beforehand what point yielded, what resolution made or act performed, would bring relief, there would be nothing mysterious in his conversion. The sinner seeks to find out the way to come to Christ, by trying first one and then another, till he falls, in humiliation, helplessness, and dependence, upon the mercy of God. God seems not to enlighten him previously as to the way, lest it should not subserve his brokenness of spirit and humiliation. Persons often suppose that God does thus show them what precise act they must perform in order to obtain relief; but this savors of the human, and not the divine. That is the natural and false conception of conversion, not the spiritual and true. Nor does the person understand that the act which constitutes the final test is to bring relief while performing it, like a child who finally submits to some trifling requirement of the parent, wholly unaware that the act stands for universal obedience. He is obliged to submit, not knowing whether he shall ever be relieved or not. He must resign his soul into the hands of God, to be disposed of at his pleasure, according to his infinite justice or his sovereign mercy.

This is not man's natural conception of a sense of forgiveness, or of the manner in which it is to be obtained. His natural idea of it is, that he is to examine himself carefully and thoroughly, discover precisely what his sins are, then fully repent of each and all, and as he repents receive forgiveness. In such godliness there is no mystery. The very intelligibleness of it, to an unenlightened mind, is conclusive proof of its spurious nature. "God's ways are not our ways, nor his thoughts our thoughts."

## LOVE FOR GOD AND CHRIST.

Love for God and Christ is a characteristic of the regenerate state. But how shall it be determined whether we have such love? It is often stated that it is as easy to know whether we love God, as to know whether we love our earthly friends. A recent writer, of sound reputation, remarks that "we need no other method of ascertaining the nature of love to God, than the nature of love to man." "Seriously considered," he says, "there is precisely the same difficulty in conceiving of the nature of love to man, that there is in conceiving of the nature of love to God." "You may as easily know what it is to love God, therefore, as what it is to love your friends." These statements have only a seeming basis of truth. It is acknowledged that if a man love his friends, or any earthly pleasure as he ought, he would possess an affection kindred to genuine love for God and Christ. But that would be a spiritual affection. There is a love, both to God and man, that is natural, and one that is spiritual. The natural is depraved and false, the spiritual alone good and true. It is impossible, therefore, that man's depraved love for his friends should reflect the nature of holy love for God. It cannot even reflect holy love for his friends. Let the parent be converted, and he will feel that he never before loved his children, or nature, or anything else in the proper manner.[1]

Between man's natural and spiritual love for God, and his natural and spiritual love for man, there is a parallel,—the latter being the sanctification, or the spiritual engraftment of the former. But between them, also, the distinction is as vital as between life and death. The unconverted man, therefore, can have no conception of his love for God by his love for his friends; and the converted man can no more easily decide whether he loves his friends in a spiritual manner, than whether he loves God thus. How, then, is true spiritual love for God and Christ to be distinguished? We answer, that, like other gracious exercises, it is to be known by the peculiarities attendant upon its existence.

[1] The parent's natural love for his child is depraved and false, because he does not love the child as it is reasonable he should. God requires that whatever we do, whether we eat or drink, we should do all to his glory. Hence we should love our children for his glory. This is reasonable, because he gives us our children, stamped with his image, to remind us of him and make us love him for the gift. But if we love him for the gift, regardless of the giver, he will be angry with us. And the more we love the gift, without loving him, the more jealous will he have cause to be that we do not love him at all. If a child love his toy more than he loves the parent who gave it, will not the parent be offended?

We shall speak of love to God and Christ promiscuously, according to convenience, inasmuch as he who loves the one will love the other also.

First, we shall notice the peculiarities attendant upon the manner in which true love for God and Christ originates. And we remark, that it arises not from any direct effort to produce it, but is spontaneous. True love is not originally produced by contemplating the character of Christ, and what he has done and suffered, when this is done for the purpose of creating it. Contemplation serves to revive love where it has already existed, but cannot produce it. An unconverted person may take a selfish *pleasure* in thinking that Christ has died for his salvation, which is liable to be mistaken for love. He is glad an atonement has been made, but has no enlightened view of his own ill-desert, or of the condescending and loving spirit in which the cross was endured for his salvation.

This is the natural conception of love for Christ. But true love, which is produced by the Holy Spirit, is, so far as man is concerned, spontaneous. The individual is not sensible that any particular instrumentalities have produced it. He never conceives that his love arose from his examination of the atonement, and his discovery of the obligations he is under to Christ. The first love of the new-born soul springs up independently of these contemplations. He is delighted with the character of Christ, yet scarcely knowing why. This is true to nature. All true love gushes up spontaneously. That is false which is gotten up by an effort, or which is based only upon a sense of indebtedness and obligations. We may have a sense of indebtedness and obligation, without love, or any appreciation of the true spirit in which the favors were bestowed.

Sometimes persons seek to exercise love in a certain direction, because their interest so inclines them. But the result is spurious. True love will not be forced into exercise. So, if an individual seeks to love Christ merely because he knows it will be for his interest, his love will be only imaginary. Or, if he seeks to love him simply because he knows he ought to love him, the result will be similar. Men generally know they ought to love God, but they do not do it. If I do not love, no sense of duty can make me love; and if I do love, no sense of duty can make me cease to love. Love does not consult duty.

True love for God and Christ originates in a change of heart, induced by the Holy Spirit, who produces it only in harmony with reason, duty, and interest. The individual is brought into a state of reconciliation with God, and then love springs up spontaneously. He sees his obligations and interests, and the guilt of not loving, and yet loves independently.

Nor is the person conscious of the commencement of his love. He finds himself, almost before he is aware of it, in a loving state, — not realizing that he is about to love, or is beginning to love. He is absorbed in the process which is about to bring him into this state, and he cannot anticipate its results till the process is passed.

It may be asked, if we ought not to make an effort to love Christ, and pray for an increase of love. We ought rather to seek to come into a state of harmony and peace with him, when we can but love him. When the Christian prays for an increase of his love, the significance of his prayer is that he may be brought to a view of his sinfulness, to see the real nature of what Christ has done, in order that, in view of these, his heart may be affected with love. The Holy Spirit produces love in no unnatural way.

It is only by effecting such harmony, or affinity, between the soul and the object, that love will arise spontaneously.

Next we shall speak of the peculiarities of this love itself. The first is, that he who possesses love to Christ, will feel that he does not love him so much or so deeply as he ought. He will honestly declare that he *knows* he does not do so. If a man thinks he does love Christ as he ought, it is evident that he has no conception how he ought to love him. The natural man supposes the Christian feels that he has abundant love for Christ. Such a feeling would not be legitimate. No one can love Christ who has not some correct view of the value of salvation. And he who has such a view must regard his love, however great, as being exceedingly small, scarcely worth the name. The Christian's estimation of his love is low, because his standard is so high.

Where true love exists, the individual will feel that other Christians have more love for Christ than he. He esteems others better than himself. If he is told that they view themselves as he views himself, he cannot conceive it to be so. He is confident that they have more love than he, and that they estimate it more highly. This is legitimate, since the Holy Spirit enlightens as to our own hearts, and not the hearts of others.

Another peculiarity is a disposition on the part of the individual to keep to himself the feeling that his love for Christ is so small. He carries about with him a deep conviction of the meanness of his love, regretting it and mourning over it, but scarcely ever divulging the feeling to others. This is because he feels mortified and guilty on account of it.

But it may be asked if the Christian is necessarily deceived as to the amount of love he possesses. We answer, that probably he never *under*estimates his love, except in some morbid and unhealthy state. In his best estate he has the lowest estimate of it; but even then, he reckons it higher than it is reckoned by his Saviour. Yet, after all, that is a state in which he delights. If his love were put to the test in that condition, it would be found to be stronger than in any other. The Christian should infer that when he has that feeling he is in his best condition. Indeed, he values his love more highly when he thinks he has little, than when he thinks he has much. It is a state parallel to that indicated by Paul's paradox, "When I am weak, then am I strong." When he has little love, then has he much. He loves Christ because Christ's love is so much greater than his own. "We love him because he *first* loved us."

Finally, we remark, that he who loves Christ will not have the reasons why he loves him before his mind in definite form. His love will be emphatically an exercise of the heart. First-love especially exists without giving reasons. It is a matter of consciousness, rather than of the understanding. True love for Christ is more an undefined affection for him than a rejoicing because he has performed certain acts for our advantage. Affection for Christ must be distinguished from mere intellectual views of his character and office. These may foster affection, but cannot produce it. One who truly loves Christ, will appreciate the reasons why he should love him; but his love will be independent of them. He will love him because he seems lovely. That is all the reason love is necessarily required to give of itself.

Again: true love involves gratitude to Christ, which is also a characteristic of the regenerate state, and marked by similar peculiarities. If a man has gratitude to Christ, he will feel that it is very small. He will call it nothing, and be pained and mortified on the account. Sometimes, indeed, a person declares he has but little gratitude, when the object is to indicate how much Christ has done for him, on account of his superior desert. He looks upon his gifts as tokens of esteem. With the true Christian it is not so. He feels that his gratitude for the infinite and undeserved favors of Christ is not worth the name. He cannot exercise it as he ought. The reason is, he has fixed his standard of gratitude so high, that what he has appears as nothing. This is true to nature. Expressions of gratitude become less fluent and more suppressed, according to the depth and strength of the feeling.

### HAPPINESS.

Genuine happiness is a characteristic of the regenerate state. But, since there are various kinds of happiness, the question is, How shall the true be known? This is often answered by saying that the Christian has a happiness which the world knows not of. But this is not sufficient, since the deceived professor and the professors of false religion declare the same. Nor can it be determined by the fact that the source of one's happiness is *changed*, since the sources of false happiness are various; nor by the fact that whereas he once took pleasure in worldly things, he now takes delight in the things of religion; since there is a false delight in these, as unlike the truly spiritual as is the meanest pleasure of the world.

We must, therefore, seek for some more external and tangible marks, by which spiritual happiness may be distinguished. The first is, that the truly regenerate man, though conscious at times of possessing real happiness, will yet feel that he does not possess it to such a degree as he ought; and sometimes, that he does not possess it sufficiently to warrant his thinking himself a Christian. He does not feel that his cup of spiritual joy is full. The Christian may feel that his happiness is complete, when, in the glow of his first love, or when greatly revived, or after having some peculiar discipline or experience. But this is not his ordinary state of mind. When a professing Christian states that his religion makes him perfectly happy, and does it not as the outburst of feeling, but in a deliberate manner, as if perfect happiness in religion were easy to be attained, and wonders why the religion of others does not make them as happy as he, it is to be feared that his conceptions of what Christian happiness is are false.

The private experience of most true Christians will accord with these positions. Each one will acknowledge that he does not enjoy so much as he knows he might, or as it is his privilege to enjoy; and at the same time will consider his case as peculiar. He is specially imperfect. His short-coming furnishes good reason why *his* cup is not full, though he does not doubt that others live so as to feel that their happiness is complete.

The explanation of this feeling is obvious. Man's true happiness consists in the exercise of love. He is preëminently a loving being, made in the image of God, who is love. But by sin man's love has become perverted, and his happiness is lost. Christ came that his sin might be forgiven, and his love and happiness restored. In proportion, therefore, as he has a sense of forgiveness, will his love and happiness be reinstated. But it has been shown that the true Christian is conscious that he never attains so great a sense of his sin, or of forgiveness, as the occasion requires;

so that he comes correspondingly short in his love and happiness. Hence, if an individual feels that his cup of religious happiness is full, it indicates a want of enlightenment as to his sinful nature.

Another peculiarity attendant upon true Christian happiness is, that it is not uniformly the same. It is as great a mistake to suppose that the Christian is *uniformly* happy, as it is to suppose that the unchristian man is ever so. Almost every Christian has his hours, and perhaps days and weeks, of spiritual darkness and gloom: he has at least some apprehension, by experience, of what these things are.

These seasons are not to be sought, for they are the hidings of God's countenance, denoting that he is angry on account of still remaining sin. They should therefore alarm the Christian. But if he has never experienced them, and has professed religion long, he should be alarmed infinitely more, lest he never knew the grace of God. Where is the child that has not at some time felt the parent's frown? So it is spiritually. "Whom the Father loveth he chasteneth, and scourgeth every son whom he receiveth." "If ye be without chastisement, whereof all are partakers, then are ye bastards and not sons."

This peculiar experience belongs to the true Christian. The unchristian professor never complains of seasons of great gloom. He never mourns over clouds, and the hidings of God's countenance. His spiritual heavens are so dark, that the blackest cloud between himself and God cannot cast the slightest shade upon his path. Light is necessary to make clouds visible; and there is no man who has seen the light that has not also seen clouds. The Christian can and may have seasons of darkness, but the unchristian man never does or can have seasons of light.

If spiritual darkness is painful, it shows that the person is not blind. That the Christian should experience seasons of darkness and gloom while he is but partially sanctified, is legitimate. A view of sinfulness and short-coming is doubtless designed to make him unhappy, and so stir him up to a return to peace with God. At all events, this is its natural effect upon the truly pious heart.

Another peculiarity of true Christian happiness pertains to the manner in which it is obtained, or recovered when lost. And we remark, that it is never obtained by efforts put forth for the purpose of securing it. True happiness flows in like a river upon the footsteps of him who walks in the path of duty. If a person prays expressly for happiness, then what he obtains will be false and delusive, like the happiness of the world. If he prays for a broken heart on account of sin, and reconciliation with God, and obtains them, then peace which the world knows not of will come of its own accord.

Hence true happiness is obtained and recovered by the Christian when he is not looking for it. It flows spontaneously into his soul while he is adjusting his case with God. When he has once submitted to the divine terms, he finds, to his surprise, that he has peace which passeth understanding. It follows, therefore, that though a sinner may be awakened to an effort to become a Christian by the desire to be happy, yet, before the end can be realized, that motive must retire. If it retains its ascendency, or occupies any considerable place in the mind up to the point of obtaining happiness, it is not true. Just here many souls are deluded by the device of Satan, and taken captive at his will. To be happy forever, is the designed end of man's being; but it is attained only when it comes as a consequence of his relation to his Maker being restored to its original uprightness.

The laws which regulate the Christian's seasons of darkness and gloom, are the same with those which govern the production of his original peace with God. These are not removed by efforts put forth for this purpose, but depart spontaneously, as a consequence of renewed repentance and return to God. If seasons of darkness and gloom are removed by efforts put forth, or prayer offered to that effect, without any change in the individual's relation to God, they are not such as are experienced by the true believer.

From this it follows, that another peculiarity of true happiness is, that the Christian is not sensible of its origin. He is not sensible that his happiness is produced by his belief that he has been converted, — that his sins are forgiven, or his salvation secured. The true convert is generally happy *before* he believes he is converted, or forgiven. He cannot describe his happiness; and, at the first, he does not need or care to understand its causes. All true Christian experience will respond to this statement. If the young convert is asked what makes him happy, his answer is, "I do not *know;* but I am happy." That is all he knows, and just then it is enough for him to know.

Here is a test which every Christian should apply to himself: "Was my happiness originated by the belief that my sins were forgiven, or that I had found the Saviour?" If so, it must be false. The true Christian's happiness is independent of that belief. The young convert will be happy whether he believes his sins are forgiven or not. When he first begins to be happy, if asked whether he thinks himself a Christian, he sometimes answers negatively, and sometimes doubtfully.

This is peculiar. The most highly cultivated, but spiritually unenlightened reason, would dictate that the Christian should be able to assign the cause of his happiness. Hence the self-deceived person ascribes it to his belief that he is converted, or that his sins have been forgiven, which may promote true happiness, but not originate it.

The question may arise whether some persons may not have a disposition naturally so hopeful as to prevent their ever experiencing seasons of darkness and gloom. It has already been stated that, in this respect, the Christian will correspond perfectly with the man. The same varieties of cheerfulness and sadness will be found in the one as in the other. The Christian will, so far as he is spiritual, be as he was originally constituted. He will bear such fruits, in variety and form, as he would have borne if he had not fallen.

The regenerate character has the same freedom of development that belongs to the unregenerate. This is often misunderstood, and greatly abused. The fact that a professing Christian has naturally a cheerful disposition, is made an apology for his never feeling that he has occasion to mourn over his sinful character. Oftentimes what should be ascribed to spiritual blindness and self-righteousness, is ascribed to natural temperament. We are willing to accord to the Christian the same proportion of hopefulness and cheerfulness, spiritually, that he has naturally, but no greater. Where is the person of a disposition so hopeful as never to feel sad or disheartened? But many professing Christians claim never to have any spiritual sadness, discouragement, or gloom. If the man can be found who is not capable, naturally, of feeling sad when real occasion for it exists, this would be a sound reason why he, as a Christian, should never experience spiritual sadness.

Every Christian has more or less of sinfulness and shortcomings, which deserve to be lamented; and we can conceive of no constitutional reason why he should not see and deplore them. The fact that a man has naturally a hopeful temperament, is no guarantee against his ever experiencing the hiding of God's countenance. It will lead him to dwell chiefly upon the cheering aspects of religion; but, if it precludes all penitence, then he is at least exercising the graces of the gospel in a disproportionate manner, and is wanting in that sense of the divine forgiveness, of which every Christian stands in absolute need. We cannot conceive that any man can be constituted so differently from other men, as to be able to enjoy, constantly, the sweet peace of forgiveness, without ever feeling the pangs of sorrow and guilt. We have reason to fear lest the sentiment that some professing Christians are never subject to darkness and gloom, on account of the hopefulness of their natural temperament, is a device of Satan to hide from their view the truth that it is to be ascribed not to their temperament, but to their self-righteous disposition.

## ENJOYMENT OF PRAYER.

Closely allied to Christian happiness is the enjoyment of prayer, which is a characteristic of the regenerate state. The unregenerate man never really enjoys communion with God. He has what he calls happiness in prayer; but it is as corrupt and false as everything that proceeds from the natural heart. God never relaxes his anger with the impenitent sinner long enough to give him a moment of true happiness in communing with him.

The first peculiarity of true enjoyment of prayer, is, that

he who possesses it will feel that he does not have so much as he ought, and will be grieved on the account. He who feels that he has as much enjoyment in prayer as he ought, does not know what true enjoyment is. Enjoyment of prayer is unlimited in its nature, and experience is necessary to make one feel his ignorance.

Another peculiarity is, that true enjoyment of prayer is not at all times alike. The true Christian, especially in the early part of his Christian life, finds his communion with God much more sweet at some times than at others. He has his peculiarly precious seasons in prayer, and also his peculiarly dark and gloomy ones. This fact that he does not sometimes enjoy prayer, but finds it an exceedingly unwelcome task to pray, which is such an occasion of doubt, grief, and fear to the young Christian, is one of the surest signs that he is in a regenerate state. The fact that he sometimes almost believes that he does not love to pray, and distrusts the genuineness of his piety on account of it, is an unmistakable indication that he knows what the true enjoyment of prayer is. No man has ever seen the sun shine who has not also seen a shadow. If he can discern a shadow, it is evidence that he is not blind. If a dark day is painful to him, it is certain that he knows what a bright one is. A conscious want of enjoyment in prayer, which causes great grief, is by no means the product of the Holy Spirit, but the result of human infirmity. It is not to be sought, but lamented; and yet it may be regarded with favor, as a symptom that the person is in a Christian state. What more gratifying indication have we of a musical ear, than the fact that the individual sometimes hears discords; or of a delicate ear, than that discords are painful? What music is there in his soul who declares that he enjoys all music, and all alike?

This varied experience in the enjoyment of prayer belongs to the true Christian. The false professor is not troubled with seasons of great gloom in prayer, since he has never had a season of light. He believes he always enjoys prayer, because he never enjoys it at all. He is contented to be in the vale, because he was never on the mount. Blaise Pascal says, "Who mourns that he is not a king, but a king dethroned?" So it is spiritually. Who mourns his want of access to the throne of grace, but he who has once been there? If the false professor should once truly enjoy communion with God, he would call the happiness he now has real misery. The Christian's variation in enjoyment of prayer, arises from the fact, that his spiritual life, like all life, is more full, fresh, and strong at one time than at another. On account of the vitality of his prayer, it is sensitive to surrounding influences.

Kindred to want of enjoyment is the feeling which the true Christian often has that he meets with no success in praying. He has no access to God. The heavens are brass. His prayers do not rise above his head. It seems to him of no use to pray. He has no inclination; it is hard work. These are peculiarities attendant upon the praying of the true Christian. The false professor has no such trials. To him all is clear and easy. He has no such conceptions of what it is for fallen man to commune with his Maker, as to make him timid in view of the undertaking. He feels quite adequate to it, and thinks he accomplishes it very successfully. But the humility, sense of unworthiness, and helplessness of the real Christian, prevent all such self-complacence. They make him feel that for sinful man to move God by his requests, is no trifling undertaking. His sense of the greatness of it, and his unfitness for it, sometimes cause him to approach his Maker with such fear, trembling, and self-distrust, that he cannot believe his prayers are heard.

The true Christian's feeling that God hears and will answer his prayer, does not assume that definite form and confident tone which are common to the prayers of false Christians. It is more a matter of faith than of sight, or sense, or absolute knowledge. The true spirit of prayer does not incline the offerer to declare confidently that he believes he shall have the precise object prayed for, and in the particular manner desired. Nor does it incline him to take to himself the credit of having secured the object by means of his prayer, even when it seems to have been granted. True prayer presents its requests to God with earnestness and yet submission. The suppliant is not a wilful pleader. He submits his petition, saying, "Not my will, O God, but thine be done!" He who has truly gained a blessing from God by prayer, will be modest in expressing his belief that his prayer secured it.

## DOUBTS.

Every true Christian does at some time have doubts, and fears lest he may be in a state of self-deception. If one can determine that he has ever had a really spiritual doubt of his acceptance with God, it is a sign that he is a Christian. It is not asserted that doubts are to be desired, or that they are the fruit of the Spirit, or that they ought to exist: it is only meant that they are incident to the Christian state, and when found, are signs of a regenerate condition. Doubtless the Christian may, in process of time, outgrow them; or, by a certain kind of discipline or experience, become freed from them. Nor do we deny that he ought to do so; yet observation teaches that they are universally experienced at some period in the Christian life.[1]

A truly Christian doubt arises from a partly sanctified and partly unsanctified condition. Want of sanctification furnishes the occasion for doubt, and sanctification causes the occasion to be perceived and felt.

But why should not the Christian *constantly* doubt his acceptance with God, since he is constantly in a state of partial sanctification? This is because his mind is directed more to a contemplation of his sinfulness, and less to Christ and the divine forgiveness, at one time than at another. He is also more under the influence of his sinful propensities at one time than at another. Occasional indulgence in certain definite and known sins, which produces a sense of guilt and grief, leads him to fear that he may not be a true child of God. Having a greater amount of illumination at some times than at others, contributes to the same effect. This is evident from the fact, that, in times of revival, when Christians begin to be awakened to a sense of coldness and inactivity, then they begin to doubt. Self-examination, under the influence of the Holy Spirit, always produces this effect at the first, and then reäcts into a strengthening of the believer's hope.

A view of remaining sinfulness very uniformly produces doubts in the early part of the Christian life. The young convert is surprised and alarmed at the discovery that he is still sinful. His previous conceptions were that, when he became a Christian, he should feel free from sin, guilt, and self-condemnation. When, therefore, he begins to experience the contrary, it produces serious doubts of his conversion.

[1] Many apparent exceptions to this remark are originally cases of unrecognized regeneration. See Part I.

The Christian's doubts, though kindred in some respects, and produced in part by similar causes, are yet to be distinguished from his occasional seasons of darkness and gloom. He may have darkness, and yet not seriously doubt his regenerate condition; as he may have strong doubts and fears, and not feel that he is in darkness. His darkness is produced by his sinfulness; his doubts and fears, by a view of it. So far as the individual's observation is concerned, his seasons of darkness and gloom are, to a greater extent, spontaneous. He cannot give the reasons why he has them; but he can give his reasons why he doubts. The latter are connected more with reflection; while both depend, in great part, for the variety of their form and strength, on the natural temperament.

Some persons are of a doubting disposition. They doubt everything; and, of course, doubt their being Christians, let the evidence be what it may. Others are very hopeful at some times, and very doubtful at others. But we cannot conceive of a disposition such as to be incapable of doubting sincerely, where occasion to doubt is manifest. Every true Christian must necessarily see that in his character which is not becoming a child of God; and there is no reason why it should not produce the fear lest he may be deceived. If occasional doubts are incident to the Christian character, arising naturally from its very structure, no constitutional peculiarity can prevent them, but only modify their strength and form.

It may be asked, Why should the Christian doubt his conversion, because of his sinfulness, when he knows that this is common to the renewed character? We answer: this is one of the peculiarities of spiritual doubts. They have a singular vitality, which distinguishes them from those that are false. The natural man would expect that the Christian's review of his original experience, his knowledge that all Christians have remaining sinfulness, and that he does not expect to be free from sin in this world, combined with his conscious enjoyment of prayer, his love for Christ, and other evidences, would at once dispel whatever doubts might chance to arise, if it did not prevent them. This, however, does not assuage the Christian's pain and grief on account of sin, or prevent them from having the natural effect to produce the fear of self-deception. The fact that the question of his having been born again has been repeatedly settled upon a satisfactory basis, his belief that Christ shall lose none that have been given to him, and even his knowledge that just such doubts as he now has are signs of a gracious state, have no power to dispel them, or relax their grasp upon his inward life. These doubts and fears are a vital injury of the Christian's lively hope, which can be repaired only by the resuscitation of its life-principle. The application of certain considerations may serve to foster the revival of it, but they have no power to remove a genuine doubt.

This leads us to remark, as another peculiarity of the true Christian's doubts, that they are not under his control. He has no power to produce, and none to remove them. He may pray for the forgiveness of the sin which occasions them, but he can no more cast them off, than he can control his forgiveness. The removal of the true Christian's doubts is spontaneous. He does not know beforehand what considerations will effect it; nor is he, at the time, conscious that they are being removed. Under the influences of the Holy Spirit, he is occupied in being brought into a state which involves their removal, when, ere he is aware, he finds they are gone. He does not know what means will remove them, because, while doubting, he has no faith that they will ever be removed. That would destroy their genuineness. The natural man supposes the Christian removes his doubts by examining, and ascertaining that there is no just ground for them, when he doubts no more; or he supposes they are removed by praying for their removal. But this would involve no change in the believer's condition, and no reason why he should doubt less than before. If the cause of the Christian's doubts is his departure from Christ, he should continue to doubt till he returns.

## FAITH.

The next characteristic of a regenerate state is, the exercise of faith. This is a Christian grace, whose existence is most difficult of all to be determined. The Scriptures represent faith as being of a twofold nature, consisting of belief and love. "If thou shalt confess with thy mouth the Lord Jesus, and shalt believe in thine *heart* that God hath raised him from the dead, thou shalt be saved." "For with the *heart* man believeth unto righteousness." Philip said to the eunuch, "If thou believest with all thine *heart*, thou mayest." Faith is a loving belief in God and Christ, and all their attributes and acts. We may have belief without love, or, possibly, love without belief; but not faith without both. A condition of faith, therefore, is that resulting from the combined conditions of love and belief. This resultant condition has its own peculiarities, and requires a distinct description. It is like the chemical union of two substances which produces a compound unlike either.

One who is in a state of faith, has supreme love for God, and perfect confidence in all his declarations. He loves and believes, but his love controls. He loves God so well, that he can believe nothing prejudicial to him. He loves so strongly what God wills, that he can will nothing different. Hence he is in perfect harmony with the mind of God and his eternal purposes.

This faith is spiritual and true. The natural and false is composed of belief combined with a natural and false love. We shall notice, first, some of the peculiarities attendant upon the origination of genuine faith. We remark, first, that it does not originate, according to man's natural conception of it, from effort put forth for the purpose of producing it. This cannot be, since love which is not thus produced is so prominent an element in it. Genuine faith does not arise from *desire* accompanied with belief. We may desire and believe in things which are not according to the will of God. It is impossible that a person should have true faith in the fulfilment of any desire, however good, if its fulfilment is not according to God's eternal purpose. It does not matter that, in the person's judgment, there is necessity for the object desired. The judgment of God may be different. The spiritual mode of obtaining faith, therefore, is not to ask for it directly, but to ask for harmony with God's desires and eternal purposes, in which state faith can but exist. The meaning of the prayer, "Lord, increase our faith," is, "Lord, increase our confidence in thy word, and desire for the accomplishment of thy will;" and not, "Lord, increase our confidence that thou wilt do what we judge most necessary and desirable."

From this it follows that true faith does not originate in any sensible manner. A person who is coming into a state of faith, does not take cognizance of the fact. His powers are all absorbed in being brought into submission to the will of God, and desire for its accomplishment, and he can stop to consider naught else.

We shall next mention some of the peculiarities attendant upon the *exercise* of faith. First, we remark, that if one is in the exercise of genuine faith, he will not speak freely of it. He will be too deeply engaged in the exercise itself to talk about it. When a person has real faith that some desire is about to be granted, he will not be likely to announce the fact. This would interrupt, if not destroy, his faith. He would be so absorbed in the exercise that he probably would not think or care to proclaim it. This is natural. In proportion as a person is deeply absorbed in any mental exercise, are his observations concerning it diminished. When, therefore, a man is in exercise of such faith in God as will gain the blessing, he will be like to give attention to nothing else, — especially will he not be diverted to so unimportant a matter as that of announcing beforehand that he was about to receive a blessing.

One who is exercising faith, is in a state of profound humility. He is destitute of self-complacence, and pervaded with a sense of his ill-desert of the blessing sought, and of the justice of God, should he withhold it. This will check his declaration of the belief that he is about to receive it. Even when the blessing has been granted, he has little inclination to take to himself the credit of having obtained it by his faith. He feels himself too unworthy, and too dependent upon God. He regards the blessing as a perfect gratuity, and is as grateful as if he had done nothing to obtain it. In his deep humility and gratitude, the thought scarcely enters his mind that his faith was instrumental of the blessing. If he speaks of it, it is only as duty requires, and with modesty and reluctance. It is not uncommon to hear professing Christians relate, with an air of self-complacence, the remarkable answers to prayer which they have received. But it is difficult to conceive how God can regard with favor such a spirit. There is no boasting, and no self-gratulation, in the prayer of faith.

Another peculiarity attendant upon genuine faith is, the feeling, on the part of him who has it, that his faith is very weak and small. His conception of what it is to have faith, will be such that he will hardly dare to think he possesses it at all. If any one feels that he has great faith, it is indicative that his idea of true faith is very imperfect.

## HUMILITY.

Another characteristic of the regenerate state, which deserves a passing notice, is humility. True humility is a sign of regeneration. This grace has artful counterfeits. False humility is real pride. The true is distinguished from the false by certain peculiarities. And first, we observe, that he who is truly humble, does not make great pretensions to humility. He does not think he is so humble as he ought to be. He does not speak of his humility; he makes no effort to appear to possess it, and is not desirous of being credited for it. He is not so anxious to *appear* pious, as to be so. It is duty and love for Christ, not true humility, that makes one desire to profess religion. True humility produces a willingness to do what duty requires; while false humility, or pride, makes one unduly forward. True humility always involves in its production a mental struggle; false humility, seldom. The one makes a person willing to *bear* what would otherwise be a cross; the other takes the cross away. True humility has to encounter pride; false humility is in the direction of it. The one costs a sacrifice of natural feeling; the other is a gratification of it, while both may lead to the same external action. True humility originates in a breaking of soul; false humility, at most, in a counterfeit of it.

We have thus endeavored to exhibit the peculiarities of the various features of the truly regenerate character. These same peculiarities also flow out into all the outward life; and it is by these that it is to be distinguished, so far as judgment is to be based upon the external living. They will be less prominent in the outward life, in proportion as it is remote from its inward source. The true believer, and one who is self-deceived, will differ less in the outward appearance than in their real spirit. Nothing, in the general course of a person's external living, will serve as an unmistakable sign that he has been born again, except so far as it is penetrated with the peculiar spirit of the regenerate man. It is by this peculiarity, in great part at least, that the good works of the true Christian are to be distinguished from those of the false. However conscious he may be that he is endeavoring to do the will of God, he will yet feel that his good works are nothing — that he is, after all, an unprofitable servant. He can hardly see that he has ever done anything that deserves to be called a sacrifice for Christ. However much he may have endured for him, he takes to himself no credit. It is to him as nothing.

It may be said that eminent godliness will control the outward life, and show itself in the general course of living. This is admitted; though it must be remembered that we are not discussing the signs of eminent godliness, but simply of a regenerate state. It has been said that when the inward spirit is changed, it will modify even the manner in which one bows in prayer, his tones of voice, and so the outward forms of his religious acts. But, while peculiarities may and will be manifested legitimately in outward forms, yet the inward life, for want of sufficient strength, may not always throw its spirit out so far, or with such force as to make its impress upon the external action. Regeneration may not even control the *facts* of the outward history as it ought. Moral uprightness and religious exactness in form, are not, necessarily, signs of a gracious state. No inference from these can be drawn in favor of a change of heart, except by the peculiar spirit which pervades them.

# DIVISION THIRD.

## GENERAL PRINCIPLE APPLIED TO THE RECOGNITION OF REGENERATION BY OTHERS.

## CHAPTER I.

How can a regenerate person be certified of the regenerate state of others? The general basis on which this question is to be answered, has been laid down in the foregoing pages. The means by which we are to determine our own regenerate condition, and that of others, must, to a greater or less extent, be the same. We can have but one set of phenomena to examine in either case, and but one class of principles by which to judge them. The general principle which has been laid down to guide us throughout the investigation, is, that the regenerate character is peculiar, distinct from all other; and by its peculiarities and distinctiveness it is to be known. Its peculiarities have been exhibited. The only question which remains is, Has the Christian the means or ability of discovering them as they exist in others? Can he determine their existence in others to a similar degree of certainty with which he can determine their existence in himself? or, Can he do it at all?

It may be said that the Scriptures have given one simple rule, by which we are to be guided: "By their fruits ye shall know them." It has already been shown that this passage signifies that the religious character is to be known by the *kind* of its fruits. Our Saviour is showing the disciples how to distinguish between true and false religious teachers. The implication is, that they could not be known by the external aspect of their fruits, because religious teachers would come clothed like the true sheep of Christ's flock, while inwardly they would be ravening wolves. Since the fruits, therefore, cannot be known by their form, they must be determined solely by the spirit which actuates them. The Christian spirit also being marked by peculiarities, we are reduced to the question, as before, Can these peculiarities be discovered in others, either as they manifest themselves in the outward form of their fruits, or by any other means?

The position which we shall assume is, that Christians have the ability of determining these peculiarities in others, with a degree of certainty proportionate to the responsibility they are obliged to assume in regard to them. We have seen that this responsibility is very great, and hence, the degree of certainty they can possess is also very great. As the regenerate man can be certified of his own regenerate state according to the responsibility involved, and by means perfectly suited to the nature of the case, so he may, in a similar manner, be certified of the regeneration of others. It is not meant that this is uniformly done. Many Christians and Christian ministers do not become certified of the regeneration of others, to a degree at all proportionate to their responsibilities in regard to them. They do not cultivate the ability they have, or appropriate the means with which they are furnished for doing it. Because the subject is delicate, and attended with difficulties and liabilities of mistake, they are deterred; and, excusing themselves upon the ground that it is impossible to know, with infallible certainty, who are Christians, they determine to throw the responsibility upon the individuals themselves.

It might be anticipated, that, in order to be in harmony with all spiritual things, the means by which the Christian is to ascertain the regenerate state of others would be peculiar, and not such as man's natural judgment or desires would dictate. We should expect, also, that according to the superiority and perfection of spiritual things, these means would be superior to any we should choose, and also perfectly suited to the necessities of the case. We have seen that this is true in regard to the Christian's evidence of his own regeneration, and hence we might look for it here.

It is not best that the Christian should be certified of the regeneration of others by the exercise of a natural judgment, or by the use of natural means, since he is not thus assured of his own regeneration. If he were assured of the regeneration of others by a natural judgment, and they by a spiritual, it would produce disharmony between them. A person would be most unhappily affected, to be told, upon his reception into a visible church, that its members had evidence of his having been born again, diverse from their own. His spiritual nature could not appropriate so uncongenial and ill-suited an announcement; and it would not at all comfort him, or nurture his Christian hope.

Nor would it be useful to Christians themselves to be thus certified of the regenerate state of others. Were they convinced of it by sight, or sense, or by the exercise of natural reason, it would mar the spiritual bond of sympathy between them, and impair the proper spirit of their mutual efforts for each other's spiritual advancement. It is natural for Christians to desire that the character of the church of Christ should be comprehensible to the men of the world, and according to their judgment of what it ought to be, and in this way commend itself to their regard. But, so long as spiritual things are peculiar, and godliness is a mystery, this can never be. The followers of Christ will be of such a character as to convince the world of their superior nature, and cause them to stand in awe of it, while they shall be unable to comprehend it.

The purposes of the most perfect harmony, the most intimate love and sympathy among Christians, would seem to require that they should have toward each other a feeling, in respect to their being Christians, kindred to that which they have of themselves. They would then be upon a common level, and each one would be most favorably circumstanced to comfort and encourage his brethren. A little reflection will show that this is precisely the case. The Christian's certitude of his own regeneration is a matter of faith and trust, and not of sight; and so is his certitude of the regenerate state of his fellow Christians. He feels respecting them as they feel respecting him, in this particular, and as all feel respecting themselves.

The exhibition of this point requires that we should recall to mind the manner in which the Christian is certified of his own regenerate state. We have seen that the primary and essential source of his evidence is a spiritual consciousness of his new spiritual existence, corresponding to his natural consciousness of a natural existence, and engrafted upon it. This consciousness of being a new creature, is a consciousness of union with Christ, — it being legitimate that if the believer has been made one with Christ, he should be apprized of it through his consciousness. This is also equivalent to the witnessing of the

Spirit, of which Paul speaks. The Spirit, who makes us one with Christ, also creates within us a witness of the union. The secondary, collateral, and corroborative source of the believer's evidence, is that of reflection upon the peculiar phenomena of his inward and outward life, by which an inference is drawn, or judgment formed, corresponding with his consciousness, or the inward witness.

The Christian's evidence of the regenerate state of others, is similar to their evidence of their own regenerate state. This originates where that does, and is corroborated by the same means. The primary and essential source of it is an inward, spiritual consciousness of a union existing between us and them, and hence, of course, between us both and Christ. The secondary, collateral, and corroborative source, is reflection upon the peculiar phenomena of their feelings and outward lives, by which a judgment is formed, or an inference drawn, harmonizing with the spiritual consciousness.

This spiritual consciousness of a union between ourselves and other Christians, and hence a feeling that they, with us, are new creatures in Jesus Christ, must not be misunderstood. It is no other than that peculiar, indescribable sympathy which one Christian has with another, inducing in the heart of each the irresistible conviction that the other is truly born of God. It is a feeling which every true Christian is constantly experiencing, as he comes in contact with those who, like himself, have been born of the Spirit. We speak now not of a judgment which one Christian forms respecting another, nor an inference derived from one's appearance and actions that he is a Christian, but of an undefined, indescribable, and irresistible sympathy, — a felt oneness of heart and soul, — with those who have been born again, whose spiritual significance deserves regard. Though it is peculiar, yet no Christian is in danger of mistaking what the feeling is. It is one and the same, as possessed by the ignorant and the learned, by the old and the young, by all who are truly the redeemed of the Lord. It is spontaneous, independent of all reflection and reasoning, like the believer's consciousness of his own spiritual existence. And yet, like that, it is susceptible of being invigorated by exercise, and enfeebled from the want of it; and hence, in those who are most conversant with the Spirit's operations in the hearts of others, it has most positiveness and strength.

The existence of such a spiritual instinct, or intuition, cannot be ignored. Nor do we speak of the opinion we form by comparing the feelings of others with our own, but of something within that, constituting its life-principle, and holding to it the same relation that the inward spiritual consciousness of the Christian holds to the judgment he forms that he is a child of God. It is a witness which the Spirit induces within us, not only that we are one with Christ, but that we are one with the brethren, and they are one with us. The fact that it manifestly exists to so great an extent, and that in multitudes of cases its intimations are reliable, indicates that it is not a rare endowment, but a common gift of God, connected with the new creation, more or less developed according to cultivation and other circumstances.

If, moreover, the existence of this spiritual instinct cannot be ignored, it must be esteemed. If it is a fruit of the Spirit, it is given for an important end, and deserves to be cultivated and developed.

But we are not left to conjecture, nor merely to the teachings of existing phenomena. That such a spiritual apprehension of the regenerate state of others exists, is to be drawn from the instructions of the Bible. Our Saviour teaches that his disciples are as truly one with each other, as they are with him, and he with God. "That they all may be one; as thou, Father, art in me and I in thee, that they also may be one in us; that they may be one even as we are one: I in them and thou in me, that they may be made perfect in one." If we believe in the unity of the three persons in the Godhead, we must also in that of the many persons in the body of Christ. Since, therefore, Christ's disciples are conscious of being one with him, why not also of being one with each other, and so perceive each other's union with Jesus Christ? The phenomena which exist accord with this supposition. That peculiar bond of sympathy, which Paul calls the "unity of the Spirit," among the members of the body of Christ, can be accounted for in no other way.

The church of Christ is not merely a social body, composed of distinct individuals, held together by rules and covenants. These are not the basis of the tie that binds in one the people of God. This lies beneath and within them all. They are the outward expression of this inward love. The "unity of the Spirit" indicates a deeper and more vital bond than that of union or association. It denotes a oneness. The followers of Christ, in his visible church, are not simply agreed to dwell together, but are one in heart and soul: the separate individuals are merged together, constituting not a harmonious union, but an absolute unity, like the chemical union of several bodies in distinction from the mechanical mixture, where they are not simply mingled together, but are merged into one new body, distinct and indissoluble.

It may be objected that this doctrine conflicts with another which has been laid down, derived from the

Scripture. It has been stated that the Bible represents the new man as an engraftment of the old, the spiritual faculties of the one being set in the corresponding faculties of the other; while *here*, it will be said, is a faculty in the new man having no correspondence in the old — a spiritual graft not set in a natural stock. This objection, however, is only apparent. Mankind have the natural faculty of recognizing each other as possessing spirits kindred to their own. The Creator has placed in our hearts a responsive feeling, which tells us that others are moral and intelligent beings like ourselves. It is not an exercise of judgment, but an instinct of nature. In some instances this is particularly manifest. An utter stranger creates a response which tells us that he has a heart and soul preeminently like our own.

But this natural faculty in man — this loving response of heart to heart — is imperfect, lying among the universal ruins of the fall. In the apostasy, the bands of love were not only broken between man and God, but also between man and man. But for the fall, perfect unity would always have existed, not only between God and his creatures, in whom they would have lived, and moved, and had their being, in the happiest sense, but also among his creatures themselves. Having all been made in the image of God, and living and moving in him, they must have been of one heart and one soul, preserving the original "unity of the race" in its best and highest sense.

Now, this unity is broken. It is broken between man and man, as well as between man and his Maker. Hardly enough of the original, loving response remains to indicate what man was designed to be, and always would have been, but for sin. This noble faculty is scarcely recognized amid the universal ruin. Now and then we see it, struggling to reinstate itself, which it is able to do only in an imperfect manner, and for a most uncertain period. That responsive love, often discovered even between man and his nearest kindred, while it continues, is exceedingly imperfect, and is liable at any moment to suffer a sad and final rupture. The strongest love and mutual attraction are often suddenly changed to the bitterest hate and mutual repulsion.

Upon this natural, fallen faculty is engrafted the spiritual stock. The original unity of the race, which was lost in Adam, was restored in Christ. "That they all may be made perfect in one. As thou, Father, art in me, and I in thee, that they also may be one in us." That loving response which one Christian feels toward another, is the restoration of the feeling which God ordained should always exist between man and man.

Its dictates constitute the primary and essential source of the Christian's evidence of the regenerate state of others, as their consciousness of being one with Christ constitutes the primary source of the evidence of their own regeneration. It has been shown that no reasoning or inferential process, however conclusive, without this living consciousness, would be adequate to the Christian's wants; and also that this inward witness is adequate to sustain him, despite the contrary conclusions to which he might otherwise be brought. So, also, is no inferential or reasoning process able to satisfy the Christian of the regenerate state of others, without the existence of this inward sympathy. They may live such lives, and perform such outward acts, as would be becoming the Christian character; but if this sympathy is wanting, they produce no spiritual satisfaction that they are born of God. And, moreover, if such a feeling does exist, there may be much wanting in the outward life that is desirable; but it shall not destroy the conviction that they are, notwithstanding, the redeemed of the Lord. This inward feeling is not easily overcome. We say of such persons that we cannot help feeling they are Christians, though imperfect.

The conditions in which this response is awakened, are such as are rendered necessary by the twofold character of man, which is both spiritual and corporeal. The first condition is, that both parties should be in a truly regenerate state, and that one of comparative healthiness. The second is, the personal presence of the parties. The communion of the spirits of men with each other, is not independent of this physical condition, as is the communion of man's spirit with the Spirit of God. Another condition is, the opening of the natural channels of communication between the hearts of men in conversation upon spiritual things, to a greater or less extent.

This is a matter familiar to every Christian who has any considerable acquaintance with religious things. How often does the briefest interview with a young believer produce an irresistible conviction that he is born of God! If the Christian is asked for the grounds of this conviction, he is embarrassed, as are many when asked for the reason of their hope in Christ. He believes there are reasons, but he has not thought to define them. Yet the conviction is not, on that account, at all impaired, — showing that it does not arise from the exercise of the judgment or reason, but is spontaneous. Nor is this conviction grounded upon others' belief that they are Christians. It often exists in regard to those who have no hope themselves, and often does not exist when they cherish hope.

All this indicates that the true Christian has a capability, to a greater or less extent, of perceiving the spiritual state of others — that there is a reflection in his own heart of the image of Christ in the hearts of others. This feeling is as well-defined and confident as the responsibilities he is obliged to assume in regard to others require, and yet is not of such a nature as to preclude a felt necessity of praying and laboring for them that their faith fail not. He feels, with respect to them, as with respect to himself.

It may be said that we have this responsive feeling toward those who prove not to be Christians, and hence it deceives, and is not reliable. To this we answer, that it is not the genuine response, but a counterfeit of it, that deceives. The false Christian never awakens the true response. That is a fruit of the Spirit, uniting two hearts in one, and cannot exist where the union has not taken place. The mere belief that another is a Christian, excites a pleasure and an outgoing of interest toward him, which may be mistaken for spiritual sympathy; but the intimations of the genuine response are reliable, like the Christian's spiritual consciousness of his own regeneration, while both may have their counterfeits. When it is said that this response is excited by those whose lives prove them not to be Christians, it must be borne in mind that the lives of regenerate persons may be very imperfect; and the question will be, whether the testimony of their feelings or their lives shall prevail, since we may err either in deciding that we have this witness, or in deciding that others cannot be Christians from the imperfections of their lives.

It will be objected, that we lose this witness for others, when their lives become such as to excite distrust. This is not strange. This feeling does not exist toward undoubted Christians at all times alike, and sometimes not at all. They may fall into an unspiritual frame, which shall fail to excite it. If the real feeling *ever* existed, it is evidence that they are born again.

The fact that this responsive feeling has its counterfeits, which are liable to deceive, does not invalidate this source of evidence. All evidences have their counterfeits. The false Christian has a feeling which he regards as a witness of the Spirit. But this should not cause us to distrust the true witness. It only renders it important to discriminate. If we could always be certain that this response is genuine, it would be infallible evidence, which is not claimed.

It also renders it important that this kind of evidence should be cultivated. Exercise and cultivation give it definiteness and positiveness, and diminish the liability of mistake, as with the consciousness of one's own regeneration.

It is said that this is a mere feeling, and feelings cannot be trusted. Nor are our judgments to be trusted. They are as thoroughly perverted as our feelings. Faith is more an exercise of feeling than of judgment; but shall it not be trusted? The intimations of our feelings are as reliable as our judgments, if we can only determine that they are genuine.

It may be said, also, that much depends on the spiritual state of the Christian, in regard to his gaining this evidence of others. So it does in regard to his gaining evidence of himself. He must be in a somewhat healthy state to gain evidence of either. Unless he is so, he has no right to judge, especially of others. The question may arise, Do Christians who are in a healthy state have this responsive feeling toward all others, provided the conditions for awakening it duly exist? As a general rule, it must be so. But there are many obstructions to the exercise of all spiritual feelings; and this will be modified according to existing circumstances. Personal prejudice may suppress or prevent, and the natural judgment or some selfish motive may interrupt it. Or, the person respecting whom the feeling is exercised may be in an unhealthy state, and exhibit mental phenomena which may confuse it.

The rule will be, that if the parties are favorably conditioned, and no causes arise to prevent, the response will exist on the part of every Christian toward every other. The injuries to which it is exposed are only such as are incident to every Christian grace.

But it is not easy to determine whether the necessary conditions are fulfilled. We may not recognize our prejudices, or other mental states. How, then, shall we know whether we are in possession of this responsive consciousness which is of so important service? This is a feature of the regenerate character to be known by its peculiarities, which are similar to the believer's consciousness of his own regeneration, modified only by the fact that the feeling pertains to another and not to himself.

One of the peculiarities of this responsive consciousness is its *indescribableness*. We have the same difficulty in describing our conviction of the regenerate state of others, that we do of our own. Our consciousness of being one with Christ's disciples is similar to that of being one with him. A description of it always fails.

Another peculiarity is its *spontaneity*. We are conscious that it does not arise from our desire that others may be Christians, or from our efforts for them, or from our desire to *feel* that they *are* such. These causes may combine to produce a counterfeit of this spiritual conviction, but not the genuine. This arises of itself, and sustains itself in every variety of circumstance, favorable and unfavorable.

Another peculiarity is its *convincing* and *satisfying* nature. The response awakened by the falsely regenerate state is more a feeling of hope than of conviction. The Christian *tries* to feel satisfied. His *judgment* may be that the person is a Christian; and, though he does not feel precisely as he would like, yet he is inclined to be charitable and hope for the best. But, where the genuine feeling exists, the Christian has a peculiar satisfaction and an irresistible conviction. He has no occasion to be charitable. The false response has the form, but not the power of the true. The conviction is an ordinary one, destitute of unction. There is no repugnance toward the individual, but simply an absence of that peculiar satisfaction which is sometimes enjoyed. An interest is felt, but not that loving sympathy which unites pious hearts. The Christian has a disposition to excuse this deficiency in his feelings. He hopes that at another time it would be developed more fully; or that, as the individual advances, his feelings will become more satisfactory. He thinks, perhaps, that it arises from the person's ignorance, or his previous habits or associations, or from his not knowing how to express his feelings. But the genuine conviction needs no apologies. The satisfaction is complete, the conviction strong. It is not necessary to call in circumstances to their aid. This is the character of the response, though it may be, in this particular, both embarrassed and counterfeited.

Finally, this responsive consciousness partakes of that *modesty* of *expression* which is peculiar to one's consciousness of his own regeneration. Our conviction of the regenerate state of others does not express itself in naked and unqualified terms, as we speak of any matter of fact. If the Christian is asked whether another is a Christian, he answers that he *thinks* he is; or, he thinks he gives evidence of being such; or, he *trusts* he is so. He speaks thus modestly not because he has doubt. His conviction may be the strongest possible, and yet his language will be the same. His evidence of others' regeneration is similar to his evidence of his own; and his expression denotes that he apprehends it not as a matter of fact, but as a mysterious life in the soul, of which it is becoming to speak only in modest and reverential terms.

The responsive witness of which we have spoken, is only the primary source of our evidence of the regenerate state of others. The secondary, collateral, and corroborative source, and that which, practically, is perhaps the most available, is reflection upon the phenomena of their feelings and lives, by which a judgment is formed in harmony with the inward witness. These two sources are necessary to each other. The exercise of reflection and judgment constitutes the body of the evidence, which is vitalized by the spiritual sense. The latter directs the former, while the former protects and invigorates the latter. Examination of the phenomena, through the natural channels of communication, awakens the inward witness, while the witness discovers the proper temper and spirit of the phenomena. The natural judgment and the spiritual sense mingle with and penetrate each other, and thus form a spiritual judgment.

The query may arise, whether the object of hearing and examining experiences is not simply to compare them with our own, and thus judge of their genuineness; and, also, whether the responsive feeling is not merely the natural gratification of discovering a similarity between our own exercises and those of others. So far as the judgment is concerned, the object of examining experiences is to compare them with our standard. If the Christian has no other knowledge of spiritual exercises than what his own experience furnishes, then that will be his standard. But he can safely adopt this only so far as its essential spirit is concerned, and the order which its principal exercises naturally assume. If any Christian regards all his incidental exercises, in their order and apparent strength, as the proper standard, then it will be erroneous. Such a standard is formed only by a comparison of our own experience with the word of God, and the largest possible number of experiences. From all these an ideal standard will be derived, containing only the essential exercises, in their necessary order.

In reply to the query, whether what we call the responsive sense is anything more than the natural gratification attendant upon discovering that another has experienced like feelings with ourselves, we remark, that the relation which the Bible teaches Christians sustain to each other, involves something more vital than this. And, moreover, the feeling often exists, independently of a comparison of exercises, where there exists only a general acquaintance. The fact that it is natural to be drawn towards another, upon discovering in him like exercises with our own, is not an argument against, but rather in favor of, the spiritual response. This is the natural stock which receives the spiritual graft. If it be admitted that we have a faculty of perceiving and appreciating each other's natural, why not also each other's spiritual feelings? This faculty may be called merely sympathy, or a perception, or a witness. Whatever it is naturally, it is the same spiritually.

We have said, also, that, combined with this perception of the spiritual feelings of others, we exercise a judgment as to whether they constitute a genuine work of grace. That we have the faculty, not only of perceiving the feelings of others naturally, but also of forming opinions in regard to them, admits of no question. And if it be so naturally, why not spiritually? The natural faculty may be very imperfect, having shared in the general ruin of the fall; but, if such a faculty exists, it is sufficient to receive the spiritual graft. How far God ordained that his moral creatures on earth should be able to perceive, understand, and sympathize with the feelings of each other, we are not able to say. The fact that they have this ability, to some extent, in the fallen state, is indicative that, had man not fallen, it would have been nearly if not entirely perfect. At all events, it is certain that what in this respect is lost in Adam, is designed to be restored in Christ.

This perception and sympathy combine to form, as has been intimated, those peculiar and superior bonds of love which exist among the members of the church of Christ on earth. We cannot conceive how that superior love for each other, to which so much importance is attached in the Scriptures, can exist among them, except by virtue of a spiritual oneness, perceived and felt. The members might be more happy in themselves, because united to Christ. But if their love toward each other is grounded simply upon their *belief* that they have been born again, then there would be no stronger *bonds* of love among them than among the members of any other body who confidently believe the same, though without any real ground.

This, doubtless, constitutes also one of the sources of

the superior happiness of heaven. Its inhabitants are not only happy in themselves, but they most eminently love each other, which constitutes heaven a happy place. The ground of this superior love must be a superior spiritual perception of each other's holiness and blessedness. And the real church of Christ on earth has all the elemental principles necessary for becoming like the church in heaven.[1]

In this spiritual perception of the regeneration of others, there is nothing more mystical than in the natural faculty men have for obtaining a knowledge of the minds and hearts of other men. It is a spiritual engraftment or sanctification of this, which is designed to be sanctified and made to serve a spiritual end, as much as any one of man's natural powers. Nor can we conceive of a complete sanctification of the natural man without it. This natural capability is essential to the constitution of human society, and its elevation into the spiritual realm is essential to the constitution of the Christian church and of the society of heaven.

It is conceded that great imperfection will be attendant upon this spiritual judgment, as it is upon the natural judgment. The injury which this faculty has sustained by the fall, is but *partially* repaired in Christ. Yet it is capable of being improved to an indefinite extent, and is destined to be wholly restored when man shall be completely recovered from the effects of sin. This is a point of great importance, and sadly neglected. It is taken for granted, that because our capability of apprehending and judging of the spiritual state of others is very imperfect, therefore it is not capable of being at all increased. This is an essential error, and is attended with decisive injury to

[1] 1 Cor. xiii. 9, 12.

Christian usefulness. All spiritual attainments, in this world, are imperfect, and made with difficulty. Yet this only argues that they should be sought with greater earnestness. One reason why all the Christian graces are so imperfect, is because they are so little cultivated; and this is especially the case with the one of which we speak. If Christians have the ability to discern the spiritual state of other men to any extent, and so of administering proper encouragement and caution, it is incumbent upon them to improve the faculty to the utmost.

In this respect there are devolved upon Christians, and especially upon Christian ministers, responsibilities most delicate and solemn. How can they instruct or counsel others in regard to the exercises of their minds, unless they can perceive what these exercises are? How can Christian ministers fulfil their high commission as spiritual guides of their fellow-men, unless they seek to acquire the utmost possible facility and correctness in apprehending their spiritual condition? The merchant cultivates the faculty of discerning, at sight, the character and mental states of the men with whom he deals; and why should not the Christian minister do the same in the spiritual domain? To point inquiring souls to Jesus Christ, is the most delicate and sacred work ever entrusted to mortal hands. No man has a right to touch it with one of his fingers, without availing himself of all possible qualifications. The slightest bias given to an anxious sinner in the wrong direction, when nearing the crisis of his exercises, may be instrumental in sealing his lost condition. This bias may be given by encouraging or discouraging, by speaking or by silence, by urging or neglecting to urge. Treatment must be adjusted with the utmost spiritual wisdom. He who applies Scripture doctrines, reproofs, counsels, threatenings, and promises indiscriminately to inquiring minds, without seeking to know the precise need in which they stand, is as recreant to his trust as a physician who should prescribe to patients the most powerful remedies, without seeking to know the state of their diseases.

Similar responsibilities rest upon committees and members of churches in regard to candidates, and upon teachers and parents in regard to their pupils and children. And no one has a right to neglect to qualify himself to discharge the responsibilities which God has put upon him.

How, then, is this faculty of spiritual judgment to be improved? Man's natural faculty of perceiving the mental states of others is improved by cultivation, and the spiritual must be improved by similar means. The Christian's consciousness of his union with Christ becomes strong by exercise; and so does his consciousness of his oneness with the brethren. Both are at the first ardent, but become steady and reliable by use.

Sometimes it is said that the ability of Christians to judge of others depends upon their natural perception of character, and their acquaintance with mankind at large, — the manners and habits of men in thinking and acting in all the various relations of life. The natural faculty for discerning the characters of men, improved by acquaintance with mankind, subserves acquaintance with them spiritually. Upon this natural faculty the spiritual is engrafted. But the natural, however much it may have been improved, will of itself never qualify the Christian for forming a spiritual judgment. This constitutes altogether another realm of knowledge. To obtain facility in spiritual discernment, the Christian should be acquainted with the working of the human mind in every variety of natural circumstances. He should be able to discern its hidden springs and secret motives. But not this alone. Acquaintance with the habits of mankind, and skill in discovering their motives, in one sphere of secular enterprise, do not necessarily secure it in another. A skilful general would not necessarily be a skilful merchant. So it is, more emphatically, in spiritual things. Because a Christian man has skill in detecting the motives of men in trade, it does not follow that he would be skilful also in detecting their motives in religion. The mind here is brought into new relations, and under new bearings; and its tactics will be unlike these in every other sphere. Christians must be acquainted with the workings of the minds of men when under the influence of the Spirit. But since the Spirit operates upon men in every variety of condition, a knowledge of mental phenomena in these various conditions will facilitate the spiritual end by preventing too much or too little influence from being ascribed to mere circumstances, habits, education, or association.

The requisite mental qualifications for exercising a spiritual judgment respecting others, are, first, the natural endowment of ordinary intellectual and moral perception; and secondly, personal piety, or spirituality. The natural endowments are requisite as the receptacles of the spiritual, but without the spiritual they are nothing.

And not only is spirituality necessary, but also a cultivated spiritual perception. The former is necessary to the latter, but the latter is not necessarily the fruit of the former. A person may be very pious, and yet not be a good judge of the piety of others; as a person may be very moral, and have little facility in discovering the motives of men.

Some will say that but few can attain facility in discovering the spiritual state of others. It must be expected that there will be every conceivable variety of attainment here, as in every other department of knowledge. No two persons possess, either naturally or spiritually, the same capabilities. God endows some for one service, and others for another. "There are diversities of gifts." While God endows some for giving impulse to this work, he endows others for discriminating between the true and the false; and so of effecting its greater purity. But he does this according to the constitutional laws of the mind. Though spiritual attainments in this direction, as well as in others, are made with greater facility by some, yet they are not made by any without diligent use of means, and earnest cultivation of the faculties God has given. Nor has he withheld from any the means requisite for making *some* attainment in this, as in every other necessary direction; and when the means have been faithfully improved on the part of all, every degree of facility and correctness will exist, except perfection. Every one will be prepared for the responsibilities God has laid upon him. Some will possess great facility and correctness of judgment, some less, and some the least possible. And hence, after all has been done that can be done, the churches of Christ will be composed in part of unregenerate materials, yet to a far less extent than at present; while multitudes of souls will be saved from an eternal disappointment at the judgment-day, and the purposes of God, by human instrumentality, be duly accomplished.

# CHAPTER II.

SUMMARY.

THERE are certain *principles* involved in the foregoing, which we shall enunciate here, as important guides to forming a judgment in regard to the regenerate state of other persons.

1. It must be remembered that all depends upon the temper of the heart, as to whether a man has been born again. "With the *heart* man believeth unto righteousness." Intellectual views are nothing, except as they indicate the state of the heart. The views may be right, while the heart is wrong. The heart may be right, while many of the views are wrong. The views in regard to many doctrines, and the way of salvation, may be indistinct, while the temper of the heart is true. A child may not have distinctly defined it in his mind that Christ is the grand agent in his salvation, and yet be truly born again. He may be thoroughly convinced that there is a way in which he can be forgiven and justified, if he repents, without clearly understanding that Christ is the way. His heart may be broken on account of sin, and he receive forgiveness through Christ, without recognizing the medium. Or there may be an understanding that salvation must be through Christ, and yet no change of the heart.

This is a point of the utmost importance. It is too often supposed that clear intellectual views involve a change of heart, and that a change of heart involves clearness of intellectual views. Just here is most liable to exist either a false charity or a want of charity. The ultimate aim must be to ascertain the exact frame of the feelings. If these are right, the views will ere long harmonize.

In no particular is greater error committed than in this. Head-conversion is taken for heart-conversion. Many Christians and Christian ministers are thorough in doctrinal teaching, but fail in determining the compliance of others with their instructions. They do not discriminate between intellectual views and the temper of the feelings. More false conversions, probably, are received by the churches through this error than any other.

The prevailing temper of heart to be sought for as evidence of regeneration, are mingled feelings of self-distrust, unworthiness, timidity, humility, fear of self-deception; fear lest the work of grace is not thorough, lest Christ is not loved as he should be; feeling that one's faith is weak; that prayer is not enjoyed as it should be; that the life is not what it ought to be; — all mingled with a desire for greater attainments in these respects. These are to be sought, not as being the best and most healthy states of mind, but as feelings indicating a regenerate state least liable to be mistaken. These mingled feelings produce a general frame which is quite easy to be recognized, and which exists, to a greater or less extent, in every regenerate person, but is more especially prominent in young Christians. Great happiness, confidence, strong hope, and professed love for Christ, though equally desirable states, are more liable to have their counterfeits than the frame of which we speak.

2. Reliance cannot be placed upon the individual's honest view and account of his own feelings. It must not be supposed that a person necessarily feels as he thinks he does. If it were so, self-deception would be impossible. A man's

views of himself must be taken, not as a criterion of his true condition, but only as symptoms. If he is still unenlightened by the Holy Spirit, he does not understand his true condition. It is no more appropriate to take the sinner's word that he has repented of sin and is forgiven, that he loves Christ and is really happy, or that he is not so, than it is for a physician to take his patient's word that he is better or worse. The principle that guides the physician is, that the patient is diseased, and while so he is not a competent judge of himself. He obtains the patient's opinion only to aid in forming his own. Oftentimes he takes the patient's opinion that he is better, as a symptom that he is worse, and his opinion that he is worse, as a symptom that he is better. He treats his opinions and feelings about himself as he does the state of the pulse, of the skin, or the expression of the eye.

In this manner must the Christian form his judgment in regard to the regenerate state of others. Men are naturally, in a spiritual sense, patients, suffering under the effects of sin, which disqualify them to be judges of their own condition. When the patient is restored to perfect health, he knows it. Like the woman healed of the bloody issue, he feels the glow of health in all his frame. He does not need a physician to tell him he is well. But while he is sick his opinion is of little worth. So it is in spiritual things. When the sin-sick soul is brought into a state of spiritual health, he feels in himself that he is well. He does not need to be told it. But while he is sick his opinion is of little value. His moral perception, his reason and judgment, are so impaired that they cannot be trusted. He who is appointed to guide the sin-sick soul to Christ, must examine his symptoms in connection with his opinion of himself, and form an independent judgment.

3. In forming a judgment in regard to the regenerate state of others, it must be borne in mind that man naturally possesses capabilities of wonderful religious development, and that he is surrounded on every hand by influences whose direct tendency is to develop his religious susceptibilities, and that, too, in the form of a gracious work. The fact, therefore, that a man is awakened religiously, to a very great extent, and in the proper form, must not be taken as evidence that he is born again. The question must be whether he has been awakened by the Holy Spirit, or by other causes, which have no power to change the heart.

4. Again: it must be borne in mind, that if a counterfeit of a work of grace exist, it will be likely to have a close resemblance to a work that is genuine. A counterfeit is an imitation of the genuine, calculated to deceive. It must not be expected that every one who is born again will have hope, and that every one who has hope is born again. Our evidence of others is not necessarily coincident with their evidence of themselves. It is too common to regard others as being Christians only as they regard themselves so; whereas, young Christians often give the best evidence to others, when they have none themselves.

5. Another point is, that all persons are either regenerate or unregenerate, whatever they profess; or, in other words, if they profess to be Christians, all their exercises may be explained upon the supposition that they have experienced a true or a false conversion. Their characters are unique. Every feature of one's exercises ought to be so well understood that it can be classed with those of the renewed or the unrenewed heart, before a final judgment in regard to them is formed. Sometimes it is said that farther instruction will make the person's case more clear.

But, if all depends upon the temper of the heart, instruction will not improve the condition, since it does not change the heart. Sometimes it is hoped that the individual will become clearer as he advances. But no advancement can produce this effect, if one has not been born again.

6. Care must be taken that the judgment is not biased by circumstances, — by the age, or intelligence, or upright character, or naturally honest or dishonest appearance of the person. Both too much and too little allowance is liable to be made for these things. No inference can be drawn from mere circumstances, as to whether one is truly converted. Nor is there in these any guarantee against self-deception. The mature, sound-minded, moral, and religiously educated, are as much exposed to it as the young, the ignorant, and the wicked.

7. No reliance can be placed upon the fluency, or want of fluency, of an individual in the relation of his experience. If a person has been truly born again, it does not necessarily follow that he will be able to express himself freely in regard to it; and because he speaks freely, it does not necessarily follow that he is born again. Fluency, or want of fluency, will depend upon the time or place, age, or disposition, or education of the person, but not upon the question whether he is a new creature.

8. A natural judgment must not take the place of the spiritual. Due deference must be paid to the spiritual sense. The inward sympathy must pervade the exercise of the judgment and reason. The tendency is strong to judge of persons as being Christians in a natural way, according as they appear so to the world, to the neglect of the fact that the regenerate character is peculiar and inexplicable to natural men. Caution must be exercised, also, against an *abuse* of the spiritual sense. The impulses of

Christians must not be relied upon without careful exercise of the judgment. Both the neglect and the abuse of the spiritual sense are equally fatal errors. Because it is abused by some, it should not be neglected by others; nor because it is neglected by some, should it be abused by others. Spiritual phenomena must be apprehended, and then reflected upon in a natural manner, according to the laws of the Spirit's operation.

9. In the crisis of a gracious work, a brief space must be sought for, in which the person does not recognize the change he is undergoing. Such a space must occur in the exercises, whether it can be discovered or not. The turning-point in conversion must not be assigned to a period in which the individual has a full sense of what he is experiencing.

10. Finally: it is of the utmost importance, in judging of an experience, to remember that God's Spirit is the sovereign agent of conversion, but that his sovereignty is unobservable, in consequence of its perfect harmony with man's free moral agency. He acts in perfect accordance with the laws of mind and the use of means. Suitable means are to be employed with the same diligence, as if the Spirit were not connected with the work; and the same dependence upon the Spirit is to be recognized, as if means were not needed.

We shall next present some *suggestions* as to the practical application of these principles.

First, we remark, that a perfectly *spontaneous* expression of the person's feelings must be sought. No outward circumstances must be allowed to influence. If the expression is drawn forth by interrogations, they must not be of the nature of leading questions, but such, if possible, as the person can answer only as his feelings dictate.

If the expression is spontaneous, it must be taken as indicating the true state of the heart, whether favorable or otherwise. If the expression is modified upon the discovery that it is unfavorable, it denotes a hypocritical state of heart.

Again: such questions should be employed as will lead to the expression of the individual's feelings, and not his views. The views are to be ascertained only as indexes of the feelings. But these must not be exclusively relied upon, since they may or may not indicate them.

Again: to form a just judgment of a Christian experience, especially if it is of long standing, discrimination must be exercised as to whether the person is relating his experience as he conceived it to be at the time it occurred, or whether he is relating his present views of it. An individual's view of his exercises at the time they occurred, constitutes a part of his experience, which is important to be ascertained. His present views are only remote signs of what his original exercises were. Nor must they be taken as an actual representation of those. This would be equivalent simply to taking one's word whether he has been converted. The false Christian's view of his original exercises are too favorable, while those of many true Christians are too unfavorable.

It must be remembered, finally, that the object of relating an experience is not to describe the experience itself, but only to present the incidental exercises which denote it. The experience itself is indescribable.

For the convenience of those who have occasion to examine the experiences of others, the following summary of *test-questions* is submitted, as growing out of the previous discussion.

*Conviction of sin.* — This is the first feature in the natural order of Christian experience to be ascertained. Genuine conviction is likely to find expression in a voluntary account of one's exercises. If it is entirely wanting, the symptom is unfavorable. If the relation generally is suppressed, and this feature only equally with the rest, it is not unfavorable. If conversion took place in early childhood, convictions are not likely to be represented as very deep and strong. The statement that the person felt he was a great sinner, is not conclusive evidence that he was truly convicted. It must be ascertained why he felt so, — whether he thought he was very wicked, or only meant that he had very proper convictions. Were the convictions of a general nature, or confined to particular sins? If there was great distress, was it on account of some affliction or disappointment, or source of alarm, or on account of the person's view of his corrupt and guilty nature? Was the distress of a growing character, feeble in the beginning, and increasing until it suddenly passed away? Was there not only a view of sin, but also deep grief on account of it? Or was there grief, or a burden or distress, for which no cause could be ascertained, unless it were an indistinct sense of sin, as in case of a child?

*Removal of convictions.* — Did this take place when the person was seeking it and expecting it, or to his surprise? Did he rejoice at once that his burden was removed; or was he alarmed lest he had lost his convictions, and gone back? Or was he in a state of indifference or quiet, and then distress, lest that quiet was hardness of heart? Was this state soon followed by enjoyment of prayer, views of

Christ, love and happiness? Did the person feel more and more encouraged, while under conviction, that he should soon be relieved? Did he feel determined to persevere, and seek more and more earnestly, believing he should soon find? Or did he have an increasing feeling of discouragement, believing he was growing worse and worse, that his prospect of ever becoming a Christian was diminishing, — his discouragement being greatest just before relief? Does the person still have a sense of sin? Does he feel more or less sinful than before he thought he became a Christian, or before he had any convictions? Has he ever had just such a sense of sin since, as when under conviction? Though he may have had clearer and deeper views of sin, yet has he ever had that *peculiar* distress which he then experienced?

*Repentance.* — Does the person feel that he has repented of *all* his sins? Does he speak as though he had deliberately resolved to perform the work of repentance, and had done it accordingly? Or does he speak of the fact of having repented, with not much distinctness and positiveness; as if, while he hoped he had had repentance, he would not dare to say that he had repented of all his sins, but had need of a much deeper exercise of repentance?

*Sense of forgiveness.* — How does the individual conceive of forgiveness? Does he say, in definite and positive terms, that he believes his sins have been all forgiven, as though he had received an announcement or a revelation of it through some passage of Scripture, or some sensible sign? Or does he speak of it as a matter of faith and trust? Did the individual suddenly and confidently conceive that his sins were forgiven, from some phenomena in his mental history? Or did his hope of forgiveness arise in the form of a feeble consciousness, for which he could assign no definite cause? Was he conscious that his sins were forgiven, at the *time* of forgiveness? Or did his sense of it arise in a gradual and imperceptible manner, so that he could not tell when he first began to cherish it? Does he feel that his sins have been *all* forgiven, or does he speak of it in a modest, qualified, and reserved manner? Did his sense of forgiveness and peace with God occur when he was expecting it, and praying expressly for it; and does he think he understands the causes which produced it? Did he think he perceived beforehand what acts of his, the giving up of what points, or what resolutions made, would produce it? Or was he brought to Christ at last, in a way that he knew not, after all his own conceptions of the manner in which he was to come utterly failed, and he found himself helpless, lost, and perishing?

*Love for Christ.*—Does the person freely and confidently declare that he loves Christ very much, as if he thought his love somewhat adequate to the demands of the case? Or does he express himself modestly and doubtfully, fearing that he does not love him as he ought, and sometimes, that he does not love him at all? How does he view the goodness of God? Does he speak of it as if he thought God had been specially good to him on account of his desert? Is his gratitude mingled with self-complacence, on account of being thus distinguished above others? Or are his sense of God's goodness and his gratitude mingled with humility and a sense of great unworthiness and ill-desert? Does he feel that it is a pleasant thing to be thus distinguished on account of God's favors, and receive them freely and with gratification; or does he regard it as solemn, and receive them with fear and trembling, lest he shall not fulfil the obligations thus imposed?

*Happiness.*—Does the individual express himself as being perfectly and uniformly happy? Does he declare that he takes great pleasure in the duties of religion at all times; or does he express himself hesitatingly, feeling that he does not have all the pleasure in religious things he ought to have,—that he does not probably have as much as other Christians? Is he at some times very unhappy? Does he occasionally have seasons of gloom and darkness, and of the hidings of God's countenance, which cause him to mourn and grieve? Did his happiness arise when he was expecting it, or when he was laboring or praying for it? Or did it arise spontaneously, after his efforts to obtain it proved in vain? Was he happy because he believed he had found the Saviour; or was it a happiness for which he could not assign the cause? Did he begin to be happy before he thought he had become a Christian; or was it subsequent to that belief, and the result of it?

If the individual has seasons of darkness and gloom, does he speak as if it were easy to rid himself of them, that they are removed at once by prayer? Or does he find it difficult to recover his happiness and peace with God? Does he say that he always knows how to obtain relief in his hour of darkness and gloom; or when in these states, does every effort seem to fail him, and cause him to fear lest he shall never again realize the happiness he once enjoyed? And when at last his happiness is restored, is it by the means which he believed would restore it, and at the time he was expecting it; or was it restored spontaneously and imperceptibly, while he was absorbed in other exercises?

*Enjoyment of prayer.*—Does the individual profess to enjoy prayer equally well at all times? Or does he at some times enjoy it much better than at others? When asked if he enjoys praying, does he answer with a naked, unqualified affirmation; or does he reply that he does enjoy it at *times* very much; or, he does not always enjoy it, or he does not enjoy it so much as he would like to? Does he profess that it always does him good to pray, and that God always hears his prayers; or does he confess that at times he finds it a difficult task to pray—feels that it does him no good, and that God does not hear him?

*Faith.*—Does the person feel that he has very strong faith, or that his faith is weak compared with what it should be? Does he speak of it confidently and freely, or in a modest, distrustful, and humble manner? Did his faith originate sensibly or imperceptibly? Did he obtain it by a direct effort made to produce it, and was he sensible that he was obtaining it; or was his attention absorbed in the process of coming into a state of faith, so that he had but little to say of it?

*Hope.*—In what manner does the individual express his hope that he is a Christian? Does he do it in unqualified, positive, and confident terms; or in partially suppressed and modest language? Does he speak of his conversion in a business-like manner, or is it a matter of faith and trust? Does he never doubt that he is a Christian; or does he at times greatly fear lest, after all, he shall come short? In what manner did his hope originate? Did he obtain it by seeking for it, or when looking for it; or did it spring up spontaneously? Did he believe he had become a Christian immediately when his convictions passed away, and he found peace; or did he come to that belief subsequently, and by degrees? Did he immediately announce his conversion to other Christians, or was it previously discovered? Does he desire to make his hope appear to be a good one; or does he evince a tendency to distrust its genuineness, and a readiness to abandon it if it shall appear to be unsound?

Enough has been said in other connections to indicate to what extent the outward life may determine whether one is in a regenerate state. The judgment is ordinarily, of necessity, formed before any considerable portion of the life is witnessed. And facts teach that observation of a portion of it does not warrant any certain conclusion respecting the remainder.

## CHAPTER III.

### TREATMENT OF INQUIRERS AND YOUNG CONVERTS.

In the previous parts of this volume we have discussed the treatment appropriate to the classes of persons therein considered. A corresponding procedure in this part will embrace a discussion of the general principles pertaining to the treatment of inquirers and young converts.

The first duty, in the treatment of a religious inquirer, is to ascertain his exact condition, before any specific appliances are made. The religious teacher should put himself in the attitude of the physician when called to visit a patient. His first endeavor will be to ascertain whether the person is really under spiritual influence; and, if so, what is the precise aspect of his present feelings. It will then be important to ascertain whether he has previously been the subject of religious exercises. Some knowledge of the past history of a religious inquirer is frequently essential to a proper understanding of his present state. In case of persons who have come to years of maturity, it will often disclose examples of unrecognized or of unrecognizable regeneration, the treatment of which has before been described. Nor must it be supposed that an inquirer, any more than a patient, necessarily understands his past history, or his present state. These must be determined by the symptoms he exhibits, in addition to his representation of himself.

The immediate end uniformly to be sought, in the treatment of an inquirer is, a realization by him of his lost condition as a sinner. This is the condition in which the soul passes from death unto life, and toward it all treatment must tend. All the other features of a gracious work, such as submission, repentance, faith, love, and acceptance of Christ, under the influences of the Holy Spirit, arise spontaneously when the sinner is brought sufficiently low before God. The production of these graces is not promoted by a direct endeavor to exercise them, or by urging others to do so, but by seeking to induce the state out of which they spring.

To urge the sinner to submit to God, before he becomes sensible that he is a rebel against him, must, in the nature of the case, be ineffectual. He never can submit till he apprehends his rebellion, and he never will, till he realizes, to some extent, the danger to which it exposes him. To exercise repentance is impossible, till the sinner has a sense of sin. No man can love God till he becomes convinced of the justice of God in his condemnation. Nor can he exercise faith in Christ, or accept of him as his Saviour, until he realizes his lost and hopeless condition without him.

The question will arise whether the sinner, when brought to a sense of his condition, will not need to be urged to submit to God, to repent of sin, to exercise faith, and accept of Christ. To this we answer, that when he is brought to the requisite degree of self-abasement on account of sin, every instinct of his nature under the control of the Holy Spirit will impel him to these things. Let it not be said that this gives to the work too much of a human aspect. Conviction of sin, and all the features of a work of grace which arise as a consequence of this, are the product of the Spirit, but yet occur in a manner as strictly natural as if the Spirit were not connected with the work. The parent, in addition to punishing a rebellious child, does not plead with, and urge him to submit to his authority, to love him, and accept forgiveness. When he is made to realize the consequences of disobedience sufficiently to cause his stubborn heart to break, he will only need to know what the terms of reconciliation are, in order to comply with them. Urgency will be as needless now as it was useless before. So it is with the sinner. Means must be employed to bring him to a sense of his guilt; and when this is sufficiently accomplished, it will be indicated by his actual submission, repentance, and compliance with the terms of pardon. Instances may occur in which an inquirer will seem to be brought under such distress as not to warrant the use of means to increase still farther his sense of sin; but, even then, it will be unsafe to urge him to put his trust at once in Christ *just as he is.* The fact that he does not do it spontaneously, indicates that some farther change in his condition is required, — a change which none but the Holy Spirit, it may be, is able to discover. The actual yielding of the sinner, is the only sure indication that his convictions have attained to sufficient maturity. In many instances this will occur much earlier than would be anticipated by a watchful observer, while in others it will be strangely deferred.

The main question, therefore, in the treatment of inquirers is, What means are to be employed to induce conviction of sin? In answer to this, only some general suggestions can be made, since specific treatment for any given case cannot be determined beforehand. Arguments to show the sinner his sinfulness, may be drawn from the requirements of the law, or the higher platform of the gospel. He may be shown how he has abused the goodness of God, or how he has neglected the love of Christ, either or both, according to the effect which promises to be produced. He must not be allowed, however, to regard any new *views* of his obligations to God and Christ, and of the imperfect manner in which he has fulfilled them, as genuine conviction of sin. Indeed, such means are seldom recognized as directly producing conviction, whatever unobserved influence they may have to that effect. The most important impression to be produced upon the mind of the inquirer, is, a sense of his absolute dependence upon the Holy Spirit, who alone has power to convince the world of sin. No hesitation must be felt in teaching inquirers their entire helplessness, as the most efficient means of causing them to cry to God for mercy. They should be taught, too, that, notwithstanding their dependence, they will have no excuse for remaining in an unregenerate condition, until, in addition to making the most diligent use of all the means of grace within their reach, they have exhausted every power they possess, in pleading with God to renew their hearts.

It should be remembered that the end of all treatment of inquirers is not instruction, but the production of a certain state of *feeling*, since regeneration is emphatically a change of *heart*. Conviction of sin, or sense of guilt, is not a matter of judgment or understanding, but of feeling. Whatever instruction is imparted, must be used as a means to this end. If it do not tend to produce the state of feeling in which the soul passes from death unto life, it must be withheld, since the diversion of mind which it produces must retard the work. This remark is particularly applicable to adults, in whom a merely intellectual exercise is quite likely to predominate and supplant a change of heart.

Alarm, rather than encouragement, is best suited to produce the condition desired. Expressions of encouragement to the inquirer that he will soon be successful, promote self-reliance, rather than sink him farther and farther in the depths of his own conscious helplessness and ruin. He should rather be made to feel that his case is critical and dangerous, and that there is no hope for him except through a special manifestation of God's mercy, in compassion for his most earnest importunity. Any treatment which indicates a belief, or even a hope, that the inquirer is advancing, or which will allow him to cherish such hope, has the tendency to produce the opposite of the condition desired — to raise him up, rather than cause him to fall helpless and broken-hearted into the dust, and cry to God for help. Hence the reason why rising for prayers, or taking the anxious seats, or a public acknowledgment of one's determination to seek to become a Christian, so often results unfavorably. The inquirer interprets the act as a step of advancement, and often as the turning-point in his case, whereas it should serve only to expose to him the pride of his heart, or cause him to tremble in view of having committed himself to the solemn duty of seeking his salvation.

Sometimes inquirers are requested to pray audibly, in the presence of Christians or of each other, in the inquiry-room. Sometimes they even pray for each other, and are encouraged to do so. The tendency of this is likely to be unfavorable. The fact of their praying in company, and in turn with real Christians, and perhaps for each other and the cause in general, is in danger of leaving upon their minds the impression that they have some ability to perform a Christian duty, or that they have done something meritorious. They will be likely, like the Pharisee, to make capital of the act, and feel strengthened and built up by it, instead of being reduced to the condition of the publican, when he could not so much as lift up his eyes unto heaven, but smote upon his breast, saying, God be merciful to me a sinner! A person under real anxiety for his own soul, will not think to pray for others; or, if he does so, it will dissipate his anxiety for himself. An inquirer is sometimes found in a condition in which it may be serviceable to request, or even to urge him, in the presence of a Christian, to attempt to pray audibly for himself, — the object being a breaking of his pride, which may be needful as the final turning-point in his feelings. In such a case, he will be reluctant to comply with the request. If he is ready and willing, it is indicative that nothing will be gained.

Sometimes Christians have an ambition to see the sinner with whom they are laboring converted before they leave him, — a desire which is seldom realized in a genuine manner, especially if it is made known to the inquirer. The effect is to divert both parties from the vital work of the Holy Spirit; and thus the desire defeats itself. Sometimes the person is asked if he does not feel relieved, which has the tendency to dissipate whatever feeling he may possess. This is in direct violation of the position that when the sinner passes from death unto life, he is unconscious of the change he is undergoing.

A not unimportant duty, in the treatment of inquirers, is that of watchfulness, to prevent tares from growing up and choking the fruits of the Spirit. This is especially important when the inquirer is approaching the crisis of his exercises. Then Satan is most busy in attempting to defeat a work of grace; and unfavorable influences, also, are more harmful, than when the person is less deeply awakened. Hence any premature tendency to cherish hope, or to be hopeful, must be promptly checked. If the person conceives that he is slowly advancing, or is gradually obtaining light, or has gained a little faith and is expecting more, while he has not yet been slain on account of sin, these erroneous views must be corrected. A heart under the influences of divine grace, is to be watched like a garden of flowers. The noxious weeds of error will be constantly springing up from its native soil, while nothing that is good and true will be produced except as it is implanted by the Holy Spirit.

The earliest and most simple state of religious inquiry is that in which a person deliberately comes forward of his own accord, and states, with apparent honesty, that he has no special anxiety, but he thinks, as he always has done, that he ought to be a Christian; and, having determined to give his attention to the subject, he wishes to be directed. Concerning such a case, we remark, that it is not of a promising nature. A work of grace seldom originates in this state of mind. It bears none of the marks of the peculiar manner in which God's Spirit begins his work, and hence fails to inspire confidence in a happy result. Such an inquiry, however, cannot be treated with neglect; it must, in some way, be met. Whatever specific means are used, the general aim should be to show the person his real condition; that he is under no special concern, and that he has no real desire to be a Christian, as is manifest by his coolness and deliberation; that his attempt, moreover, to become reconciled to an offended God in such an indifferent and thoughtless manner, is proof of his blindness and hardness of heart, and an indication of the improbability that God will regard his efforts with any favor. Congratulation of the individual upon having begun to seek his salvation, or the manifestation of pleasure or of satisfaction in view of it, would be likely to cause him to think he had made a good beginning, which would be unfavorable. Offering to assist the person, or to instruct him, or pray with him, in any such manner as to allow him to draw a similar inference, would also be unpropitious. He must be made to see that he has no sense of his lost condition, or of his need of a Saviour, and that the work he contemplates is infinitely more difficult than he supposes. This kind of treatment, however, must not be carried too far, else he will abandon the undertaking. Effort should be made to fasten and deepen, if possible, the little interest he professes to have. This will be best accomplished by inducing fear and trembling in view of the greatness of the undertaking and the danger of his condition, and not by producing a feeling of hopefulness. But, as has been said, such a beginning is not a favorable one, and it is difficult to suggest treatment for it which shall give any promise of success. Cases of this kind commonly result in a premature and spurious conversion, or, in a little period, vanish altogether.

Another condition in which inquirers are often found, is that of desire to become Christians, awakened by some strongly selfish motive, such as that arising from the conversion of a very dear friend. It has been shown that such awakening does not commonly result in true conversion. Its tendency is to come to a crisis prematurely, and deceive the observer as to its genuineness. Such a case requires not to be stimulated, but to be made more thorough, and prevented from a premature development. It is better that the process should be checked entirely, than that it should come to a false issue. The selfishness of the individual's motives, and of his anxiety, may be exposed to him as a means of preventing his indulgence of a false hope; care being taken, at the same time, not entirely to check his efforts. Such a case, however, we are not able, even in imagination, to trace to a happy result, under any kind of treatment.

Another condition of inquiry is produced by deep and sore affliction. This has also been shown not to be a favorable kind of awakening. Appropriate treatment will be similar to that suggested in case of an awakening caused by selfish motives. It must, if possible, be prevented from coming to a spurious development. It is less hazardous for man to put his hand to a false religious exercise, and check or attempt to mould it, than to attempt to guide a real work of the Spirit. No damage is done by arresting a false experience. In cases of this kind, special care must be taken to ascertain the precise nature of the exercises, to determine the cause of the distress, and to show the person that it arises from his affliction, and not from a sense of sin. We cannot follow a case of this kind to spiritual maturity, having never witnessed the transmutation of a false work to a genuine one.

Examples of persons who seem to be suddenly "*struck*" under deep conviction, require cautious treatment.[1] The first and most important aim should be, to determine whether the apparent convictions are genuine, of which their strength must not be taken as proof, as is too often done. If the convictions appear to be merely the result of excitement or alarm, the endeavor should be to instruct the person as to their nature, and especially to arrest their

1 Genuine cases of this kind are rare. We do not mean instances in which persons are suddenly alarmed by some providential occurrence, from which they subsequently date their awakening; but examples in which persons are instantaneously shown the deep iniquity of their hearts, and are at once greatly distressed in view of it.

strong tendency to a false development. If the exercises are genuine, and also very deep and violent, little aid from man is needed. There is no occasion to attempt to allay the person's feelings. If they are the product of the Holy Spirit, they will be no more violent than the case requires. Nor will it be necessary to attempt to bring them to a speedy termination. The Spirit's work will not be unduly protracted. Effort to relieve the person of his distress is dangerous.

The commencement of a genuine and promising case of inquiry is frequently referable to some trifling incident; or, more commonly, to nothing sufficiently definite to be recalled, but to the combined influences by which the person is surrounded. Accordingly, such a case will not ordinarily be discovered at its beginning. When first recognized as an inquirer, the individual will be found to have cherished, for a time, some special feeling. He will not have made up his mind at once to seek to become a Christian, and at the same time have announced his determination to others. This is according to the human, unspiritual idea of the work; but it is not the divine method. The Holy Spirit commences his work in the deep silence of the mind. The person scarcely recognizes himself as having begun to seek his salvation. He begins, at first, to be wrought upon, but not to work. Under the enlightening influence of the Holy Spirit, a deep seriousness and alarm are produced, which cause him to fear lest he shall never be brought to know the truth. His choked utterance will indicate that a vital work is begun. In proportion as he expresses himself freely, professing openly and frankly to be very anxious to become a Christian, is it indicative of a superficial work. In a truly enlightening process, the inquirer, on account of his increasing sense of guilt and shame, will not freely make known his feelings until compelled to do so, which will be only after a period of time has elapsed.[1]

Such a case must be treated with solemnity. The work must be viewed as being preëminently that of the Holy Spirit. Man may watch its progress with a prayerful heart. He may endeavor to shield it from unhallowed influences; but he must be careful how he attempts to mould or guide it. It is safer to seek to deepen than to hasten it. In order that the individual may feel that his case is to be adjusted with God alone, he should be left *mainly to himself*, under the influence of the ordinary means of grace. Christians must not be so anxious to give their advice and aid with their prayers, as to cause him to rely upon their efforts. He must be taught to seek for no prescribed form of experience, either as defined by others or conceived by himself, but to plead for the Holy Spirit to perform in him his own peculiar work, in his mysterious way.

Christians sometimes attempt to assist the inquirer to discover the hinderances which lie in his way; or they urge his submission to certain requirements; or his yielding certain points, which they conceive to be the terms on which he can receive salvation. This is an unsafe procedure. It is the Holy Spirit's work to enlighten the sinner, and bring him to the terms of salvation. Our Saviour could point out to the young ruler the ultimate test of his unwillingness to comply with the requirements of the gospel; but for man to attempt it, is presumptuous; and for

[1] That a work of the Holy Spirit should ordinarily commence thus, is according to the constitution of the human mind. All thorough and abiding mental changes, with rare exceptions, will be found to have had such a beginning. Under this general aspect of the manner in which real conversions most commonly commence, we have room for that unlimited variety of manifestation which has been spoken of in another connection. See page 238.

the sinner to yield such points as are indicated by others or imagined by himself, to constitute the final test in his case, can result in nothing better than a counterfeit of a gracious work. All genuine experience shows that the sinner never knows beforehand what point yielded will bring him true relief. It may not be imprudent for a Christian, in an indirect manner, to endeavor to discover what particular obstacle prevents the sinner from obtaining pardon, and treat him accordingly. It must, however, be done without allowing the inquirer even to suspect his aim. But such a procedure will, after all, be likely to fail entirely, or be followed by a spurious result. When the sinner is brought to the requisite sense of his guilt, helplessness, and ruin before God, the Holy Spirit, who can control all minds, will order instrumentalities by which to bring him to yield the final point at issue, without any direct endeavor on the part of man.

Nor is there occasion to congratulate the individual, when the change seems to have occurred. This is not only uncalled for, but unsuited to the tender, child-like state of the new-born soul. Better suppress manifestations of joy, or even of confidence that the event has taken place; and, while watching with fear and trembling, regard the occasion as one calling for humiliation before the mighty hand of God. The spiritual infant is not prepared to appropriate the naked statement that he has passed from death unto life. The new creature must be allowed a little opportunity for his renewed nature to develop and strengthen itself, under the nurturing influences of the Holy Spirit, instead of being forced to receive the strong nutriment which Christians are often in over-zealous haste to administer. He must first learn to breathe the atmosphere of his new condition, and then receive food of the simplest kind, that he may grow thereby. Testimony from others, that one has just been born again, is uncongenial and harmful. If a person has been born of the Spirit, he will find sufficient evidences to feed upon, in the smiles of God, in nature, and in the incidental manifestations of satisfaction on the part of others, which will providentially occur.

No more delicate, solemn, and responsible duty is ever committed to mortal hands, than that of guiding inquiring souls to Jesus Christ. He who would contribute to such a work, must himself be under the Spirit's control. His endeavors must be not so much the acting of his own will, as the appointed medium of the Spirit's efficacious working.

In regard to the treatment of the persons under consideration, subsequently to conversion, and prior to a public profession of religion, it may be suggested that they are to be regarded not as religious prodigies, but as tender babes in Christ. It should be remembered that they are but partially sanctified, and are still susceptible of being injured by the unhallowed influences of flattery, or of overmuch congratulation. They are ill-prepared to be put forth at once as heroes and champions for Christ. They stand in need of Christian nurture and watchfulness, instead of being thrust forward into the front ranks of Christian service, as if, in their infantile existence, they had attained to larger growth than Christians of maturer years. They should be encouraged to the performance of Christian duty gradually, and in harmony with the position that a little space is needed for the attainment of experience and spiritual strength.

Effort should not be made directly to remove the doubts to which young converts are commonly subject. These should rather be allowed to have their course, as being suffered of God, and probably required for the purposes of discipline. Young Christians should not be told that they ought not to doubt, but should be led to self-examination, prayer, and humiliation. Thus removed, doubts result in Christian nurture and experience.

But one question remains to be considered. Should young converts be urged immediately to make a public profession of religion, and unite with a Christian church, or should they be required to wait a given period in order to test the reality of their change? According to the sentiments submitted in the foregoing pages, the reality of conversion is *not* a question of time. It is to be determined by the religious experience of the person, his temper of heart, and his apprehension of spiritual things. There is no occasion, therefore, to require that the duty of uniting with a Christian church should be deferred farther than to give opportunity for the person's views and feelings to become so developed as to enable him to go forward somewhat trustfully and intelligently. Christians who are entrusted with the responsibility of admitting members to the churches, must become better acquainted with the legitimate phenomena of an initial experience, and seek for greater facility in detecting the peculiarities of a regenerate state; and according to their judgment thus formed, they must act.

THE END.

# VALUABLE WORKS.

**Diary and Correspondence** OF THE LATE AMOS LAWRENCE. Edited by his son, WM. R. LAWRENCE, M. D. Octavo, cloth, $1.25; also, royal 12mo. ed., cl., $1.00.

**Kitto's Popular Cyclopædia** OF BIBLICAL LITERATURE. 500 illustrations. One vol., octavo. 812 pages. Cloth, $3.

Intended for ministers, theological students, parents, Sabbath-school teachers, and the great body of the religious public.

**Analytical Concordance of the Holy** SCRIPTURES; or, The Bible presented under Classified Heads or Topics. By JOHN EADIE, D. D. Octavo, 836 pp. $3.

**Dr. Williams' Works.**

**Lectures on the Lord's Prayer — Religious Progress — Miscellanies.**

☞ Dr. Williams is a profound scholar and a brilliant writer. — *New York Evangelist.*

**Modern Atheism.** Considered under its forms of Pantheism, Materialism, Secularism, Development and Natural Laws. By JAMES BUCHANAN, D. D., LL. D. 12mo. Cloth, $1.25.

**The Hallig:** or the Sheepfold in the Waters. A Tale of Humble Life on the Coast of Schleswig. From the German, by Mrs. GEORGE P. MARSH. 12mo. Cl., $1.

**The Suffering Saviour.** By Dr. KRUMMACHER. 12mo. Cloth, $1.25.

**Heaven.** By JAMES WM. KIMBALL. 12mo.

**Christian's Daily Treasury.** Religious Exercise for every Day in the Year. By Rev. E. TEMPLE. 12mo. Cloth, $1.

**Wayland's Sermons.** Delivered in the Chapel of Brown Univ. 12mo. Cl., $1.00.

**Entertaining and Instructive Works** FOR THE YOUNG. Elegantly illustrated. 16mo. Cloth, gilt backs.

*The American Statesman.* Life and Character of Daniel Webster. — *Young Americans Abroad;* or Vacation in Europe. — *The Island Home;* or the Young Cast-aways. — *Pleasant Pages for Young People.* — *The Guiding Star.* — *The Poor Boy and Merchant Prince.*

THE AIMWELL STORIES. Resembling and quite equal to the "Rollo Stories." — *Christian Register.* By WALTER AIMWELL. *Oscar;* or the Boy who had his own way. — *Clinton;* or Boy-Life in the Country. — *Ella;* or Turning over a New Leaf. — *Whistler;* or The Manly Boy. — *Marcus;* or the Boy Tamer.

WORKS BY Rev. HARVEY NEWCOMB. *How to be a Lady.* — *How to be a Man.* — *Anecdotes for Boys.* — *Anecdotes for Girls.*

BANVARD'S SERIES OF AMERICAN HISTORIES. *Plymouth and the Pilgrims.* — *Romance of American History.* — *Novelties of the New World, and Tragic Scenes in the History of Maryland and the old French War.*

**God Revealed in Nature and in** CHRIST. By Rev. JAMES B. WALKER, Author of "The Philosophy of the Plan of Salvation." 12mo. Cloth, $1.

**Philosophy of the Plan of Salvation.** New enlarged edition. 12mo. Cloth, 75 c.

**Christian Life:** SOCIAL AND INDIVIDUAL. By PETER BAYNE. 12mo. Cloth, $1.25.

All agree in pronouncing it one of the most admirable works of the age.

**Yahveh Christ;** or the Memorial Name. By ALEX. MACWHORTER. With an Introductory Letter, by NATH'L W. TAYLOR, D. D., in Yale Theol. Sem. 16mo. Cloth, 60 c.

**The Signet Ring,** AND ITS HEAVENLY MOTTO. From the German. 16mo. Cl., 31 c.

**The Marriage Ring;** or How to Make Home Happy. 18mo. Cloth, gilt, 75 c.

**Mothers of the Wise and Good.** By JABEZ BURNS, D. D. 16mo, Cloth, 75 c.

☞ A sketch of the mothers of many of the most eminent men of the world.

**My Mother;** or Recollections of Maternal Influence. 12mo. Cloth, 75c.

**The Excellent Woman,** with an Introduction, by Rev. W. B. SPRAGUE, D. D. Splendid Illustrations. 12mo. Cloth, $1.

**The Progress of Baptist Principles** IN THE LAST HUNDRED YEARS. By T. F. CURTIS, Prof. of Theology in the Lewisburg University. 12mo. Cloth, $1.25.

**Dr. Harris' Works.**

The Great Teacher. — The Great Commission. — The Pre-Adamite Earth. — Man Primeval. — Patriarchy. — Posthumous Works, 4 volumes.

**The Better Land;** OR THE BELIEVER'S JOURNEY AND FUTURE HOME. By Rev. A. C. THOMPSON. 12mo. Cloth, 85 c.

**Kitto's History of Palestine,** from the Patriarchal Age to the Present Time. With 200 Illustrations. 12mo. Cloth, $1.25.

An admirable work for the Family, the Sabbath and week-day School Library.

**The Priest and the Huguenot;** or, PERSECUTION IN THE AGE OF LOUIS XV. From the French of L. F. BUNGENER. Two vols., 12mo. Cloth, $2.25.

This is not only a work of thrilling interest, but is a masterly Protestant production.

**The Psalmist.** A Collection of Hymns for the Use of Baptist Churches. By BARON STOW and S. F. SMITH. With a SUPPLEMENT, containing an Additional Selection of Hymns, by RICHARD FULLER, D. D., and J. B. JETER, D. D. Published in various sizes, and styles of binding.

This is unquestionably the best collection of Hymns in the English language.

☞ In addition to works published by themselves, they keep an extensive assortment of works in all departments of trade, which they supply at publishers' prices. ☞ They particularly invite the attention of Booksellers, Travelling Agents, Teachers, School Committees, Librarians, Clergymen, and professional men generally (to whom a liberal discount is uniformly made), to their extensive stock. ☞ To persons wishing copies of Text-books, for examination, they will be forwarded, per mail or otherwise, on the reception of *one half* the price of the work desired. ☞ Orders from any part of the country attended to with faithfulness and dispatch.

# WORKS FOR BIBLE STUDENTS.

**KITTO'S POPULAR CYCLOPÆDIA OF BIBLICAL LITERATURE.** Condensed from the larger work. By the Author, JOHN KITTO, D. D. Assisted by JAMES TAYLOR, D. D., of Glasgow. With over five hundred Illustrations. One volume, octavo, 812 pp. Cloth, $3.00 ; sheep, $3.50 ; cloth, gilt, $4.00 ; half calf, $4.00.

A DICTIONARY OF THE BIBLE. Serving, also, as a COMMENTARY, embodying the products of the best and most recent researches in biblical literature in which the scholars of Europe and America have been engaged. The work, the result of immense labor and research, and enriched by the contributions of writers of distinguished eminence in the various departments of sacred literature, has been, by universal consent, pronounced the best work of its class extant, and the one best suited to the advanced knowledge of the present day in all the studies connected with theological science. It is not only intended for ministers and theological students, but it is also particularly adapted to parents, Sabbath-school teachers, and the great body of the religious public.

**THE HISTORY OF PALESTINE,** from the Patriarchal Age to the Present Time ; with Chapters on the Geography and Natural History of the Country, the Customs and Institutions of the Hebrews. By JOHN KITTO, D. D. With upwards of two hundred Illustrations. 12mo, cloth, $1.25.

☞ A work admirably adapted to the Family, the Sabbath, and the week-day School Library.

**ANALYTICAL CONCORDANCE TO THE HOLY SCRIPTURES;** or, the Bible presented under Distinct and Classified Heads or Topics. By JOHN EADIE, D. D., LL D., Author of "Biblical Cyclopædia," "Ecclesiastical Cyclopædia," "Dictionary of the Bible," etc. One volume, octavo, 840 pp. Cloth, $3.00 ; sheep, $3.50 ; cloth, gilt, $4.00 ; half Turkey morocco, $4.00.

The object of this Concordance is to present the SCRIPTURES ENTIRE, under certain classified and exhaustive heads. It differs from an ordinary Concordance, in that its arrangement depends not on WORDS, but on SUBJECTS, and the verses *are printed in full.* Its plan does not bring it at all into competition with such limited works as those of Gaston and Warden ; for they select *doctrinal* topics principally, and do not profess to comprehend as this THE ENTIRE BIBLE. The work also contains a Synoptical Table of Contents of the whole work, presenting in brief a system of biblical antiquities and theology, with a very copious and accurate index.

The value of this work to ministers and Sabbath-school teachers can hardly be over-estimated ; and it needs only to be examined, to secure the approval and patronage of every Bible student.

**CRUDEN'S CONDENSED CONCORDANCE.** A Complete Concordance to the Holy Scriptures. By ALEXANDER CRUDEN. Revised and Re-edited by the Rev. DAVID KING, LL. D. Octavo, cloth backs, $1.25 ; sheep, $1.50.

The condensation of the quotations of Scripture, arranged under the most obvious heads, while it *diminishes the bulk* of the work, *greatly facilitates* the finding of any required passage.

"We have in this edition of Cruden the *best* made *better.* That is, the present is better adapted to the purposes of a Concordance, by the erasure of superfluous references, the omission of unnecessary explanations, and the contraction of quotations, &c. It is better as a manual, and is better adapted by its price to the means of many who need and ought to possess such a work, than the former large and expensive edition." — *Puritan Recorder.*

**A COMMENTARY ON THE ORIGINAL TEXT OF THE ACTS OF THE APOSTLES.** By HORATIO B. HACKETT, D. D., Prof. of Biblical Literature and Interpretation, in the Newton Theol. Inst. ☞ A new, revised, and enlarged edition. Royal octavo, cloth, $2.25.

☞ This most important and very popular work has been thoroughly revised ; large portions entirely re-written, with the addition of *more than one hundred pages of new matter ;* the result of the author's continued, laborious investigations and travels, since the publication of the first edition.

www.ingramcontent.com/pod-product-compliance
Lightning Source LLC
LaVergne TN
LVHW010150110826
845151LV00002B/473